TRANSFER BETWEEN
SEA AND LAND

T0396712

Sidestone Press

TRANSFER BETWEEN SEA AND LAND

*Maritime vessels for cultural exchanges
in the Early Modern Period*

edited by
SIMONE KAHLOW

Published by Sidestone Press, Leiden
www.sidestone.com

Lay-out & cover design: Sidestone Press
Photograph cover: A Ship on the High Seas Caught by a Squall, known as 'The Gust', Willem van de Velde (II), c. 1680. Oil on canvas, H 77cm × W 63.5 63.5cm, SK-A-1848 collection Rijksmuseum, Amsterdam.

ISBN 978-90-8890-620-6 (softcover)
ISBN 978-90-8890-621-3 (hardcover)
ISBN 978-90-8890-622-0 (PDF e-book)

Contents

List of Figures, Sources and Permission

Introduction (Simone Kahlow)
Figure 1: View of a Dutch (?) harbour in 1647. Etching by Wenzel Hollar (14.3 x 23.7 cm). Metropolitan Museum of Art. http://www.metmuseum.org/art/collection/search/361525. This file was donated to Wikimedia Commons by as part of a project by the Metropolitan Museum of Art. CC0 (https://commons.wikimedia.org/w/index.php?curid=60876355).

Asien Objects in Europe (Gerson H. Jeute)
Figure 1: Mechanisms of Distribution of Goods. Work of Gerson H. Jeute, after Drauschke 2011.
Figure 2: Map of Asian objects in Europe (black: Early Middle Ages, gray: High and Late Middle Ages, white: Early Modern Period). Work of Gerson H. Jeute.
Figure 3: Trade route of early medieval dirhams. Source: Bálint 1981, fig. 1; additions: Gerson H. Jeute.
Figure 4: Map of evidence of oriental spices in Europe (black: Early Middle Ages, gray: High and Late Middle Ages, white: Early Modern Period). Work of Gerson H. Jeute.
Figure 5: Potential value of things imported into Europe. Work of Gerson H. Jeute.

'Nuremberg Ware' from Venetian Shipwrecks in the Eastern Adriatic (Patrick Cassitti)
Figure 1: Location of the shipwreck sites of Gnalić and Drevine. Work of Patrick Cassitti.
Figure 2: Brass finds from the Gnalić shipwreck in the Town Museum of Biograd na Moru. Photo by Patrick Cassitti.
Figure 3: Coils of wire in the Town Museum of Biograd na Moru, stacked as they were found during excavation at the Gnalić shipwreck site. The diameter of the large coils is approx. 50 cm. Photo by Patrick Cassitti.

Figure 4: Rolled brass sheet from the Gnalić shipwreck site in the Town Museum of Biograd Na Moru. The diameter of the roll at the center is approx. 7 cm. Photo by Patrick Cassitti.

Figure 5: Folded brass sheet from the Gnalić shipwreck site in the Town Museum of Biograd Na Moru. The overall length is approx. 73 cm, the width approx. 18 cm. Photo by Patrick Cassitti.

Figure 6: Rod-shaped brass ingots from the shipwreck of Gnalić in the Town Museum of Biograd na Moru. The length of the rods is approx. 60 cm. Photo by Patrick Cassitti.

Figure 7: Merchant's sign on the lid of a barrel containing brass rods from the shipwreck of Gnalić, marked with an arrow. Photo by Patrick Cassitti.

Figure 8: Small wooden box with coils of thin wire from the shipwreck of Drevine in the Maritime Museum of Dubrovnik (top) and one of the coils of fine wire from the same site stored in the International Centre for Underwater Archaeology in Zadar (bottom). Work of the author. Merchant's sign on the lid of a barrel containing brass rods from the shipwreck of Gnalić, marked with an arrow. Photo by Patrick Cassitti.

Figure 9: Knives with papier – mâché scabbards from the shipwreck of Drevine, currently stored in the International Centre for Underwater Archaeology in Zadar. Photo by Patrick Cassitti.

Figure 10: Places of print of the identified printed sheets used for the manufacture of the knife sheaths from the shipwreck of Drevine. Work of Patrick Cassitti.

With the Warship Kronan in the Wake of Paracelsus (Björn Lindeke, Bo Ohlson)

Figure 1: First page of the requisition of *Materia Medica* from Amsterdam ordered by *Carl Gustaf Wrangel* in 1655 (AKP 1655). Photo by Björn Lindeke.

Figure 2: The medicine chest being excavated at the wreck of the *Kronan*. Photo by Lars Einarsson, Kalmar county museum.

Figure 3: A number of medicinal flasks of various shapes and sizes have been retrieved from the *Kronan*. Some flasks are square to fit into the wooden casing. Photo by Max Jahrehorn, Kalmar county museum.

Figure 4: Wooden box fragments with denoted texts; 4a, *Sem Foenicúl* (fennel fruit), 4b, *Pl Rharb Tost* (toasted root of medical rhubarb), 4c, *pl fumal* (incense). Photo by Max Jahrehorn, Kalmar county museum.

Figures 5: 5a, the clyster pipe designed to be attached to a bladder; 5b, the application of a clyster according to the English surgeon John Ardene in 1412. Photo by Max Jahrehorn Kalmar county museum (5a) and Gertie Johansson, the Hagströmer library (5b).

Figures 6: 6a, the forceps for teeth-extraction found in 2014, 6b, dental instruments depicted in Dionis 1708, 6c, Saint Appolonia the patroness of dentistry holding a forceps in her left hand. Painting by *Albertus Pictor* (†1509) in Härnevi Church, north-west of Stockholm. Photo by Karin Adriansson (6a), Björn Lindeke (6b) and Christa Malmberg (6c).

Thoughts about Supply and Demand of Exotic Animals (Simone Kahlow)

Figure 8: Remains of the Barbary macaque, wreck of the Dauphine, 1704, Natière 1. Reconstruction by Philippe & Magali Migaud, drawing Marie-Noëlle Baudrand (Adramar), photo by Frédéric Osada (Images Explorations) © ADRAMAR / DRASSM.

The Lloyd´s Lists (Stefan Geissler)

Figure 1: Handwritten report about a wrecked ship and the entry in a Lloyd's List, Minutes 1805. Courtesy of The Corporation of Lloyd's. Photo by Stefan Geissler.

Cultural Exchange in Early Modern Age Shipbuilding (Anne Kathrin Piele)

Figure 1: Design drawing of the first ship build by Hepp in Vienna 1769. Source: Schäfer 1985, 103.

Figures 2 and 3: Similar types of the Rhine: Samoreus and Keulsche Aak. Source: Dessens 1995, 109-110. For Fig. 3 Groenewegen 1789.

Figure 4: Local ship type used for the salt transport in Gmunden, Austria. After an original sketch by G. Arnold in 1874. Source: Das Buch für Alle 31, 1896.

Figure 5: Hepp ship and local ship types. Source: Slezak 1971, table 16.

Figure 6: Depiction of a 'Zille', Vilshofen on the Danube, Stadtplatz 16. Photo by High Contrast, CC BY 3.0 de, via Wikimedia Commons (https://commons.wikimedia.org/w/index.php?curid=28061048).

Figure 7: Wreck of Kehlheim-Kehlheimwinzer. Drawing by Franz Herzig (Bayrisches Landesamt für Denkmalpflege). Source: Herzig and Weski, 2009, 86, fig. 18.

Figure 8: Cockle boat at Strassbourg. 'Reinbruck Zollhauss' by Wenceslaus Hollar, circa 1630, copper engraving (7 x 11 cm). Thomas Fisher Rare Book Libary, Wenceslaus Hollar Digital Collection, Toronto. Photo via Wikimedia Commons (https://commons.wikimedia.org/wiki/File:Wenceslas_Hollar_-_Reinbruck_Zolhaus.jpg).

Figure 9: Wreck of Kehlheim-Kehlheimwinzer. Photo by Archäologische Staatssammlung München. Source: Herzig and Weski, 2009, 85, fig. 17.

Notes of contributers

Patrick Cassitti

Patrick Cassitti studied Prehistoric and Historical Archaeology at the Universities of Bologna, Innsbruck and Kiel. He completed his PhD in Innsbruck in 2009. He was member of scientific staff at the Foundation Pro Monastery of St. John – UNESCO World Heritage site, adjunct lecturer at the Department of Archaeologies of the University of Innsbruck, and from 2011-2015 lecturer at the Chair of Medieval and Post-Medieval Archaeology of Bamberg University. In 2015 he was appointed Scientific Director of the Foundation Pro Monastery of St. John – Unesco World Heritage site.

Stefan Geissler

Stefan Geissler has been a doctoral student since March 2014 under the supervision of Prof. Dr. Roland Wenzlhuemer (Heidelberg, now Munich). Following his Master of Arts in History, German and Political Science at the University of Heidelberg (2014), he initially received a start-up funding from the German Historical Institute in London and began working with PhD-Thesis under the working title 'The Lloyd's List – A global information system?'. He is currently Team-Leader for the online exams & public student labs at ETH Zurich. His research focus is on digital humanities, historical geography and global history.

Gerson H. Jeute

Gerson H. Jeute is a specialist in settlement and environmental archaeology. He is also very interested in transcontinental and transcultural interrelationships during the Middle Ages and early modern times. After his study and research at the Humboldt University in Berlin, he worked as PostDoc fellow at the Roman Germanic Central Museum (RGZM) in Mainz as well as leader of the project 'Harbours in the Bremen Basin at the 1st millennium A.D.' at the University Bremen as part of the Special Research Programme 'Harbours from the Roman Period to the Middle Ages' of the German Research Foundation.

Simone Kahlow

Simone Kahlow is a research scientist in the area of cultural studies and humanities. Her research interests mainly focus on medical archeology and material culture of the Middle Ages and the Early Modern Period. In her doctoral thesis on welfare institutions from the eighth to the nineteenth century, she already dealt with diseases of seafarers and thus came to the German Maritime Museum in Bremerhaven. There she initiated the research topic 'Cultural exchange through shipping'. Since then she has been engaged in interdisciplinary research on the transfer of exotics and medicine in the Early Modern Time.

Björn Lindeke

Björn Lindeke is Professor Emeritus and Docent in Medicinal Chemistry University Hof Uppsala, former Executive Director, of the Swedish Pharmaceutical Society and former President of its section for the History of Pharmacy. From 1991 and onwards his engagement devoted to the history of medicinal drugs and the trade and development of drugs throughout centuries.

Bo Ohlson

Bo Ohlson is a licensed pharmacist and member of the board of the Swedish Society for the History of Pharmacy. He has been working thirty-eight years in quality control by chemical and physical methods of pharmaceutical starting materials. Ohlson is active at the pharma-historical museum of the Academy of Pharmaceutical Sciences and at the Museum Pharmacy in the Skansen Open-air Museum.

Anne-Kathrin Piele

Anne-Kathrin Piele studied prehistoric archaeology in Berlin. Her research focus is directed towards ship archaeology and ship construction. In her Master's thesis, Piele compared the technique of different types of sewn ships within Europe from the Bronze Age to the Iron Age. In the Future, she wants to continue research in historic ship construction techniques and ship types of the late middle age and the early modern age.

Foreword by the State Archaeologist of Bremen

Uta Halle

In 2015 an international workshop for humanities and natural science about maritime vessel as evidence for cultural exchange in the Early Modern Time was held at the German Maritime Museum in Bremerhaven, Institute of the Leibniz Association. As state archaeologist of Bremen, I was pleased to support this topic because the cities and ports of Bremen and Bremerhaven look back on a varied history of shipping, in which the transfer of knowledge, goods, and people went hand in hand for centuries.

Bremerhaven is the smaller city of the two-town federal state Bremen at the mouth of the river Weser. In the year 1827 the city of Bremen needed a new, more navigable harbour, because ships became bigger and bigger and the port in the city had been silted. The merchants, shipbuilder as well as the mayor and senat of Bremen decided to buy a piece of land near the mouth of the river from the King of Hanover, only a short distance from the deep water of the North Sea. They bought 122 hectares of land for the purpose of constructing a harbour and some houses for the dockworkers.

During the nineteenth and twentieth century the new harbour-city Bremerhaven developed to an important embarkation point for most emigrant leaving Germany or some other parts of Europe to the new world America.

Today Bremerhaven is the largest city on the German North Sea coast. The maritime character of the location is reflected in the scientific landscape, which is recognized internationally as well as nationally. In basic research, renowned institutes in the city are active in the fields of oceanography, climate research, port industry, sea transportation and logistics, wind energy and others, *e.g.* the food and fish industry. The cooperation with industry is of great significance for all institutes and scientists of different disciplines work together.

The famous research institute the German Maritime Museum in Bremerhaven, Leibniz Institute for German marine history (DSM) was opened in 1975 with one of the highlights, the cog, excavated 1962 at a harbour-expansion in Bremen. The DSM is one of eight research museums in the Leibniz Association combining research and education in a special way. It is the largest of its kind in Germany and focusses on the eventful and momentous relationship between human being and the sea. The research program is engaged in the use of ships in the context of marine economy and maritime research. The objects and sources form the beginning point of historical perspectives on the links between maritime history, archeology and related practices, through invention, use, research and reflection on marine technologies. This book provides results on one of these research areas.

Uta Halle

Introduction: Maritime Vessels and Their Significance for Early Modern Cultural Exchange

Simone Kahlow

If you want to build a ship, don't drum up the men to gather wood, divide the work, and give orders. Instead, teach them to yearn for the vast and endless sea.' Antoine de Saint-Exupéry (1900-1944) about the interaction of desire and motivation in *'Citadelle'*.

Cultural exchange is ubiquitous. The world in which we live today is shaped by global interconnectedness. Change through innovation, novel ideas, and communication strategies, and the exchange of consumer goods and products are everyday occurrences. Cultural exchange is invariably linked with interconnectivity, mobility, communication, adaptation as well as social and economic interconnectedness, and cannot be understood without ships as bearers of global transfer. Sea shipping is thus the carrier and motor for processes of global cultural exchange and interconnectivity. Only through sea shipping can the increase in worldwide adaptation and enculturation processes become possible.[1]

The far-reaching exchange of traded goods, ideas, and cultural expressions is not a modern phenomenon. *'Wide-ranging interconnectedness coupled with great historical depth'* can be observed early on. The oldest relevant evidence dates to the Stone Age and therefore can only be observed in the archaeological record. During the Aurignacian, for example, stones, decorative snails, and shells were sought-after trade goods (*cf.* Rähle 1978; Kompatscher and Kompatscher 2011). During Antiquity, the focus lay, amongst other things, on spices. During the Middle Ages, mostly northern Italian merchants from Venice, Genoa, and Pisa traded in East Asian goods. They procured them from the Levant, the end point of the Silk Road, shipped them across the Mediterranean and sold them across large parts of Europe (Wendt 2007, 22.). The networks under

---

1 Regarding opening up seaways, see de Barros 1910.

in: Kahlow, S. (ed.) 2018: *Transfer between sea and land. Maritime vessels for cultural exchanges in the Early Modern Period*, Sidestone Press (Leiden), pp. 15-22.

Figure 1: View of a Dutch (?) harbour in 1647. Etching by Wenzel Hollar.

observation here were restricted to geographically and culturally defined areas. Cultural exchange became truly 'global' in the strict sense of the word only at the beginning of the Early Modern Period, facilitated by sea shipping.

The desire for valuable goods for trade and prestige necessitated leaving dry land and taking to the open seas. This in turn brought about innovations in shipbuilding and navigation. These were equally the results of Arabian, Mediterranean and northern European achievements that can be observed since the late Middle Ages and benefitted processes of European expansion during the early modern period (Hundsbichler 1994; Phillips 1998; Feldbauer *et al.* 2001). Replacing the terrestrial link of the Silk Road by opening up the sea routes to India, the (European) discovery of the Americas, and the acquisition of Africa as an important trade partner all happened within one century. The world's interconnectedness took off – with ships as bearers of reciprocal cultural exchange (Fig. 1).

Current state of research

Cause and effect of cultural exchange regarding religions, cultural groups, and diseases have been the subjects of interdisciplinary research since the 1980s. Central to this research are the different phases of exchange, the balance or shift in balance of reciprocal relationships as well as the transfer or distribution of knowledge, ideas, and artefacts, amongst others. However, the main focus of research rested on economic aspects of reciprocal cultural exchange during the early modern period especially (Emmer and Beck 1988). Socio-historical studies are clearly in the minority and are mainly concerned with the analysis of written sources. Studies of archaeological artefacts from shipwrecks and their potential for making statements about cultural transfer are desirable but so far lacking. This seems rather strange, as ocean-going ships enable global trade on a big scale.

TRANSFER BETWEEN SEA AND LAND

'The ship was regarded as an essential engine of consolidation: be it a means of provision, exploration, and expansion as well as a transport medium for budding trade relationships' (Marboe 2009, 136).

Objects that obviously document cultural exchange from the sixteenth to the nineteenth century, when ships sailed the whole world, are known from collections and archaeological finds.[2] They are the material remains of occurrences that are represented in written and art historical sources. Collections have long been subjects of research, although the topic of sea shipping seems to play a minor role. However, the interrelation with cultural exchange is immediately obvious. Contrary to this, relevant finds from archaeological contexts have been highlighted in individual case studies and in relation to urban excavations. The itinerary of those exotic goods and the duration of transport are usually intangible. Finds from shipwrecks are usually different. They represent a so-called sealed deposit, *i.e.*, several objects that have been deposited simultaneously during a singular event and remained untouched until the time of discovery.

Since the invention and development of diving technology from the mid-20th century onwards, shipwrecks have increasingly become the subject of extensive investigations. The ships of the leading agents of European expansion can therefore be used for an appraisal of cultural exchange between Europe and other continents on a large scale. The focus is on ocean-going trade and war ships of leading maritime nations such as Portugal, Spain, the Netherlands, England, and France, as well as river barges enabling trade between the coast and the European hinterland. They sank due to highly diverse circumstances, such as hostile attacks or bad weather.

Special objects such as ship's bells, together with additional written sources, often allow the identification of the wreck and statements regarding age, time of sinking, crew, and cargo. Interdisciplinary investigations can thus enable extensive insights into cultural exchange during the early modern period.

Sea shipping during the Early Modern period: exchange and agents

The age of the European expansion began with Spanish and Portuguese expeditions during the fifteenth century (here and ff. see especially Wendt 2007). They sought a seaway to Asia in order to procure spices, precious stones, and textiles at lower cost, and thus discovered the Americas. Their increase in trade relationships with Africa, Asia, and the Americas meant that states and cities that had previously held monopoly positions, such as Italy, Venice, and Genoa, lost their supremacy. Instead, Lisbon and Antwerp became the most important trans-shipment hubs. Antwerp represented the most important hub for spices. All the pre-eminent European commercial establishments of the sixteenth century kept a branch in Lisbon. From there, European goods were shipped around the whole world, and here the well-known Augsburg merchant family Fugger also kept a business branch. The Fuggers recognised the importance of metals for global trade early on and bought copper and silver mines. They finally

---

2   Regarding collecting and collections *cf.* Findlen 1996; 2013; Auer *et al.* 1996; Daston and Park 1998; Förschler and Mariss 2017, amongst others.

managed to establish copper, silver, mercury, cinnabar, and tin monopolies. Indeed, the Fuggers' reciprocal cultural exchange activities are evidenced by archaeological finds. An archaeological investigation of the trade vessel Bom Jesus, wrecked on the coast of Namibia in 1533, revealed 1845 semi-spherical copper ingots bearing the Fugger trademark. They were intended to pay for spices, precious stones, and cloth. Non-European trade goods came from the Bom Jesus too (Knabe and Noli 2012). They are presumed to have been destined for Asian markets. Among these are whole elephant tusks – objects that are known as trade goods from the ships of other seafaring nations.[3] Ivory was coveted in India. And to obtain it, contacts with Africa were important. Here, communication between negotiators and local people, an understanding of language and culture as well as knowledge about demand were indispensable components of exchange. The crew aboard the Bom Jesus were aware of this too. The braids of horsehair, contained in the wreck, suggest as much. Horsehair braids served as a symbol of authority in West-African Benin. They therefore had a high prestige and commercial value on the West-African coast. It is assumed that these horse braids served as a medium for exchange, perhaps for ivory. Ivory originally came from the country's interior. Therefore it must have been brought to the coast specifically for the purpose of exchange. The afore-mentioned example supports the hypothesis that, during that time, exchange of knowledge or goods happened in a reciprocal manner. The Bom Jesus serves as an example for many aspects of cultural exchange and sea shipping presented in this volume: 1 – knowledge of have and want, 2 – trade via stopover points, 3 – presence of negotiators and knowledge of cultural habits in other countries, 4 – accumulation of knowledge through interdisciplinary investigations.

During the latter half of the sixteenth century, further European actors entered the stage. The northern part of the Netherlands separated itself from Spain in 1566. Amsterdam became Antwerp's successor as trans-shipment centre and stock market as well as a marine hub connected to nearly every part of the then known overseas world. At the start of this phase the Netherlands was partly still in Iberian service. During their dependency they accumulated knowledge and experience and gained access to Portuguese nautical charts. Subsequently the Netherlanders, too, set sail for the 'Spice Islands', competed against each other and thereby drove up the market prices. The founding of the *Vereenigde Oostindische Compagnie* (VOC) in 1602 remedied the situation. In contrast to the Portuguese, the VOC was better financed, organised more effectively, and had modern technological equipment. They maintained stopover points, *e.g.*, at the Cape of Good Hope in Africa, to offer travellers rest and provisions. The sea route from the Cape of Good Hope to Batavia, the domicile of the VOC in Asia, was particularly dangerous. Poor weather conditions were responsible for many ships drifting off too far east and shattering on the western coast of Australia.

Batavia was the trans-shipment centre for goods coming from the hinterland and destined for the European markets as well as for those for the country trade. Batavia was of strategic importance: For a long period of time, the 'Spice Islands' as well as China, Japan, and India were linked to Europe only via Batavia. These regions exported goods such as sugar, later also coffee, from the area around Batavia, nutmeg and cloves from the 'Spice Islands' and pepper from Sumatra. Additionally, there were pep-

---

3 Ivory tusks are known from the Vergulde Draeck (1656), amongst others (Green 1973).

per and cinnamon from Sri Lanka. Japan exported silver. Textiles, precious stones and luxury goods came especially from India. As a general observation, the spice business initially dominated the trade between Asia and Europe. Trade in textiles increasingly replaced the spice trade, until coffee and tea became the dominant trade goods (Denzel 1999; Edelmayer *et al.* 2001).

The chronological development in trade goods, and their transportation, that the VOC and its associate firm, the *Geoctroyeerde West-Indische Compagnie* (WIC), brought to other continents should also be investigated. For example, ivory, gold, and slaves were exported from Africa. Incidentally, archaeological finds of ivory in shipwrecks place an emphasis in trade on the seventeenth century. The WIC acted mainly in the Americas. There it traded in sugar, cotton, and coffee. The latter came originally from Asia and was cultivated by African slaves.

When, with England, another global player entered the stage, alliances shifted within the competition for profits. The Netherlands once again entered an alliance with Spain. England allied themselves with France and Portugal. It came to a major confrontation in 1651 when England started issuing the '*Navigation Acts*'. As a result, only English ships were allowed to deliver goods from overseas to the British Isles. This led to many conflicts. England built up its fleet and emerged victorious from a number of clashes with the Netherlands. The *East India Company* (EIC) was fundamentally more flexible than its competitors. For example, they did not buy and operate their own ships, which could potentially incur high losses. Instead the EIC hired the ships. In Asia, the EIC traded mainly in textiles and tea. They sourced slaves from Africa who were in turn indispensable for the plantations in the Caribbean and in North America. Just like their competitors, the EIC traded in cash crops. In America, these were mainly tobacco, cotton, sugar, and indigo, fetching high prices on the European markets.

Since the seventeenth century, France traded mainly in African slaves and American cane sugar. During the eighteenth century, the afore-mentioned maritime nations were struggling for the supremacy of certain trade monopolies. The associated European conflicts were felt in North America, the Caribbean, Africa, India, and even in Australia. The Netherlands finally joined the English side, and the VOC was dissolved in 1799. In 1815 the British Empire emerged victorious. French and Dutch settlements and monopolies were largely transferred into British hands.

Cultural exchange through transport of objects and shipwrecks

Cultural exchange on early-modern ocean-going ships and barges manifests itself in various areas, in shipbuilding, navigation and the military, as well as in everyday life at sea through material culture, nutrition, clothing, and medicine. Navigation and cartography are fundamental preconditions for any journey at sea, as soon as a ship lost sight of the coast and with it visual orientation. The same is true for ship building technology that, as Anne-Kathrin Piele shows in this volume, had already been of major importance for inland water navigation. Piele demonstrates a dynamic knowledge transfer since the early modern period, for optimising the construction of trade ships. Northern European shipbuilding technology in particular had a strong influence on shipbuilding in the Mediterranean.

The most striking indicators of cultural exchange are, above all, trade goods or non-domestic, exotic goods. These were already part of exchange processes before the so-called European expansion and were, in particular, given away or traded as prestige objects among others, as Gerson H. Jeute is able to show in this volume by means of a number of medieval objects. Based on the examined objects, Jeute also states that the 'East' was more familiar to the 'West' than had previously been assumed.

The relatively early detection of 'foreign' goods may also be responsible for the fact that more and more disciplines are investigating the question as to when the process of 'globalization' can first be observed.[4] Undoubtedly, an increase in interconnectedness was a prerequisite for the global exchange of objects, knowledge, plants, and animals. Patrick Cassitti, for example, demonstrates in this volume the diversity of goods and agents aboard, drawing on the case study of brassware from Nuremberg. Demand for these objects has grown steadily around the world since the Middle Ages. Corresponding finds are known from several shipwrecks on the coasts of England, Spain, Croatia, Africa and America. Cassitti's work impressively illuminates the connection between archaeological finds and written sources. It was thus possible to link the wreck of the Gagliana Grossa, which had been recovered from the Adriatic (wrecked in 1584), with documents and files in the state archives of Venice, and to obtain information on the owners, the cargo and the merchants. This large assemblage of Nuremberg brassware is so far unique and stands in stark contrast to the individual finds that are otherwise known through collections and excavations on land.

Björn Lindeke and Bo Ohlson firmly state on the basis of medical objects that trading goods presupposes knowledge exchange and at the same time documents changing attitudes. They show this with the case study of a Swedish warship wrecked in 1676. The Kronan yielded a hitherto unique assemblage of more than 30,000 objects. Of these, 180 entries were of a medical nature, evidence of a shift in medical science from pure Galenism to Paracelsianism.

The author's own contribution to this volume clarifies the diachronic and regional change in trade goods by looking at selected exotic animals. Simultaneously, different types of sources give an idea of the roles played by different agents (clients, merchants, negotiators, and people with specialist knowledge) in transporting these animals over months aboard trade ships.[5]

The path of research from wreck to written sources can also be done in reverse. Evidence for this is Stefan Geissler's investigation presented in this volume. His subject is Lloyd's List, an eighteenth century London business newspaper, offering economic facts about the contemporary merchant navy. The List is a global source of maritime history and the maritime trade network. It allows the making of statements about age, crew, cargo, departure and destination ports and the sinking dates of merchant ships mentioned by name. In addition, reasonably accurate temporal and local coordinates about individual wrecks provide the possibility to search for new sources in nearby port cities.

---

4   For instance recently in Hodos 2017 as well as the volume ‚Globalisierung‘, Mitteilungen der Deutschen Gesellschaft für Archäologie des Mittelalters und der Neuzeit 30.2017.
5   Meadow 2002; Harkness 2002; Parrish 2006; Neuwirth 2009; Becker-Braun 2012.

TRANSFER BETWEEN SEA AND LAND

The results presented in this volume provide evidence for the longstanding discussion of questions of historical cultural exchange within the humanities and cultural sciences. However, they also show that time and bearers of the increase in reciprocal transfer have hitherto been almost disregarded in interdisciplinary studies, even though they have significance for a more objective method of approach. Bringing together different sources in navigation history and maritime archaeology can now provide preliminary answers to the following questions:

1. How does cultural exchange manifest itself in sea shipping in Early Modern times?
2. Which evidence can be provided in this context?
3. What aspects of continuity and discontinuity are identifiable both regionally and temporally?

Overall, it becomes clear that in order to investigate ships as bearers of reciprocal cultural exchange during the Early Modern period a much larger database is essential. Moreover, the divergence between written and archaeological sources is proof that we can approach a true depiction of historical reality only through interdisciplinary research.

References

Auer, A., Sandbichler, V., Schütz, K. and Beaufort-Spontin, C. 1996. *Schloß Ambras*. Mailand und Kunsthistorisches Museum Wien: Electra.

Becker, J. and Braun, B. 2012 (eds.). *Die Begegnung mit Fremden und das Geschichtsbewusstsein*. Göttingen: Vandenhoeck & Ruprecht.

Daston, L. and Park, K. 1998. *Wonders and the order of nature, 1150-1750*. New York, Cambridge: Mass, Zone Books; Distributed by the MIT Press.

de Barros, J. 1910. *Auf dem alten Seewege nach Indien: Beschreibung der Entdeckungs- und Eroberungsfahrten der Portugiesen in den Jahren 1415 bis 1503, insbesondere die Fahrten des Generals Vasco de Gama / erzählt nach der Asia des João de Barros*. Köln: Schaffstein.

Denzel, M.A. 1999 (ed.). *Gewürze. Produktion, Handel und Konsum in der frühen Neuzeit : Beiträge zum 2. Ernährungshistorischen Kolloquium im Landkreis Kulmbach 1999*. St. Katharinen: Scripta-Mercaturae-Verlag.

Edelmayer, F., Landsteiner, E. and Pieper, R. 2001 (eds.). *Die Geschichte des europäischen Welthandels und der wirtschaftliche Globalisierungsprozess*. Wien, München: Verlag für Geschichte und Politik, Oldenbourg.

Emmer, P.C. and Beck, T. 1988 (eds.). *Wirtschaft und Handel der Kolonialreiche*. München: C.H. Beck.

Feldbauer, P., Liedl, G. and Morrissey, J. 2001 (eds). *Vom Mittelmeer zum Atlantik: Die mittelalterlichen Anfänge der europäischen Expansion*. Wien, München: Verlag für Geschichte und Politik, Oldenbourg.

Findlen, P. 1996. *Possessing Nature: Museums, Collecting and Scientific Culture in Early Modern Italy*. Berkeley: University of California Press.

Findlen, P. 2012 (ed.). *Early modern things*. New York: Routledge.

Förschler, S. and Mariss, A. 2017 (eds.). *Akteure, Tiere, Dinge: Verfahrensweisen der Naturgeschichte in der Frühen Neuzeit*. Böhlau: Böhlau Verlag.

Green, J.N. 1973. The wreck of the Dutch East Indiaman the Vergulde Draeck, 1656. *The International Journal of Nautical Archaeology and Underwater Exploration* 2.2, 267-289.

Harkness, D.E., 2002. 'Strange' Ideas and 'English' Knowledge: Natural Science Exchange in Elizabethan London, in: Smith, P.H. and Findlen, P. (eds.). *Merchants & marvels: Commerce, science and art in early modern Europe.* New York: Routledge, 137-160.

Hodos, T. and Geurds, A. 2017 (eds.). *The Routledge handbook of archaeology and globalization.* New York: Routledge.

Hundsbichler, H. 1994 (ed.). *Kommunikation zwischen Orient und Okzident, Alltag und Sachkultur: Internationaler Kongress, Krems an der Donau, 6. bis 9. Oktober 1992.* Wien: Verlag der Österreichischen Akademie der Wissenschaften.

Knabe, W. and Noli, D. 2012 (eds.). *Die versunkenen Schätze der Bom Jesus: Sensationsfund eines Indienseglers aus der Frühzeit des Welthandels.* Berlin: Nicolai.

Kompatscher, K. and Kompatscher, N.M. 2011. Mittelsteinzeitliche Fernverbindungen über den Alpenhauptkamm, in: Schäfer, D. (ed.). *Das Mesolithikum-Projekt Ullafelsen: The Mesolithic project Ullafelsen.* Darmstadt: von Zabern, 205-244.

Marboe, A. 2009. Das Schiff als Träger der spanischen Expansion in Amerika, in: Marboe A. (ed.). *Seefahrt und frühe europäische Expansion.* Wien: Mandelbaum-Verlag, 123-152.

Meadow, M.A. 2002. Merchants and Marvels: Hans Jacob Fugger and the Origins of the Wunderkammer, in: Smith, P.H. and Findlen, P. (eds.). *Merchants & marvels: Commerce, science and art in early modern Europe.* New York: Routledge, 182-200.

Neuwirth, M. 2009. Diplomatischer Austausch und globaler Kunsthandel um 1600, in: North, M. (ed.). *Kultureller Austausch: Bilanz und Perspektiven der Frühneuzeitforschung* Köln: Böhlau, 391-408.

Parrish, S.S. 2006. *American curiosity: Cultures of natural history in the colonial British Atlantic world.* Chapel Hill: University of North Carolina Press.

Phillips, J.R.S. 1998. *The medieval expansion of Europe.* 2nd ed., Oxford, New York: Clarendon Press.

Rähle, W. 1978. Schmuckschnecken aus mesolithischen Kulturschichten Süddeutschlands und ihre Herkunft, in: Taute, W. and Boessneck, J. (eds.) 1978. *Das Mesolithikum in Süddeutschland: Naturwissenschaftliche Untersuchungen.* Tübingen: Archaeologica Venatoria, 163-168.

Wendt, R. 2007. *Vom Kolonialismus zur Globalisierung: Europa und die Welt seit 1500.* Paderborn: Schöningh.

| TRANSFER BETWEEN SEA AND LAND

Asian Objects in Europe

Ways of Transcontinental Intertwining in the Middle Ages and the Early Modern Period

Gerson H. Jeute

Abstract

Long time before the discovery of the sea routes to India, a more or less intensive relationship existed between the continents. During the Early Middle Ages there has been a brisk exchange between the Orient and Northern Europe, and from there southwards. In the High Middle Ages and Late Middle Ages the relations slowed up but never stopped entirely. It was a pre-condition that a direct connection between West and East was sought in order to escape the dangerous paths along the Silk Road during the transition from the Middle Ages to the modern era. Asian objects which reached Europe at these times travelled by both ships and boats on large rivers as well as overland. This paper shows which objects reached Europe between the eighth and eighteenth centuries. It also shows in which social environment we find these objects today. It will attempt to trace the transport routes from Asia to Europe and the routes of distribution within Europe.

Keywords: cultural exchange, distribution, changing values, ceramics, faience, raqqa ware, Chinese porcelain, celadon, glass, oriental gold enamel glass, coins, dirham, spices, pepper, Early Modern Period, Middle Ages

Introduction

Objects that found their way from Africa or Asia to Europe in the Middle Ages and the Early Modern Period are often regarded today as very precious and as a rule assigned to a higher social class (Kerr 2004a; Spieß 2008; 2010; Ertl 2008). This results from the fact that such objects are usually only known to come from larger collections of art and rarities, that is, from a manorial context (Auer *et al.* 1996; Corrigan *et al.* 2015; Krahe 2016). Archaeological research has dug up numerous finds in the past decades which

in: Kahlow, S. (ed.) 2018: *Transfer between sea and land. Maritime vessels for cultural exchanges in the Early Modern Period*, Sidestone Press (Leiden), pp. 23-42.

can qualify and substantiate this. What is significant, is the way in which these archaeological objects are handed down. The often fragmented pieces come from settlement contexts, for example from waste pits and latrines, or they were lost in other ways by previous owners. The finds give us clues that they were once actually in use and not just served as precious objects. Thereby, the archaeological finds differ from the objects from the collection holdings, in which the artistic aspect is emphasized more.

The following is intended to provide some initial insight into this comprehensive topic. The focus is on the question of which finds and groups of finds have so far been brought forth by archaeology. Furthermore, both the temporal and social context will be examined in which these findings arise. Finally, the paths that these objects took on the way to their final owners will be questioned. All this could only be done fragmentarily as of yet, but nevertheless, some statements can be made.

State of research

The question of Asian objects in the European context is not yet very old in medieval and post-medieval archeology. John G. Hurst and David Whitehouse were the first to discuss archaeological finds from the Middle East and East Asia in Western Europe at the beginning of the 1970s (Hurst 1968; Whitehouse 1973). At the same time, presentations of Turkish finds in Hungary appear (Gyürky 1974). Then at the end of the 1980s, Ingmar Jansson dealt with Oriental objects in early medieval Scandinavia in a larger essay (Jansson 1988). For the first time ever, a larger region was processed comprehensively. With the increase in excavation activity throughout Europe from the 1990s, the number of finds in the form of smaller communication or a short mention in several essays continues to rise. Here one must particularly refer to the series of the *Lübecker Kolloquium zur Stadtarchäologie im Hanseraum* (a colloquium on urban archeology in the territory of the Hanseatic league).[1] In addition to that, there is the first monographic presentation of a find complex from the Buda Castle Palace by Imre Holl (Holl 2005; last Komori 2014). Another monography is a study by Jörg Drauschke on the distribution of objects from the Orient and Byzantium during the Merovingian period (Drauschke 2011). All these larger and smaller studies are usually limited in space and time, a cross-regional investigation or even a consideration of a *longue durée* has been missing so far (see Jeute 2013; 2017).

Methodical approach

On the question of how the objects came from Asia to Europe, the scheme of Jörg Drauschke (Fig. 1) based on ethnological models for the exchange of goods can be used (Drauschke 2011, 201-208). Objects in the inland that are known, say little about the way they were transferred. It is therefore important to include findings in the sense of a finding's context as well as the overall distribution. A great advantage of archaeological finds lies in this aspect, compared to the realities of the rarities collections.

---

1   The volumes follow thematically the meetings of the same name. Especially the volumes 'Der Handel' (volume II) and 'Luxus und Lifestyle' (volume VI) are the results.

Mechanisms of Distribution of Good (DoG)						
Exchange			Subsistence Economy	Robbery and War Booty	Tribute and Subsidy Payments	Mobility
Reciprocity	Redistribution	Market Exchange	DoG from Cooperative Works			Migration
						Exogamie
						Hiking Crafts
		Custom Work	DoG from Indivudual Work			Exile
		Interest and Fees				Travels
		Trade				

Figure 1: Mechanisms of Distribution of Goods.

Thus, distribution always means a flow of goods or services. The mechanism of exchange involves reciprocity, that is goods and services are exchanged within the framework of close social relations and under the principle of reciprocity. Market exchange, including trade, is also part of the exchange. It usually runs between equal partners. They exchange goods or services which they consider to be equivalent. We can accept trading especially for larger quantities. From an archaeological point of view, this means that there are several similar pieces in one place or a uniform regional distribution pattern of similar pieces. In the early Middle Ages, one may have had to accept several intermediate stages for trade, but later on it would be more and more direct. However, redistribution is also possible as a third form of exchange. It runs from hierarchically subordinate up to mostly political, higher-level headquarters. Ultimately, goods are then returned to the bottom.

In addition to the exchange, another form of distribution is gift exchange among rulers. Robbery and spoils of war were also conceivable for outstanding individual pieces. Here too, depending on the region of intermediate stages and not just directly, contact can be assumed. On the other hand, migration, exogamy, and exile are difficult to prove archaeologically, but there are at least written sources which indicate travelling and hiking crafts.

It should be noted, however, that especially in complex societies, as we already find them in medieval and post-medieval Asia and Europe, there is also a coexistence of different mechanisms.

Objects according to find groups

In the following, the Asian objects in Europe (Fig. 2) are divided into different groups. The group of ceramics will be subdivided again.

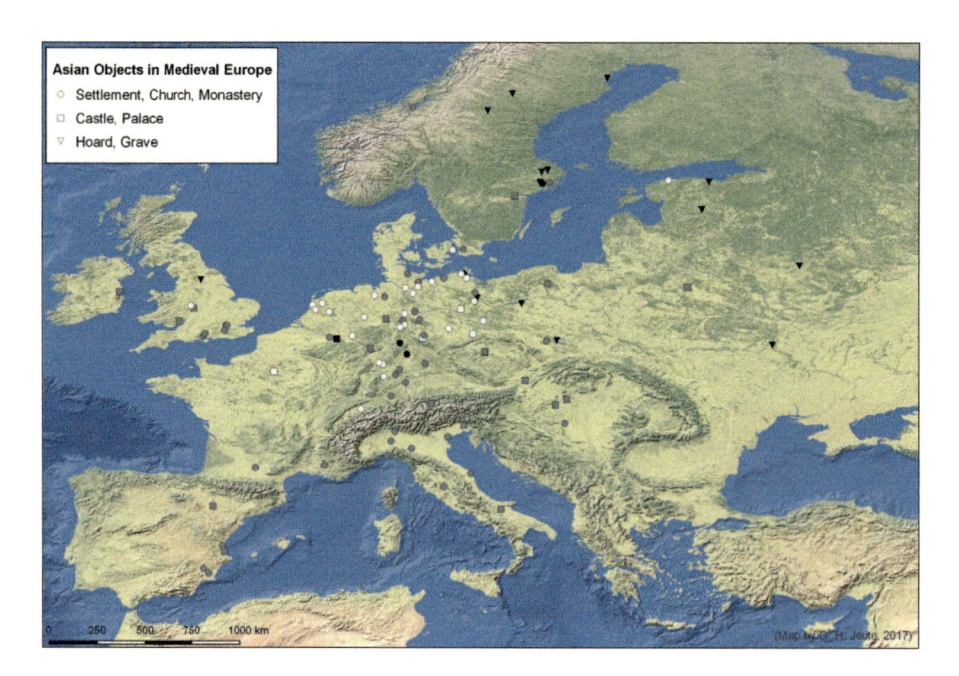

Figure 2: Map of Asian objects in Europe (black: Early Middle Ages, gray: High and Late Middle Ages, white: Early Modern Period).

Faience

Faience belongs to the early ceramic objects which reached us from the east in various quality. Two glazed and polychrome painted vessel fragments of a large plate of Islamic luster faience, were found in the former Benedictine abbey of Fulda, right next to the cathedral (Ludowici 1994). This product from the ninth to the eleventh century is rarely found outside the Mediterranean and the Islamic world (Mason 2004, 219-233; Falk 2001). The early dating suggests that the piece is from the Middle East. At the end of the High Middle Ages, the luster production was carried out for the first time on the Iberian Peninsula. Evidence is shown by several brightly-toned fragments of small shells found in Almería, Spain, originally from China (Heidenreich 2007, 243, 458, plate 6.a, Al – 30-33). They date between the tenth and twelfth centuries. They all have a golden lustre decoration, some even an Islamic inscription. Written sources of the first half of the twelfth century call the port of the city as a hub for oriental goods, which were exported to North Africa. Likewise, the production of chandelier faience in Almería for the thirteenth century is documented in writing. It is therefore conceivable that in Almería, the imported Chinese objects were adorned with Arabic script decoration in gold luster technique, and then further traded to North Africa or other regions.

Further Central European faience finds belong to the beginning of the late Middle Ages. During excavations at the castle complex of Falkenburg at Detmold, a small shard of Raqqa ware, amongst other things, came to light. It is a quartz frit ceramic, with polychrome underglaze painting. It dates back to the thirteenth century. The excavator assumes that it came to Westphalia through crusaders (Peine 2010, 80). From the Cucagna castle in the Italian Friuli come several fragments of light-clay pottery with cobalt blue and brown paint and hanging Kufi inscription. They date back to the third quarter of the thirteenth century. Due to the type of goods, decoration and glaze, they probably came from a Persian workshop (Grönwald 2013/2014, 200-211). No less than 11 albarelli from alkaline-glazed fritwares came from Plantation Place, London (Mincing Lane and Fenchurch Street; see Blackmore 2013, 65-68). They were probably imported from Syria as containers for spices or other exotic goods. They are identical to pieces from the late twelfth to the early thirteenth century, but could also belong to the fourteenth or fifteenth centuries due to the situation of lost property.[2]

Alfred Falk (Falk 2001, 619) names further sites of Persian faience in connection with John G. Hurst (Hurst 1968, 196): Stockholm (around AD 1300, with luster painting), Trondheim (with blue glaze and unclear dating) and Lund (probably fourteenth century). These pieces show how far north such objects have come. Here, certainly the East Atlantic trade and activities of the Hanseatic League contributed to the spread. In addition, this corresponds to the trade of exotic spices, such as pepper (see below, and Jahnke 2017), which already belonged to everyday life at this time. Whether the corresponding vessels, mostly Albarelli, can be regarded as transport vessels for these spices, cannot currently be determined. At least it can be said that they were probably more than just souvenirs of travellers and crusaders (so Falk 2001, 619). That such ceramics not only reached the coastal cities but also reached the hinterland, is shown by a similar piece from Erfurt, which belongs to the fifteenth century (Böhme and Ullrich 2004, 95-99). It belongs to the typical Raqqa goods and originates from the Middle East, presumably Syria. There are also four fragments of the Valencia product in Erfurt.[3]

Various pieces of the Turkish Iznik goods come from the Dominican monastery in Buda and date back to the first half of the sixteenth century (Gyürky 1974, 417-418). Fragments of light-colored, blue-painted Persian faience, came to be found in various places in Hungary in the seventeenth century, such as the in the city of Baja (Holl 2005, 156).

Porcelain

When one thinks of objects that have come to Europe from Asia, one probably thinks of Chinese porcelain first. Though, this arrived relatively late in the West, it then began to arrive in large numbers. These circumstances have shaped our present picture a great deal.

China held the monopoly on porcelain production for a long time. Arab traders negotiated the goods to the Middle East and Africa. Places such as Cairo, the most important port of transshipment in the South-Eastern Mediterranean, was also able to supply the cities of the Balearic Islands, Liguria and the Adriatic Sea. Therefore, in the area around Italy the earliest evidence appears in written sources (Kerr 2004b, 47; Whitehouse 1973, 63). From the seventeenth century onwards, Europe was able to trade directly with China through the establishment of trading companies and shipping routes. Yet it was not until the beginning of the eighteenth century, that the invention of the European hard-paste porcelain made production in Europe possible.

David Whitehouse names a fragment of a Yüeh-ware bowl from Lucera in Italy, which dates back to the eleventh century (Whitehouse 1973, 67). Yüeh-ware also

---

2   Furthermore, Iznik-Ware, which dated at the end of the fifteenth century (Blackmore 2013, 68).
3   Incidentally, Iberian ceramics are widespread in Western and Northern Europe.

comes from Valencia and was found there in the urban context of the ninth/tenth century (Heidenreich 2007, 243, 458, plate 6.a, Va – 45-49). However, this is not classic porcelain but a pre-form of porcelain. The oldest evidence of classical porcelain could be a fragment of a white porcelain dish from the Spanish town of Cullera dating back to the late Tang period, which is the tenth century (Heidenreich 2007, 458, plate 6.a, Cu – 8-9). A fragment of classic blue and white porcelain was found in Winchester, England in the late fourteenth or early fifteenth-century (Whitehouse 1973, 68).

Chinese porcelain, mostly of the seventeenth/eighteenth century, comes from numerous archaeological sites in Europe. On the one hand, there are fragments from the urban areas of Hamburg, Wolverhampton in England, and countless other cities. They stand opposite the finds from the Thuringian castle of Neideck, as well as the almost 200 vessels containing debris from the palace of Buda.[4] It is probably the largest archaeological ensemble of imported porcelain ever found in Europe.

Another small find complex comes from Hirsau in the Black Forest (Brand, 2003). It was rescued from the kitchen of a clerical school or from the living rooms above it. In addition to a few Chinese pieces, these are mainly Japanese imitations with polychrome enamel painting and blue-white background glaze. These imitations were usually of a slightly lower quality than the Chinese originals, but can be dated, in this case, to the second half of the seventeenth century.

Porcelain soon reached popularity, especially in the circles of the middle-class. However, this was not found in such high numbers as in manorial environments. In addition, for reasons of cost, more common people had to be take imitations.

The masses of porcelain that came to Europe from the seventeenth century onwards are shown in traditional study collections of major European museums or salvaged shiploads. At the auction of the wreckage of the Geldermalsen, more than 150,000 pieces were sold, including 19,535 coffee cups with saucers, 25,921 slop bowls, and 63,623 teacups with saucers (Ledderose 2000, 90 passim).

According to the studies of Lothar Ledderose, mass production in China was based on a modular system used in various spheres of life long before the appearance of Europeans. In ceramic production, however, European demand increased the modular system from the late sixteenth century (Ledderose 2000, 86).

European demand even changed the style of the products and adapted to the western taste. Customers, especially the Portuguese and the Spanish, were able to express their individual wishes and had their coats of arms or inscriptions affixed, or they combined their orders with catalogue-like templates (Ledderose 2000, 98-100). A fragment of a Portuguese faience vessel in Hamburg, for example, has no Asian origin but a Hamburg coat of arms and bears the year 1649 (Först 2006, 57-58; Falk 2007). The

---

4   Finds from the urban area at: Wedemeyer 1989, 48-60 and 52, Fig. 27 (Göttingen, Germany); Barry 1994 (London); Rötting 1999, 335-336 (Brunswick, Germany); Boschetti-Maradi 2006, 150-151 (Bern, Swiss); Först 2006; 2008, 235-236 (Hamburg); Bitter 2008, 159, 161 (Alkmaar, The Netherlands); Veeckmann 2008, 128 (Antwerp, The Netherlands); Krabath 2008; 2011 (Dresden, Germany, municipal and stately area); Mulsow 2008, 389 (Rostock, Germany); Hewitson et al. 2010, 45 (Wolverhampton, Great Britain); Nurk et al. 2011, 133 (Tallinn, Estonia); Schrickx and Duijn 2012; Bartels 2014 (Hoorn and Enkhuizen, The Netherlands); Wirth 2013, 94-95 (Mannheim, Germany); Søndergaard Kristensen 2014 (Copenhagen). Finds from the domain at: Lappe 1978, 145 and plate XXVI (Neideck, Germany); Ravoire 1998 (Roissy-en-France castle near Paris); Holl 2005 (Castle of Buda/Budapest, in addition also at last extensively Komori 2014 with further literature).

piece shows the tradition of adding owner brands to commissioned works. At the same time, such finds clearly show the trade route along the West Atlantic and North Sea coasts (also Böhme and Ullrich 2004, 101, fig. 15, in connection with John G. Hurst).

As a consequence of mass production and trade, traders were able to lower their prices while increasing their profits, so that larger sections of the population could participate in this luxury. Whenever a luxury object was too expensive, customers could soon fall back on imitations. It was even cheaper to use European imitations, initially with tin-glazed, light-toned earthenware and later also with domestic porcelain.

Porcelain is clearly a product that came to Europe via maritime vessels, firstly only across the Mediterranean, then later by sea directly from Southeast Asia. It reached the port cities and major centres but quickly reached the wider hinterland. As regards the question of ceramic transport from the German low mountain regions to Northern Germany, Stefan Krabath pointed out that river transport was more suitable for fragile freight than transport by land (Krabath 2008; 2011). This is even more true for valuable porcelain but was always dependent on the quantity.

Celadon

A special feature among the Asian objects is the material Celadon. This delicate, pale green glazed Chinese stoneware was always considered very valuable, such as the so-called Fonthill Vase (Kerr 2004b, 46; Whitehouse 1973, 70, plate XA) or the so-called Katzenelnbogen Bowl and therefore, is usually only found in stately collections. It reached Europe before AD 1500 (Ledderose 2000, 88; Kerr 2004b, 48; Whitehouse, 1973, 71, plate X.B). Both artworks have varied object biographies, with some reworking and some well-handled owner credentials. Thus, they are also interesting for cultural transfer research. The Fonthill Vase once had silver-gilt and enamel mounts. In the fourteenth century, the vase was a gift from the Hungarian King Louis to Charles of Durazzo, King of Naples. It was probably forty years earlier that it was brought to Europe by an embassy of Nestorian Christians from China, possibly even directly to the Pope in Rome. The Katzenelnbogen Bowl still has a silver-gilt mount embellished with the coat of arms of Count Philip of Katzenelnbogen, which he probably purchased on a trip to the East. The artificial rework probably took place in a Rhenish workshop in the middle of the fifteenth century. Until the end of the sixteenth century, the bowl was owned by the Landgraves of Hesse (Whitehouse 1973, 70-71). However, Celadon occasionally emerges even on excavations, as in the Italian city Lucera (Whitehouse 1973, 67). The pieces probably date back to the twelfth century. The Buda Palace contains parts of a jug, a plate and a bowl from the first half of the sixteenth century (Holl 2005, 174, plate 6.4, 151-152, figs. 103, 104). Individual fragments also come from a manorial context, for example from the city of Zaragoza of the eleventh/twelfth century. Besides this, there are pieces of the ninth/tenth centuries from an Islamic house in Valencia, both in Spain (Heidenreich 2007, 243).

Glass

Far more common in Europe than the aforementioned group, was oriental glass. Oriental gold enamel glasses used as lamps, derived from the Middle East, have mainly come to find themselves in museums- and art collections. In the meantime, they too are becoming more and more archaeological, as Andrea Wolf has established (Wolf

2003). Only recently Uwe Gross was able to assign further fragments to this group of objects (Gross 2012). Several colourless wall fragments from the Vestgasse in Ulm, Germany also with colourless or blue eyelet, once had the function of hanging devices. Thus there were at least two different hanging lamps. The Islamic models are painted with enamel and often have religious inscriptions. Evidence of glass oil lamps north of the Alps are rare. The late medieval piece from Ulm was probably not used in a household, but in a private chapel (Gross 2012, 51). It was a place in which the representation always stood strongly in the foreground.

Some glass finds from London are significantly older. From the city district around Mincing Lane and Fenchurch Street, for example, come fragments of blue sprinklers. They date from the middle of the eleventh century and the first quarter of the thirteenth century. Other fragments are known from further parts of the city (Tyson 2013, 71). The use of perfumes increased in Western Europe, especially in the late Middle Ages. It is still unclear whether the flasks came from the East to London as the containers for a specific liquid or if they were they valued as vessels in their own right.

It is the largest assemble of Islamic-style glass found in the UK. It is believed that some pieces arrived in England by crusaders or as diplomatic gifts. For pieces that came through trade, it is presumed that this trade was done through Italian dealers (Tyson 2013, 74). Due to a large number of finds, however, one can probably assume that the flasks were brokered by dealers.

What shows up in the English medieval metropolis is also confirmed on the continent. Since it is known that Oriental glass was found in Europe in castles, as well as in city centres and monasteries, nobles and wealthy citizens were amongst their owners.[5] The increased use of gold-enameled glass from the thirteenth century onwards goes hand in hand with the general increase in glassware for drinking at this time (Wolf 2003, 527). The locations of enamel-painted glass vessels from the High and Late Middle Ages have significantly increased in recent decades. It turns out that they were mass-produced products, some of which were series-produced and intended for a relatively broad, albeit wealthy, consumer class. From Lübeck, 22 Kleine Burgstraße ('*Kranenkonvent*'), comes a rather thick-walled piece of Islamic gold enamel glass. It is probably a drinking vessel, but it is also conceivable that it was part of a mosque lamp. There were at least five places of such findings in the thirteenth century in Lübeck. A piece from 32 Königstraße carries three human figures in the middle decoration. The musicians and dancers are bounded by two volumes whose transcriptions from the Arabic Naskh style reads: '*to be well for our Lord Sultan and King, the knower, and connoisseur [...]*' as well as '[...] *the king of the [...]*' ('*Wohl sein für unseren Herrn Sultan und König, den Wissenden und Kenner [...] der König der [...]*', see Steppuhn 2016, 45).

Already Andrea Wolf (2003, 526) pointed out that there are probably more archeological finds than specimens in the collections. Many of the finds date from the end of the thirteenth century and the beginning of the fourteenth century, including London, Stockholm, Brunswick, Maastricht, Opole, the Old Town of Prague, as well as the Castle in Prague. Finds are also known from ecclesiastical areas such as the monastery

---

5   In the fourteenth century, this also included the councilor family Pleskow from the Hanseatic city of Lübeck, mentioned by name (Wolf 2003, 527).

of Gnadental in Southwest Germany. While Wolf mentions finds in Spain, there are only a few in France (Wolf, 2003, 527).

The production period was between AD 1250 and 1350, but even in the sixteenth century, oriental glass was still produced. Imitations came out in the nineteenth century (Steppuhn 2014, 201-202; 2016, 45; Wolf 2003, 527).

After the decline of the Syrian and Egyptian production sites, Venice took over the production of high-quality glass and not only supplied Europe, but also the Orient with goods.[6] Above all, the shipping routes across the Mediterranean Sea served to intensify contact between the production centres. There was a close exchange of raw materials and manufacturing techniques between the Levant and Venice.

For Peter Steppuhn (2016, 49) the spread of Islamic gold enamel glasses from the thirteenth/fourteenth century in Central Europe does not show a clear focus and thus he assumes less of a targeted trade and more of a random distribution. He favours distribution mechanisms such as gifts, dowries, inheritance, booties or souvenirs, which were carried out in particular during pilgrimages and crusades. On the other hand, for Wolf's European-wide perspective, the growing number of finds of gold enamel glasses from a middle-class milieu concludes that these were also negotiated (Wolf 2003, 561). Another reason is that the prevalence of oriental glasses resembles that of European glass and is therefore probably the result of comparable commercial structures. It was also shown that this oriental glass often had a European metal or precious metal mount.

In addition to other commercial cities in Italy, Venice played a prominent role in the Oriental trade, because the trade routes led across the Mediterranean and the Atlantic to Northern Europe or via countless paths across the Alps to Nuremberg and Augsburg.[7] There was a trade route along the rivers from the Black Sea to the Baltic Sea as well. That route had already been active in early medieval times and used by the Vikings and Byzantines (see below). In this regard, Wolf refers in this context to the so-called Hedwig's cups for the High and Late Middle Ages, whose production regions were Egypt, Syria, or cities in Iraq (Wolf 2003, 561). The products were primarily negotiated to the north and later distributed by the Hanseatic League along the Baltic Sea. Since the motifs are not specifically Islamic, European dealers are presumed to be the contracting authorities (Wolf 2003, 561).

Further groups

The most impressive group of Eastern objects in the West are the Arab dirhams (Bálint 1981). A few decades ago, there were about 200,000 dirhams in Central, Eastern, and Northern Europe (Fig. 3). Due to the extensive use of metal detectors on excavations and in the field, new coins are constantly being added. While they used to come primarily from hoards or central locations, they are now more common in simple rural settlements.

Thomas Noonan and especially Sebastian Brather (1995/1996) have been intensively involved in the import of dirhams. This distribution was part of the Eastern Central and Northern European weight monetary system in the tenth century and was also intended to cover the regions' silver needs. It reached a peak between AD 940 and

---

6 At the same time, there was a considerable change and a reciprocity of cultural exchange.
7 For the distribution routes from northern Italy to southern Germany see the contribution of P. Cassitti in this volume.

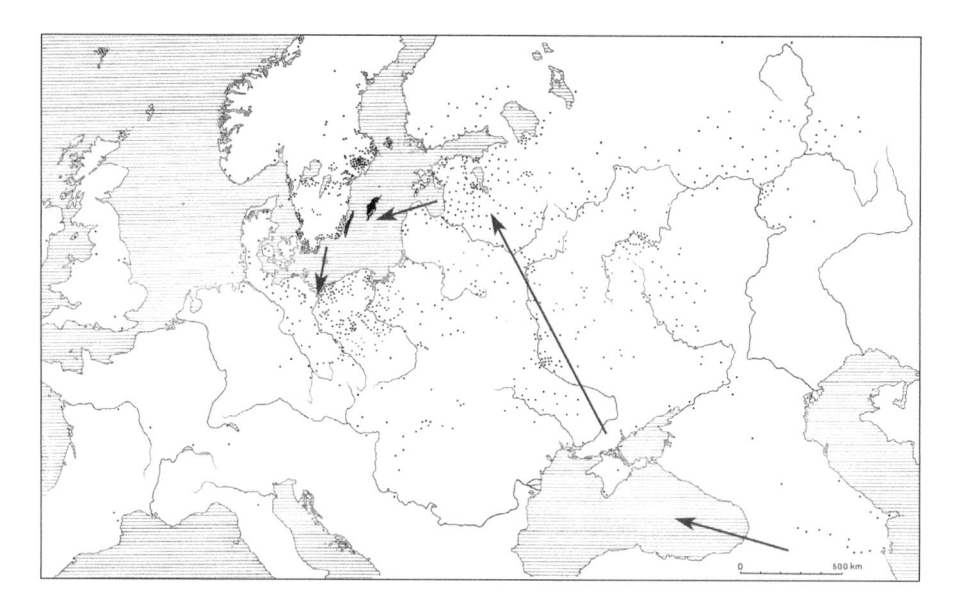

Figure 3: Trade route of early medieval dirhams.

970, then decreased and was replaced by coins of other origins. *'Hacksilver'* deposited in hoarding, probably served as a kind of savings deposit and was therefore, albeit at the lowest level, similar to the later known treasury, although the composition here was less intentional. The same may be true of Oriental tableware (Jansson 1988, 621-627), which appears occasionally in Scandinavia and in the British Isles.

One of the westernmost pieces of evidence of oriental coins is the discovery of an Indian Dramma in Lower Franconian Essleben (Bavaria) dating around AD 900 (see Abels 2001). This rural settlement was also connected to Eastern Central Europe via the River Main and important places like Bamberg. Similar coins can be found in Russia, Ukraine, Estonia, Poland and East Germany. However, these Indian coins cannot be considered detached from Arabian dirhams. Both varieties were part of the money-weight economy. They were used in the form of coins as well as hacksilver.

The route of the dirhams mainly followed along the Silk Road to the Black Sea, from there over the large rivers north through the Kievan Rus, away from the Baltic States over the Baltic Sea to Eastern Sweden, in particular to Birka and Gotland, and ultimately from there again to the south coast of the Baltic Sea towards the hinterland of East Central Europe (East Germany, Poland, Czech Republic).

Another group of objects brings us to the subject area of jewellery. Almandine garnet can be found as a gemstone, especially in the Merovingian period on many Southern German sixth century burial grounds. Archaeometric studies prove an origin from India and Sri Lanka. Almandine in larger quantities appears there in almost every cemetery and marks the outstanding burials. Therefore, the import of almandine to Europe must have taken place on a larger scale by traders (Drauschke 2011, 38-39; Greif 1998). The stone itself may have a lower value, which was only increased by craft-artful jewellery. Nevertheless, in the high and late Middle Ages, stones, especially gems still had a certain importance, for example as a means of exchange and payment for traders and travellers. Above all there is reference here to Marco Polo and his report (Marco Polo 1983, 68-69, 263).

While only a larger bag was needed for transporting gems, the raw materials of another exotic material required larger transport capacities. The most striking objects made of ivory are undoubtedly the Olifants, which today are mainly in art and treasure collections (Shalem 2004). In addition, ivory was used in the sacral field, such as for fittings of boxes and the like which was has been found so often since the early Middle Ages. Tusks of African and Asian elephants served as raw materials. As is known, Asian elephants have smaller tusks and live in less accessible habitats. This could also be an explanation for the archaeometrically proven African origin of the Merovingian leg discs (Drauschke 2011, 113-124). Where the high and late medieval ivory material comes from still has to be investigated archaeometrically. The same origin of the raw material can be assumed. However, there has been a change in the number of ultimate buyers, as ivory now hardly appears as a burial object, and even less so in the ecclesiastical and liturgical field.

The teeth of hippos, walruses and narwhales as well as sperm whales were used as substitute for ivory. Such a substitute is shown by a knob-like object from the sixteenth/seventeenth century at the London Globe Theatre which was made of elephant ivory (Bowsher and Miller 2009, 213). Tokens from the eleventh century-castle of Oldenburg are made of walrus teeth (Gabriel 1988, 229-236). This was certainly a material frequently used in the North and Baltic Seas, where it was readily available. By contrast, hippopotamus teeth were also used for human dentures, as a find from Antwerp shows. This piece dates back to the seventeenth/eighteenth century. It has single, simulated teeth, held together by a gold wire (Kahlow 2009, 209; Veeckmann 2008, 127).

Ivory came to Europe both by land and by sea, and the importance of the latter increased over time, as shown by the example of the shipwreck of the Vergulde Draeck, which had loaded numerous elephant tusks (Kahlow 2013; 2017 with references).

Live imports

The importation of live animals into Europe is also expected throughout the investigation period.[8] One famous animal I would like to mention here as an example is Abul-Abbas, the white Indian elephant, which was given to the Franconian ruler Charlemagne as a present from the Caliph of Baghdad (Hack 2011). King Matthias of Hungary rode through his country in AD 1485 with 24 camels, which can also be proven archaeologically by camel bone finds in Hungary (Bartosiewicz 1996), and the Tower of London had a menagerie with exotic animals in the thirteenth century (Parnell 1999). The preciousness of these animals also in the areas of origin and not only in the target areas is also apparent from the fact that as gifts, apparently large and white animals were preferred, which were certainly rarer than animals with the usual color.

The importation and keeping of exotic animals became more and more popular in the early modern period but remained a passion of the upper social class, similar to

---

8   This aspect is only briefly mentioned here. For a detailed treatment of the topic see the article of S. Kahlow in this volume.

curiosity cabinets. Sometimes it was only a short-term pleasure, as many animals rarely grew used to the climatic conditions in Europe. Added to this was the stress of transportation. The most famous of these innumerable victims was the so-called pygmy of Tyson, a chimpanzee that died shortly after crossing from Africa to Europe in AD 1698, becoming one of the earliest collection objects of the Natural History Museum in London. Some animal species were even extinct before they became well known in Europe, such as the dodo (*Raphus cucullatus*).

Spices and fruits

Botanical remains of oriental origin are rarely handed down, since they are strongly dependent on conservation conditions (Wiethold 2007). Meanwhile, in several North German Hanseatic cities, including Bremen (Rech 2004, 361), individual grains of black pepper from the thirteenth century have appeared (Fig. 4). The Bremen peppercorn was in a pot that was recovered from a sewer. According to the shape of the pot, it dates to the first half of the thirteenth century. Written sources confirm such findings. Thus, before AD 1288, individual citizens of Bremen had to deliver taxes in the form of pepper (*ibid.*). Another find, also from the thirteenth century, comes from an upscale district of the Hanseatic city of Rostock (Wiethold 2007, 212).

The use of pepper was widespread and was part of everyday life in larger cities (Jahnke 2017). But even in rural areas, pepper must have played a previously unimaginable role. This is indicated by tithes, which are recorded in the land register ('*Landbuch*') of the Mark of Brandenburg from AD 1375. Mills mainly had to deliver grain or money (Peschke 1937). Other taxes often came in its place. So different mills had to deliver wax or pepper. The mills in Waltersdorf (Teltow region), Sandfurt and Syppelinghe had to pay one pound of pepper each. Likewise, the village of Fischeribbe

Figure 4: Map of evidence of oriental spices in Europe (black: Early Middle Ages, white: Early Modern Period).

TRANSFER BETWEEN SEA AND LAND

in the region of Altmark had to pay the same (*'Molendinum dat 1 libram piperis illis de Luderitz'*, after Peschke 1937, 28). But also the fisheries had taxes in the form of pepper, for example for the eel catch.

Other spices and fruits are so far rare. Finds of nutmeg come from the Slovak Brno and the Northern Polish Elbląg (Wiethold 2007, 214), and evidence of fig kernels (*Ficus carica*) are also found in Bremen (Rech 2004, 362).

In addition to spices, exotic fruits were also very popular. The last remnant of a charred rice grain was found in the Danish municipality of Sorø and dated back to the fifteenth/sixteenth century (Karg 2008, 100). It is definitely an import according to the Danes, and 'only' comes from Southern Europe. According to Carsten Jahnke, rice appears in Northern Germany in layers of the late thirteenth century, but, in England it appears much earlier (Jahnke 2017, 35). Rice is, therefore, a medieval everyday commodity that can be detected almost everywhere. It should be noted that the grains were imported mostly unpeeled in the Middle Ages and were husked shortly before preparation. Thus, they were better to transport and more durable. This is why, in particular, husks are found in the find (Jahnke 2017, 36).

As is similar for figs, the cultivation area for rice in the thirteenth century was mainly in the Western Mediterranean. Later, there were also fields in the Italian Po Valley and in the area of today's Turkey (Jahnke 2017, 33-35). The rice, which was always negotiated with almonds, reached England as well as Bruges and Amsterdam by sea.

It should also be mentioned that raisins were also produced in the Mediterranean for export and were mainly negotiated to Northern Europe. Other growing areas were in the Levant.

That non-native plants and fruits – whether from Asia or later from the New World – which were in high demand in broad social circles, show early modern pumpkin seeds, that could be detected at several sites in London (Bowsher and Miller 2009, 149), for example.

As a result of the commercial growth of Europe from the thirteenth century, there was a strong demand for Mediterranean products in Northern Europe. This changed the economic structure in the growing areas. Religious boundaries between Christianity and Islam hardly played a role in trade relations. Imported food was already part of everyday life in a broader urban middle and upper class as well as in the aristocracy (Jahnke 2017, 37).

Optional extras

A few special features for which parallels are largely missing should be mentioned here. A belt bag, which is said to be made of the skin of an Indian or Indonesian Varane lizard, was found in Rösta, Central Sweden in a late Viking grave (Jansson 1988, 613). A bronze Buddha of the Viking era, which was probably produced in the sixth or seventh century in Northern India and was found together with other singular objects on the site of the trading settlement in Helgö (Jansson 1988, 629-630). A vessel from Venice may be associated with one of the most famous Oriental travellers. The so-called Marco Polo Jar (Whitehouse 1973, 71-72, plate IX. C) has parallels in Malaysia that belonged to the sixteenth or seventeenth century. Therefore, the allocation of the known travelling salesman has so far been uncertain. However, a recent study (Meicun and Zhang 2018) comes to the conclusion that the vessel from Qingbai porcelain dates back to the thirteenth century and can therefore be connected with Marco Polo.

A Polynesian fruit steamer made of reddish stone was on its way to Europe, but never arrived there (Gesner 1991, 43). A member of the crew of HMS Pandora had apparently brought it as a souvenir, but had to let it go when the ship sank off Australia. The same applies to a set of fishing hooks from this ship (Gesner 1991, 55). Here is an example of how foreign objects slowly reached the lower social strata as a result of the growing together of the continents, whether as a souvenir, barter or commercial object or a gift.

Finally, it should be mentioned that a fragment of a late medieval bell, that was found in medieval London apparently came from Japan (Egan 2004). It obviously got there even before the island state officially opened to the then-known world.

Cultural exchange from the point of view of the objects

The aspect of cultural exchange is once again particularly clear when one looks at the reworking and the potential value of the objects (see Fig. 5). Various Asian objects in the collections often have gold or silver surrounds made in Europe (Kerr 2004a, 225). The artistically designed feet, lids etc. give the object a quality that goes beyond the already existing one. On a smaller scale, this is also conceivable for the abovementioned Chinese stoneware fragment, which was provided with the Arabic script decoration in Almería (Heidenreich 2007, 243) or for an Indian Dramma, which became an earring near Smolensk (Abels 2001, 148).

The value of objects could change through cultural exchange. Most of the objects from the East had a higher value in Europe than in their areas of origin. However, the

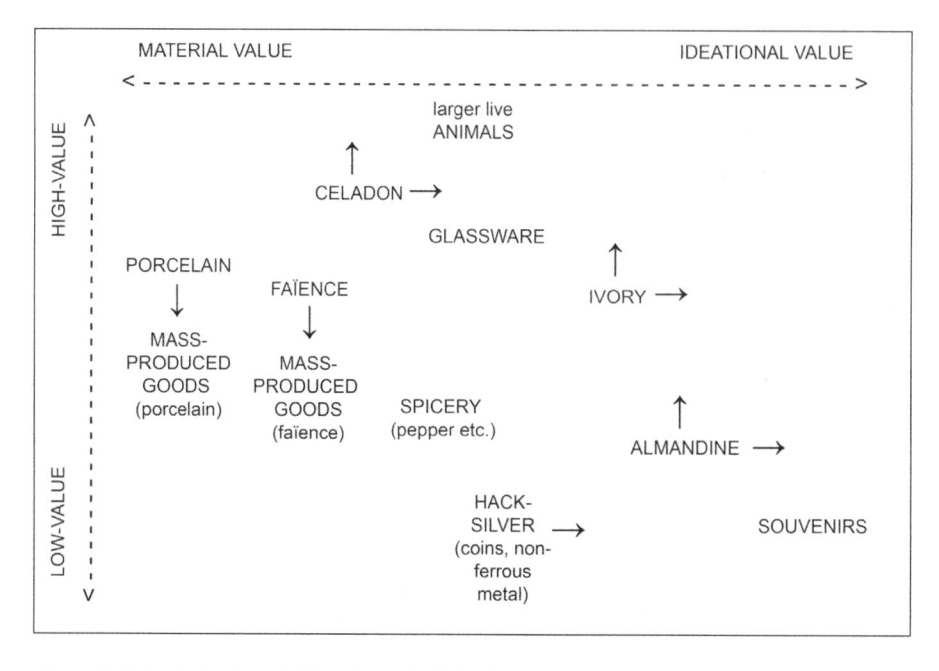

Figure 5: Potential value of things imported into Europe.

TRANSFER BETWEEN SEA AND LAND

value could decrease if objects were mass produced and negotiated. This made them accessible to a wider public. Other objects, as mentioned, had an increase in value if they were adapted. In addition to the purely material value, there was also a change of value in other ways, because souvenirs or processed pieces could also have an artistic and emotional side, which could not be balanced out with material counterparts.

Despite there being fragmentary references to imported objects, the connection between Asia and Europe can be seen. The almandine trade between Southern Asia and Central and Western Europe in the sixth century had a certain level, which fell slightly in the following century and only completely collapsed later. During the period of Charlemagne, there was, for a short time, intense contact with the Orient, which did not continue in the same intensive manner in the ninth and tenth centuries in Western Europe. Nevertheless, there were contacts from Central and Eastern Europe to the Middle East as the early medieval weight monetary system of that time clearly shows. The Crusades from the eleventh century onwards brought the East closer to the West and certainly increased the import of objects a little, but even more so were the activities of the travelling missionaries and merchants of the twelfth and thirteenth centuries. The latter moved spatially beyond the Middle East to East and Southeast Asia. The Mongol invasions initially reduced development slightly but also brought contacts in an opposite direction. However, the intensive search for a sea route to India brought a hitherto unknown upswing in relations between East and West. Even if it was initially to the South, always along the West African coast or even west towards America, so their destination was always the Indian subcontinent and the immediate adjacent regions. With the establishment of trade companies in East Asia, this development was to culminate for the time being. The connections and routes between Asia and Europe existed at all times and contact never really ceased.

References

Abels, B.-U. 2001. Eine indische Dramma aus Unterfranken, in: Pohl, E., Recker, U. and Theune, C. 2001 (eds.). *Archäologisches Zellwerk. Beiträge zur Kulturgeschichte in Europa und Asien. Festschrift für Helmut Roth.* Internationale Archäologie, Studia honoraria 16. Rahden/Westf.: Leidorf, 145-152.

Auer, A., Sandbichler, V., Schütz, K. and Beaufort-Spontin, Chr. 1996. *Schloß Ambras.* Mailand: Electa.

Bálint, C. 1981. Einige Fragen des Dirhem-Verkehrs in Europa. *Acta Archaeologica Academiae Scientiarum Hungaricae* 33, 105-131.

Bartels, M. 2014. *Portugese pracht uit de Westfriese Gouden Eeuw.* Archeologie in West-Friesland 12. Hoorn: Archeologie West-Friesland.

Bartosiewicz, L. 1996. Camels in antiquity: the Hungarian connection. *Antiquity* 70, 447-453.

Barry, J. 1994. Eighteenth century Chinese export porcelain from three London sites. *London archaeologist* 7, 150-156.

Bitter, P. 2008. Wealth and Waste – Aspects of a luxurious Lifestyle in Alkmaar, in: Gläser, M. (ed.). *Luxus und Lifestyle. Lübecker Kolloquium zur Stadtarchäologie im Hanseraum VI.* Lübeck: Schmidt-Römhild, 151-168.

Blackmore, L. 2013. Imported ceramics, in: Pitt, K. with Blackmore, L., Dyson, T. and Tyson, R. *Medieval to early post-medieval tenements and Middle Eastern imports. Excavations at Plantation Place, City of London, 1997-2003*. MOLA Monograph 66. London: Museum of London Archaeology, 64-71.

Böhme, M. and Ullrich, B. 2004. Mediterrane Keramik im spätmittelalterlichen Erfurt. *Alt-Thüringen* 37, 83-108.

Boschetti-Maradi, A. 2006. *Gefässkeramik und Hafnerei in der Frühen Neuzeit im Kanton Bern*. Schriften des Bernischen Historischen Museums 8. Bern: Verlag Bernisches Historisches Museum.

Bowsher, J. and Miller, P. 2009. *The Rose and the Globe – playhouses of Shakespeare's Bankside, Southwark. Excavations 1988-91*. MOLA Monograph 48. London: Museum of London Archaeology.

Brand, B. 2003. Ostasiatisches Porzellan des 17. Jahrhunderts aus Hirsau im Schwarzwald, in: Ericsson, I. and Losert, H. (eds.). *Aspekte der Archäologie des Mittelalters und der Neuzeit. Festschrift für Walter Sage*. Bamberger Schriften zur Archäologie des Mittelalters und der Neuzeit 1. Bonn: Habelt, 81-85.

Brather, S. 1995/1996. Frühmittelalterliche Dirham-Schatzfunde in Europa. Probleme ihrer wirtschaftsgeschichtlichen Interpretation aus archäologischer Perspektive. *Zeitschrift für Archäologie des Mittelalters* 23/24, 73-153.

Corrigan, K.H., Campen, J.v., Diercks, F. and Blyberg, J.C. 2015 (eds.). *Asia in Amsterdam. The culture of luxury in the Golden Age*. New Haven: Peabody Essex Museum.

Drauschke, J. 2011. *Zwischen Handel und Geschenk. Studien zur Distribution von Objekten aus dem Orient, aus Byzanz und aus Mitteleuropa im östlichen Merowingerreich*. Freiburger Beiträge zur Archäologie und Geschichte des ersten Jahrtausends 14. Rahden/Westfalen: Leidorf.

Egan, G. 2004. A japanese bell from medieval London?, in: Grabowski, M., Mührenberg, D., Schalies, I. and Steppuhn, P. (eds.). *Curiosa Archaeologica. Ungewöhnliche Einblicke in die Archäologie. Eine Festschrift für Alfred Falk*. Archäologische Gesellschaft der Hansestadt Lübeck, Jahresschrift 5, 2002/2003. Lübeck: Archäologische Gesellschaft der Hansestadt Lübeck, 28-31.

Ertl, Th. 2008. *Seide, Pfeffer und Kanonen. Globalisierung im Mittelalter*. Geschichte erzählt 10. Darmstadt: Primus.

Falk, A. 2001. Fayence, in: Lüdtke, H. and Schietzel, K. (eds.). *Handbuch zur mittelalterlichen Keramik in Nordeuropa*. Schriften des Archäologischen Landesmuseums 6.1. Neumünster: Wachholtz, 613-631.

Falk, A. 2007. Portugiesische Fayence in Lübeck. *Mitteilungen der Deutschen Gesellschaft für Archäologie des Mittelalters und der Neuzeit* 18, 93-100.

Först, E. 2006. Zerbrochen und weggeworfen, in: Weiss, R.-M. (ed.). *Der Hamburger Hafen – Das Tor zur Welt im Spiegel archäologischer Funde*. Veröffentlichungen des Helms-Museums, Hamburger Museum für Archäologie und Geschichte Harburgs 93. Hamburg: Helms-Museum, 39-76.

Först, E. 2008. Archäologische Zeugnisse luxuriösen Lebensstils in Hamburg, in: Gläser, M. (ed.). *Luxus und Lifestyle. Lübecker Kolloquium zur Stadtarchäologie im Hanseraum VI*. Lübeck: Schmidt-Römhild, 225-240.

Gabriel, I. 1988. Hof- und Sakralkultur sowie Gebrauchs- und Handelsgut im Spiegel der Kleinfunde von Starigard/Oldenburg. *Bericht der Römisch-Germanischen Kommission* 69, 103-291.

Gesner, P. 1991. *Pandora. An Archaeological Perspective.* Brisbane: Queensland Museum.

Greif, S. 1998. Naturwissenschaftliche Untersuchungen zur Frage der Rohsteinquellen für frühmittelalterlichen Almandingranatschmuck rheinfränkischer Provenienz. *Jahrbuch des Römisch-Germanischen Zentralmuseums Mainz* 45.2, 599-646.

Grönwald, H. 2013/2014. *Archäologie und Geschichte des hoch- und spätmittelalterlichen Landesausbaus im Friaul. Rolle und Entwicklung der Burg Cucagna und ihrer Ausstattung im Nordosten Italiens.* Inaugural-Dissertation. Freiburg.

Gross, U. 2012. Luxusleuchte aus der Latrine. Eine gläserne Lampe orientalischen Typs aus dem spätmittelalterlichen Ulm. *Denkmalplege in Baden-Württemberg* 41.1, 50-51.

Gyürky, K.H. 1974. Venezianische und türkische Importartikel im Fundmaterial von Buda aus der ersten Hälfte des 16. Jahrhunderts. *Acta Archaeologica Academiae Scientiarum Hungaricae* 26, 413-423.

Hack, A. Th. 2011. *Abul Abaz. Zur Biographie eines Elefanten.* Jenaer mediävistische Vorträge 1. Badenweiler: Franz Steiner.

Heidenreich, A. 2007. *Islamische Importkeramik des hohen Mittelalters auf der Iberischen Halbinsel. Unter besonderer Berücksichtigung der frühen Goldlüsterproduktion im Untersuchungsraum.* Iberia Archaeologica 10. Mainz am Rhein: Philipp von Zabern.

Hewitson, Chr., Ramsey, E., Shaw, M., Hislop, M. and Cuttler, R. 2010. *The Great Hall, Wolverhampton: Elizabethan Mansion to Victorian Workshop. Archaeological Investigations at Old Hall Street, Wolverhampton, 2000-2007.* Birmingham Archaeology Monograph Series 5/BAR British Series 517. Oxford: Archaeopress and Birmingham Archaeology.

Holl, I. 2005. *Fundkomplexe des 15.-17. Jahrhunderts aus dem Burgpalast von Buda.* Varia Archaeologica Hungarica 17. Budapest: Archäologisches Institut der Ungarischen Akademie der Wissenschaften.

Hurst, J.G. 1968. Near Eastern and Mediterranean Medieval Pottery Found in North West Europe. *Res Mediaevales, Ragnar Blomqvist. Archaeologica Lundensia 3*, 195-204.

Jahnke, C. 2017. Globalisierung in der Vormoderne. Die globalisierte Welt des Mittelalters – die Hanse, Norddeutschland und der Mittelmeerraum. *Mitteilungen der Deutschen Gesellschaft für Archäologie des Mittelalters und der Neuzeit* 30, 33-40.

Jansson, I. 1988. Wikingerzeitlicher orientalischer Import in Skandinavien. *Bericht der Römisch-Germanischen Kommission* 69, 564-647.

Jeute, G.H. 2013. Materielle Hinterlassenschaften aus Fernkontakten und der Versuch ihrer sozialen Interpretation. *Mitteilungen der Deutschen Gesellschaft für Archäologie des Mittelalters und der Neuzeit* 25, 225-234.

Jeute, G.H. 2017. Zur Frage einer Globalisierung im Mittelalter im Hinblick auf transkontinentale Verflechtungen. *Mitteilungen der Deutschen Gesellschaft für Archäologie des Mittelalters und der Neuzeit* 30, 25-32.

Kahlow, S. 2009. Prothesen im Mittelalter – ein Überblick aus archäologischer Sicht, in: Nolte, C. (ed.). *Homo debilis. Behinderte – Kranke – Versehrte in der Gesellschaft des Mittelalters*. Studien und Texte zur Geistes- und Sozialgeschichte des Mittelalters 3. Korb: Didymos, 203-223.

Kahlow, S. 2013. Archäologische Erkenntnisse zu medizinischen Tätigkeiten auf Schiffen der Frühen Neuzeit, in: Nolte, C. (ed.). *Phänomene der 'Behinderung' im Alltag. Bausteine zu einer Disability History der Vormoderne.* Studien und Texte zur Geistes- und Sozialgeschichte des Mittelalters 8. Affalterbach: Didymos, 125-148.

Kahlow, S. 2017. Globale Vernetzung in der frühen Neuzeit als Sprungbrett für die Entwicklung der medicina nautica. *Mitteilungen der Deutschen Gesellschaft für Archäologie des Mittelalters und der Neuzeit* 30, 163-174.

Karg, S. 2008. Diversität der Nutzplanzen im Mittelalter Nordeuropas. *Archäologische Informationen* 31, 97-102.

Kerr, R. 2004a. Asia in Europe: Porcelain and Enamel for the West, in: Jackson, A.M.F. and Jaffer, A. (eds.). *Encounters. The Meeting of Asia and Europe, 1500-1800.* London: Victoria & Albert Museum, 222-231.

Kerr, R. 2004b. Chinese Porcelain in Early European Collections. In: Jackson, A.M.F. and Jaffer, A. (eds.). *Encounters. The Meeting of Asia and Europe, 1500-1800.* London: Victoria & Albert Museum, 44-51.

Komori, T. 2014. A budavári királyi palota porcelán leletanyagának kutatása új szempontok alapján. *Budapest Régiségei* 47, 313-338.

Krabath, St. 2008. Chinesische Tradition – sächsische Innovation. Frühe Porzellanfunde aus Stadtkerngrabungen (Reinhard Spehr zum 70. Geburtstag). *Archæo* 5, 40-44.

Krabath, St. 2011. *Luxus in Scherben. Fürstenberger und Meißener Porzellan aus Grabungen.* Dresden: Landesamt für Archäologie Sachsen.

Krahe, C. 2016. *Chinese Porcelain in Habsburg Spain.* Madrid: Centro de Estudios Europa Hispánica.

Lappe, U. 1978. Ruine Neideck in Arnstadt. Ein Beitrag zur materiellen Kultur des 17. Jahrhunderts. *Alt-Thüringen* 15, 114-158.

Ledderose, L. 2000. *Ten Thousand Things. Module and Mass Production in Chinese Art.* Bollingen Series XXXV:46. Princeton: Princeton University Press.

Ludowici, B. 1994. Frühmittelalterliche islamische Fayence aus Fulda. *Germania* 72, 612-613.

Marco Polo 1983. *Il Milione. Die Wunder der Welt.* Translation by E. Guignard. Zürich: Manesse.

Mason, R.B.J. 2004. *Shine Like the Sun. Lustre-Painted and Associated Pottery from the Medieval Middle East.* Bibliotheca Iranica, Islamic Art and Architecture Series 12. Toronto: Royal Ontario Museum.

Meicun, L. and Zhang, R. 2018. A Chinese Porcelain Jar Associated with Marco Polo: A Disussion from an Archaeological Perspective. *European Journal of Archaeology* 21.1, 39-56.

Mulsow, R. 2008. Luxus und Oberschichten in Rostock, in: Gläser M. (ed.). *Luxus und Lifestyle. Lübecker Kolloquium zur Stadtarchäologie im Hanseraum VI.* Lübeck: Schmidt-Römhild, 377-394.

Nurk, R., Kadakas, V. and Toss, G. 2011. Preliminary archaeological investigations in the area of the medieval and post-medieval harbour of Tallinn. *Archaeological Fieldwork in Estonia 2011*, 125-136.

Parnell, G. 1999. *The Royal Menagerie at the Tower of London.* Leeds: Royal Armouries Museum.

Peine, H.-W. 2010. Raqqa-Ware und Wolfsangel – Alltagsleben auf der Falkenburg im 13. Jahrhundert. *Archäologie in Westfalen-Lippe* 2009, 78-81.

Peschke, W. 1937. *Das Mühlenwesen der Mark Brandenburg. Von den Anfängen der Mark bis um 1600.* Inaugural-Dissertation. Berlin.

Ravoire, F., 1998. *La vaiselle de terre cuite en Île-de-France entre la fin du XVe et la première moitié du XVIIe s. Définition d'un faciès régional.* Lille.

Rech, M. 2004. *Gefundene Vergangenheit – Archäologie des Mittelalters in Bremen. Mit besonderer Berücksichtigung von Riga.* Bremer Archäologische Blätter, Beiheft 3. Bremen 2004.

Rötting, H. 1999. Archäologische Erkenntnisse zum Handel in Braunschweig vom 12. bis zum 17. Jahrhundert, in: Gläser, M. (ed.). *Der Handel. Lübecker Kolloquium zur Stadtarchäologie im Hanseraum II.* Lübeck: Schmidt-Römhild, 331-347.

Schrickx, Chr. and Duijn, D. 2012. *Handel met sultan en sjah. Archeologische vondsten van Turks en Perzisch aardewerk uit de Gouden Eeuw in Horn en Enkhuizen.* Archeologie in West-Friesland 8. Hoorn: Archeologie West-Friesland.

Shalem, A. 2004. *The Oliphant. Islamic Objects in Historical Context. Islamic History and Civilisation.* Studies and Texts 54. Leiden and Boston: Brill.

Spieß, K.-H. 2008. *Fürsten und Höfe im Mittelalter.* Darmstadt: Wissenschaftliche Buchgesellschaft.

Spieß, K.-H. 2010. Asian Objects and Western European Court Culture in the Middle Ages, in: North, M. (ed.). *Artistic and Cultural Exchanges between Europe and Asia, 1400-1900. Rethinking Markets, Workshops and Collections.* Surrey and Burlington: Ashgate, 9-28.

Søndergaard Kristensen, R. 2014. Made in China: import, distribution and consumption of Chinese porcelain in Copenhagen c. 1600-1760. *Post-Medieval Archaeology* 48.1, 151-181.

Steppuhn, P. 2014. Emailbemalte Gläser des 13./14. Jahrhunderts aus der Altstadt von Lübeck. In: Falk, A., Müller, U. and Schneider, M. (eds.). *Lübeck und der Hanseraum. Beiträge zur Archäologie und Kulturgeschichte. Festschrift für Manfred Gläser.* Lübeck: Schmidt-Römhild, 193-206.

Steppuhn, P. 2016. *Mittelalterliche und frühneuzeitliche Glasfunde aus der Altstadt von Lübeck.* Lübecker Schriften zu Archäologie und Kulturgeschichte 30. Rahden/Westf.: Leidorf.

Tyson, R. 2013. Imported glass, in: Pitt, K. with Blackmore, L., Dyson, T. and Tyson, R. *Medieval to early post-medieval tenements and Middle Eastern imports. Excavations at Plantation Place, City of London, 1997-2003.* MOLA Monograph 66. London: Museum of London Archaeology, 71-78.

Veeckman, J. 2008. Luxury in medieval and post medieval Antwerp: an archaeological approach, in: Gläser, M. (ed.). *Luxus und Lifestyle. Lübecker Kolloquium zur Stadtarchäologie im Hanseraum VI.* Lübeck: Schmidt-Römhild, 121-129.

Wedemeyer, B. 1989. *Coffee de Martinique und Kayser Thee. Archäologisch-volkskundliche Untersuchungen am Hausrat Göttinger Bürger im 18. Jahrhundert.* Materielle Kultur: Archäologie – Baugeschichte – Nachbarwissenschaften 1. Göttingen: Edition Moderne Archäologie.

Whitehouse, D. 1973. Chinese Porcelain in Medieval Europe. *Medieval Archaeology* 16, 1972 (1973), 63-78.

Wiethold, J. 2007. '…und pfeffers ein wenig mit gestossenem Pfeffer / ist es sehr gut und wolgeschmack.' Exotische Gewürze in der mittelalterlichen und frühneuzeitlichen Küche: Quellen zur Handels- und Sozialgeschichte, in: Klein, U., Jansen, M. and Untermann, M. (eds.). *Küche – Kochen – Ernährung. Archäologie, Bauforschung, Naturwissenschaften.* Mitteilungen der Deutschen Gesellschaft für Archäologie des Mittelalters und der Neuzeit 19, 207-226.

Wirth, K. 2013. Archäologischer Kontext und seine Interpretation unter sozialen Aspekten. Mannheim B4,13, C 4,8 und E6,1: Drei Parzellen mit ihren Befunden und Funden im Vergleich. *Mitteilungen der Deutschen Gesellschaft für Archäologie des Mittelalters und der Neuzeit 25,* 89-96.

Wolf, A. 2003. Orientalische Goldemailgläser im mittelalterlichen Europa. *Jahrbuch des Römisch-Germanischen Zentralmuseums Mainz* 50.2, 489-611.

A Contribution to the Study of Global Trade Routes in the Post Medieval Period

'Nuremberg wares' from Venetian Shipwrecks in the Eastern Adriatic

Patrick Cassitti

Abstract

'Nuremberg ware' is a term used to denote common and everyday items produced in large quantities in Nuremberg and other Central European manufacturing centers. They include wooden dolls, pins, thimbles, bells, reckoning tokens, tableware and tools, scales and weights, and so on. These items were exported in great numbers and over long distances thanks to what can be termed a pre–industrial economy of scale. Even though they were clearly of economic importance, very few systematic studies exist on their production, distribution, and consumption. Archaeology is in an ideal position to expand our knowledge on this type of objects. Preliminary results from the study of Nuremberg wares from two Venetian shipwrecks in the Eastern Adriatic show that the trade with copper alloy objects from Central Europe, including Nuremberg wares, was an important economic and cultural factor in the Mediterranean across changing political landscapes between the twelfth and the eighteenth centuries.

Keywords: Nuremberg, Venice, Croatia, Gnalić, Drevine, Africa, Ottoman Empire, shipwreck, copper, brass, wire, ingots, metal sheet, knives, printed sheets, books, trade, material culture, underwater archaeology, Nuremberg wares

Trade is an important motor for cultural transmission. It can be seen both as a consequence of and as a motive for contacts between different regions and cultures. It is only one aspect of cultural contact, but one which can be studied through the material record, and which therefore plays an important role in Archaeology and Material Culture Studies (Renfrew 1975, 3-4). Few historical periods are associated with trade more

in: Kahlow, S. (ed.) 2018: *Transfer between sea and land. Maritime vessels for cultural exchanges in the Early Modern Period*, Sidestone Press (Leiden), pp. 43-62.

strongly than the early modern period. From the fifteenth century onward, European traders gradually expanded their reach in a process for which the term 'globalization' is commonly used. Trade per definition involves the mutual exchange of goods, but historical and archaeological studies on this era usually have focused only on one side of the exchange, namely on the imports to Europe and European consumption of goods from the new markets and how this influenced European societies (for example recently Berg 2015 on the material culture of trade between Europe and Asia).

The extension of the trade routes from the sixteenth century onward coincides with the beginnings of the 'consumer revolution' postulated for England (McCracken 1988), the 'golden age' of the Netherlands (Schama 1988), and the 'industrious revolution' in Anglo–Saxon countries (de Vries 2008). It is no coincidence that these terms were coined and adopted by scholars focusing on the Atlantic trade since this period plays an important role in the history and self–perception of the territories involved. On the other hand, they are rarely used in countries such as France or Germany. In Germany, in particular, the seventeenth century is associated with stagnation and loss of wealth and power (see for example Vierhaus 1984, 26-27). This supposed decline, however, did not leave obvious traces in the archaeological record, and it is possible that theories on revolutions, golden ages and periods of decline are influenced by idealized national discourses on the past as much as by empirical data.

The 'golden age' of Nuremberg and of southern Germany is usually considered to have been in the late fifteenth and sixteenth century, a period associated with famous names like Albrecht Dürer, Veith Stoß and Peter Vischer (Grieb 2007, VII). From the fifteenth century onward, an increasing regulation and specialization of crafts can be observed in Nuremberg. The theory that the division of labor and specialization is dependent on the extent of the market has been first suggested by Adam Smith, using as an example the production of pins, which not coincidentally was an important Nuremberg product (Smith 1776, 18). Depending on whether interpretation is focused on consumerism or on production, the extension of the market accessible to craftsmen in Nuremberg can be attributed to a growing demand for consumer goods in different parts of Europe and beyond, or by an increase of production and therefore the supply of goods. The first mechanism would be typical for the 'industrious revolution', while the latter is associated with the industrial revolution (de Vries 1994, 256).

In this paper, I would like to focus on the production aspect, as evidenced by so–called 'Nuremberg wares'. These are an example of items produced in Central Europe in large numbers by highly specialized and rationalized methods and traded extensively on a global scale. The production costs for the single object were very low thanks to large–scale production, and they were traded in such numbers as to gain larger economic importance. The definition of 'Nuremberg wares' varies, but mostly the term is used to denote finished or half–finished items made of different materials, like wooden dolls, pins, thimbles, bells, reckoning tokens, tableware and tools, scales and weights, lamps, chandeliers, steel, brass and copper wire, brass sheets, and so on. The main production center for these items was Nuremberg, but since these were common items other, less important centers existed in northern and southern Germany, for example in Aachen (Peltzer 1909), so that the term 'Nuremberg wares' is here used to identify the type of product, and not necessarily the place of production.

An important and early source on Nuremberg wares, and one of the few sixteenth century texts which list explicitly some of the items indicated by the term 'Nuremberg wares', is the account of Michael Heberer von Bretten, a German who travelled the Mediterranean and was enslaved as a prisoner of war by the Ottomans in 1583. He was released in 1587. During this time, he had the opportunity to travel through the Ottoman Empire. In 1610 he published an account of his travels across the Near East. In this account, he describes the markets of Cairo and the large variety of exotic goods which could be bought there. At the end of the chapter, he notes: *'Of Nuremberg wares / cheap toys / mirrors / whistles / and similar / can be found there in abundance / therefore the saying is true / Nuremberg's hand / goes through every land.'* (Heberer 1610, 135, translation by the author). This passage shows the wide distribution of Nuremberg wares in the sixteenth century. The 'abundance' of these objects in Cairo implies their large–scale and cheap production in the European manufacturing centers so that even with the added transport costs they could still be sold profitably in Ottoman markets. Michael Heberer's account also contains one of the earliest mentions of the saying *'Nuremberg's hand goes through every land'*, which is still well-known in Nuremberg to-day. Later sources supply more information on the products of Nuremberg. Compiled by Andrea Metrà in the late eighteenth century, a guide for Italian traders in five volumes contains an extensive characterization of Nuremberg manufacture. According to Metrà, production in Nuremberg is characterized by few factories worthy of that name, a great number of small artisans working *'all imaginable manners of products'*, which are exported *'in incredible numbers to Spain, Portugal, France, and all countries of Europe and other parts of the world'*. Metrà attributes this to the low cost of the products, achieved thanks to efficient production methods and the extensive use of simple water–powered machines (Metrà 1794, 446, translation by the author). What Metrà describes is essentially a pre–industrial economy of scale, which is still strong in the eighteenth century, and has its roots in the fourteenth, as shown by one of the few detailed case studies on the organization of craftsmen in Nuremberg which focused on the knife and sword makers (Keller 1981).

Even though 'Nuremberg wares' must have been of great economic importance in Europe for at least three centuries, they are rarely included in studies on early modern trade and consumption, since they are not well-represented in the historical record or in museums and collections. Most objects which have been studied therefore come from archaeological excavations. However, single finds of 'Nuremberg wares' from archaeological sites in Europe and beyond tell us little about the networks of exchange and trade which led to their presence at the excavated sites.[1] Underwater sites, in particular, shipwrecks, on the other hand, are potentially more valuable for the study of long–distance trade and communication networks. Even when Nuremberg wares are recovered from shipwrecks, however, individual finds are not enough to demonstrate trade. In order to discern between the personal belongings of the sailors or passengers and goods intended for trade, the site must be well-preserved and systematically excavated.

An area with high potential for the study of trade with Nuremberg wares can be found in the eastern Adriatic, on the Venetian shipping routes along the eastern shores.

---

1   Finds of presumed Nuremberg origin have been made on multiple continents: Eser 2002.

Since Venice and Nuremberg had very close commercial ties (Kellenbenz 1960, 308), it can be expected that Nuremberg products are to be found in this region. It is a fortunate coincidence that the eastern Adriatic offers very favorable conditions for the preservation of shipwrecks. In this region, therefore, the coast is littered with shipwrecks of every epoch. In a recent paper, Sauro Gelichi (2014) listed 12 known shipwrecks from the late medieval and early modern age in Croatia. Several of these shipwrecks contained items which can be termed 'Nuremberg wares', and can be attributed to southern Germany based on stylistic and typological considerations (Brusić 2006). This confirms what we know from written sources, namely that important quantities of Nuremberg wares were traded from Germany to Venice and then transported to the coasts of the Levant or of North Africa (Braunstein 1977, 90-91). Two shipwrecks are of particular importance for the study of the trade with Nuremberg wares between Germany and the Mediterranean, because of the importance of their cargo, their age, and the available archaeological documentation: the shipwreck of Gnalić and the shipwreck of Drevine. Selected items from the two shipwrecks are currently being studied by the author as part of a project on the production and trade of Nuremberg wares at the University of Bamberg. In the following pages, some preliminary results of this analysis will be presented.

The Shipwreck of Gnalić

The site of the shipwreck is located close to the small island of Gnalić, near Biograd na Moru, at the entrance to the Pašman-channel (Fig. 1). It was discovered in 1967 and

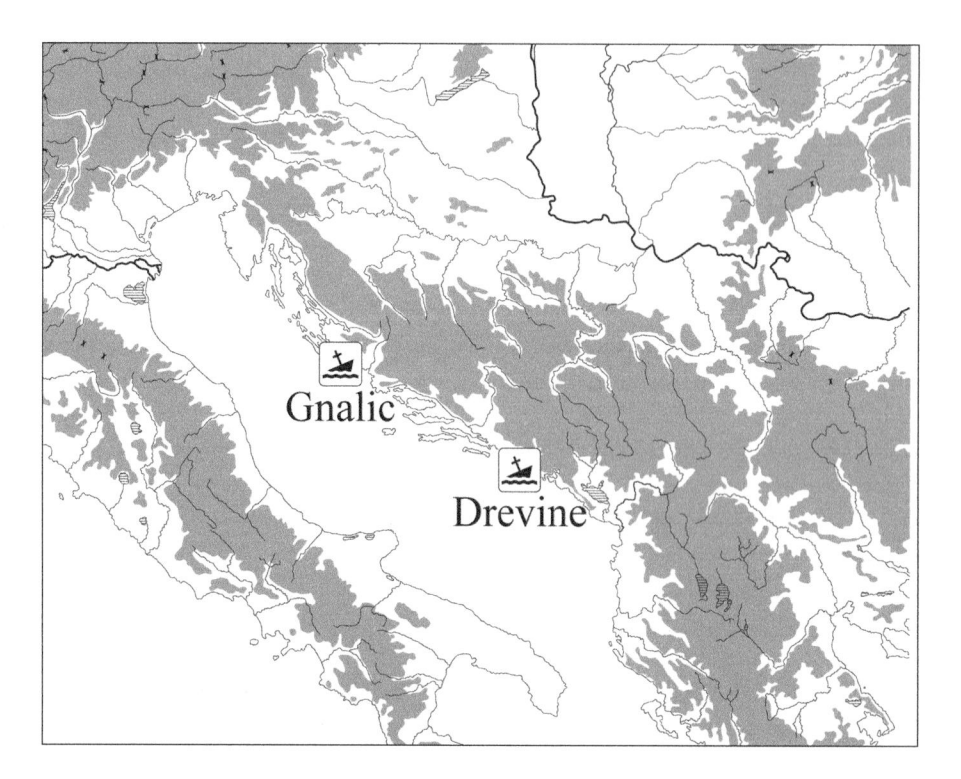

Figure 1: Location of the shipwreck sites of Gnalić and Drevine.

TRANSFER BETWEEN SEA AND LAND

Figure 2: Brass finds from the Gnalić shipwreck in the Town Museum of Biograd na Moru.

looted by divers. The Croatian authorities carried out three systematic archaeological investigations of the site between 1967 and 1996. Since 2012 the shipwreck is being studied by the international project *'The shipwreck of Gnalić – Mirror of Renaissance Europe'*, led by the University of Zadar and the Institute of Nautical Archaeology of Texas A&M University.[2] Thanks to this ongoing project, our knowledge about the ship and its cargo has increased considerably. Historians have been able to identify insurance records and other documents in the National Archives in Venice, which allowed the identification of the shipwreck as that of the Gagliana Grossa, which sailed from Venice in October 1583, bound for Istanbul (Radić Rossi *et al.* 2013, 78). Among other things, it transported window panes for the Harem of the Sultan Murad III (*ibid.*, 75-76). The documents also mention jewels and textiles, while no mention is made of the other objects categories recovered from the shipwreck, like the Nuremberg wares (Radić Rossi *et al.* 2013, 88).

Even though only the lowest portion of the hull, which was covered by seabed sediments, survives, tens of thousands of objects were recovered in the course of the excavation campaigns. According to the position inside the ship's hull these were mainly bulk wares: Among other things, over 10,000 glass vessels (Lazar and Willmott 2006), several barrels of cinnabar and lead white, and over 1,000 small and large brass objects and other products typical of Nuremberg and the surrounding region, like chandeliers, candle-holders, sconces, bells, needles, thimbles, razors, eyeglasses, candle snuffers, brass wire and sheet were recovered (Fig. 2). Thanks to the good preservation conditions for organic materials, many wooden containers of the transported wares are well-preserved, giving important insights into the transport logistics of the era (Stadler 2006, 109). Apart from the glass vessels, the finds from the shipwreck have not yet been studied systematically.

2   http://nauticalarch.org/blogs/gnalic–project/.

The brass wire, brass bars and brass sheet from the Gnalić shipwreck

The half-finished products from the shipwreck, the brass wire, brass bars and brass sheet, are of particular interest since they are very rarely found in the archaeological record. They shall, therefore, be presented in more detail.

The brass wire recovered from the shipwreck was transported in coils. These belonged to two types: small coils of wire with a diameter of approx. 13 cm and a wire thickness of approx. 1.0 mm, and large coils of wire with a thickness of approx. 1.2 mm and a diameter of approx. 50 cm. The coils were bound together with pieces of wire and stacked in barrels. Bundles of smaller coils were placed inside the larger ones (Fig. 3).

Three types of brass sheet were recovered from the wreck: Folded sheet with a width of approx. 18 cm and a sheet thickness of approx. 0.8 mm, rolled sheet with a width of approx. 10 cm and a sheet thickness of approx. 0.3 mm, and rolled sheet with a width of approx. 15 cm and a sheet thickness of approx. 0.3 mm (Fig. 4 and Fig. 5). The brass rod–shaped ingots have a length of approx. 60 cm, a width of approx. 1.2 cm and an average weight of 480 g (Fig. 6).

Historical documents of the sixteenth century show that these items were an important trade good for the Venetians. A dispatch of the Venetian Senate to Francesco Cornaro, the ambassador at the court of Charles V, dated May 1518, is one of the most explicit sources of information on the Mediterranean trade with Central European brass products in the sixteenth century. The dispatch was meant as an informative for the ambassador, who was to negotiate Venetian trading rights on the coasts of the *Barbaria*, the western Mediterranean coast of Africa. It lists the main wares being

Figure 3: Coils of wire in the Town Museum of Biograd na Moru, stacked as they were found during excavation at the Gnalić shipwreck site. The diameter of the large coils is approx. 50 cm.

Figure 4: Rolled brass sheet from the Gnalić shipwreck site in the Town Museum of Biograd Na Moru. The diameter of the roll at the center is approx. 7 cm.

Figure 5: Folded brass sheet from the Gnalić shipwreck site in the Town Museum of Biograd Na Moru. The overall length is approx. 73 cm, the width approx. 18 cm.

Figure 6: Rod-shaped brass ingots from the shipwreck of Gnalić in the Town Museum of Biograd na Moru. The length of the rods is approx. 60 cm.

traded to the North African ports by the Venetians. According to this document, the Venetians sold bread- and rod–shaped copper ingots, broad copper bands and copper wire to Djerba and Tunis, where they were then transported to *'Ethiopia'* by *'negroes'*. Furthermore, it is stated that *'for centuries'* the Venetians have also been selling spices, silken and woolen textiles, different types of cloth, silver, bread- and rod–shaped copper ingots, broad bands of copper, copper wire and worked copper objects to Oran and the Kingdom of Fes. The wares were bought by 'moors' and transported south, where they were used to produce *'things according to their customs'* (Mas Latrie, 1866, 274-275. Translation by the author).

The word for 'copper' in the original Italian text is used in its plural form: *rami*. This makes it clear that different types and qualities of copper were meant in the dispatch, and it is likely that these included brass. Until metallic zinc was discovered in the seventeenth century, brass was not regarded as an alloy, but as copper tinged yellow by the addition of calamine.[3] The dispatch to Cornaro lists types of brass items which have been recovered from the Gnalić shipwreck: wires, bands, ingots and worked items. While the 'worked copper objects' mentioned in the document are unfortunately not described in more detail, the text contains more information on the raw and half-finished materials. For example, the dispatch differentiates between rod-shaped and bread-shaped copper ingots. Archaeological finds show that since at least the early medieval period the rod-shape was predominantly used for brass ingots. Rod-shaped brass ingots have been recovered from Anglo–Saxon sites in England (Bayley *et al.* 2014), and from the Viking–age harbor of Haithabu (Meixner 2010). The 'bread'-shaped, or plano-convex ingots were a form commonly used for pure copper. No examples of plano-convex brass-ingots are known to the author. Plano-convex copper ingots on the other hand have been recovered from shipwreck sites. One of the most famous is the so-called wreck of the Bom Jesus, a Portuguese merchant ship which sunk in the early sixteenth century on the coast of Namibia, from which hundreds of ingots have been recovered (Knabe and Noli 2012). The ingots bore the mark of the Fugger family, which demonstrates their Central European origin. It is interesting to note that no plano–convex copper ingots were recovered from the shipwreck of Gnalić, nor from other shipwrecks of the same period in the eastern Adriatic.

The Venetian dispatch also mentions *'broad bands of copper'*, which probably means brass sheet like the one recovered from the Gnalić shipwreck. The Gnalić items allow us to differentiate between different types of brass sheet, which were not specified in the dispatch. The formats recovered from the shipwreck correspond to products known in Germany as 'Tafelmessing' (flat brass) and 'Rollmessing' (rolled brass). These were still being produced in the eighteenth and nineteenth century (Priesner 1997, 208; Prechtl 1830, 259).

Another good listed in the dispatch are the wires of copper alloy which were also part of the cargo of the Gagliana Grossa. It seems as though the mentioned copper items formed a typical assemblage of goods traded together on ships bound for the coasts of the Mediterranean.

Another important information which we can learn from the Venetian dispatch is that the ports and cities of the north-African coast were not the end point of the trade

---

3   For example in an alchemical treatise printed in Nuremberg in 1541: Darmstaedter 1969, 40.

TRANSFER BETWEEN SEA AND LAND

with copper alloy objects. Instead, African traders bought the products and transported them to sub–Saharan Africa. The dispatch mentions that this trade had been going on for *'centuries'*. This could be interpreted as an exaggeration with the aim of strengthening the cause for Venetian trading rights in North Africa. However, an archaeological discovery in the Mauritanian desert corroborates this claim. In 1964 Théodore Monod came across a cache consisting of 2,085 rod–shaped brass ingots and a large number of cowry–shells (Monod 1969). The objects were wrapped in bundles of organic matting, which yielded two uncalibrated BC dates: 1165 +- 110 and 1090 +- 108 AD, which have been calibrated to 1024-1329 AD and 980-1303 AD by Garenne–Marot and Mille (2007, 168). The ingots are of very similar size and weight as those recovered from the Gnalić shipwreck. Their average length is 73 cm, their average weight 470 g (compared to 60 cm and 480 g for the bars from Gnalić). The weight corresponds to the Venetian *libbra grossa* (approx. 477g), which is roughly equivalent to the pound of Cologne (468 g) (Gerhard *et al.* 2001, 22) or the Nuremberg pound for precious metals (478 g) (Diefenbacher and Endres 2000, 1246). Both the brass bars from Gnalić and from Mauritania, therefore, seem to have been made with a standardized size and weight in mind, which points to central Europe and Venice as the source of the material. In the case of brass sheet, we know from a manual written in 1780 that the products were sized according to the standards of the target market. For example, brass sheet intended to be sold to France was fashioned using the French system of measurement (Priesner 1997, 211). It is, therefore, possible that the bars from the shipwreck of Gnalić and from the Mauretanian desert were manufactured specifically for export to Venice, or were possibly manufactured in Venice itself. As shall be shown, this is unlikely for the bars from the Gnalić shipwreck. As early as the sixteenth-century manuals for traders were printed which contained detailed information on the systems of weights and measurements used in different cities and markets (for example Meder 1562). A level of standardisation which took into consideration the system of weights and measures of the target market would therefore not be surprising in the early modern era, but the find from the Mauretanian desert shows that European export of raw materials had likely already reached a high level of standardization in the Middle Ages.

Trace element analysis performed on the ingots from Mauritania also point to central and NW-Europe as the origin of the metal (Willett and Sayre 2006, 67). No analysis has been carried out on the ingots from the shipwreck of Gnalić but on one of the containers in which the ingots were transported a merchant's sign is still visible (Fig. 7). The same sign can be found in several locations in the *Fondaco dei Tedeschi,* the headquarters of the German merchants in Venice. In this building merchants from the territories of the Holy Roman Empire were required by Venetian law to live and to sell their merchandise. The merchants used signs to mark their wares, which were also used to mark the entrance to the chambers of the merchants. They can, therefore, be found as graffiti on the pillars and parapets of the porticoes of the *fondaco* (Barbon 2005). The specific sign found on the barrel is very frequent in Germany and Scandinavia (Homeyer 1870), and is shown as an example for a merchant's mark in a German manual printed in 1559 by an unknown author. In this manual the sign is attributed to 'Johann Woldran zu Genua', probably a merchant of German origin (Homeyer 1870, 131; Unknown Author 1559). While no definite proof, the fact that a merchant's sign well attested in Germany and northern Europe and present in the *Fondaco dei Tedeschi*

Figure 7: Merchant's sign on the lid of a barrel containing brass rods from the shipwreck of Gnalić, marked with an arrow.

was used on a barrel of rod–shaped brass ingots makes it likely that the brass was imported from the German territories.

The archaeological discoveries in Mauretania and at Gnalić show that the trade of brass from Europe to sub-Saharan Africa goes back at least to the thirteenth century, and was still important towards the end of the sixteenth. This corroborates the importance given to the trade with copper and brass products by the dispatch from 1518, and shows that at that time this trade did indeed go back for *'several centuries'*. Arabic and European written sources allow us to trace the trade with copper across the Sahara back even further. Copper from Moroccan mines was traded across the Sahara at least since the eleventh century, while trade with European copper can be traced back at least to the twelfth (Monod 1969, 314-315).

This fact sheds an important light on the early Portuguese expansion of trade along the coast of West Africa, which marked the beginning of early modern global trade. The main goods which Portuguese traders exchanged for slaves and gold on their travels were brass and copper objects.[4] This made the trade with sub-Saharan Africa extremely profitable. This market, however, was not created by the Portuguese in the course of their expansion, but, as shown by archaeological and written sources, was already being supplied with European products, albeit through intermediaries (Kellenbenz 1977, 337; Willet and Sayre 2006, 77). The Portuguese expansion was, therefore, able to build upon an established market for European copper, brass, and other manufactured goods, and would probably not have been as successful without this precondition. The Portuguese opened an alternative, direct route, which removed the need for intermediaries and therefore made trade more lucrative. Even though this meant competition for the Venetian merchants, it does not appear that the number

---

4   An overview in Herbert 1984 as well as Lux and Althoff 1995.

TRANSFER BETWEEN SEA AND LAND

of copper products traded in the Mediterranean diminished significantly, as merchant manuals of the late eighteenth century tell us that Nuremberg wares were still exported in *'incredible numbers'* (Metrà 1794, 446). It seems that the decline of Nuremberg and Venetian trade was more in relative profitability and importance than in absolute numbers of goods being traded.

The shipwreck of Drevine

Another important shipwreck, which sheds light on the trade with central European products termed 'Nuremberg wares', lies north of Dubrovnik, in the Koločep channel, close to the village of Drevine (Fig. 1). The site was discovered and partially excavated in 1976. During this excavation, 47 wooden crates were recovered, which are mostly still unopened and currently stored in different Croatian museums (Gluščević 2006, 75). While barrels and wooden boxes of different sizes were recovered from the Gnalić site, all the crates from Drevine are of the same size, and no barrels have been recovered. This could indicate a development towards higher standardization in transport logistics. However, only a small area of the site has been investigated, and it cannot be excluded that the homogeneity of the crates is due to this fact. Loose finds strewn across the seabed were also recovered from the site. In Drevine, just as in Gnalić, metal finds which can be attributed to the category of 'Nuremberg wares' form an important part of the assemblage. They include iron knives, brass wire, brass sheet metal, small brass bells, brass pins, and brass reckoning tokens from the workshop of Cornelius Lauffer in Nuremberg, who was active between 1688 and 1711 (Gluščević 2006, 75; Mitchiner 1988, 499). The tokens provide a terminus post quem of 1688 for the sinking of the ship. The spectrum of copper alloy objects from the Drevine shipwreck is remarkably similar to the one from the shipwreck of Gnalić. The brass sheet is of the 'Rollmessing' type. The wires from the Drevine shipwreck show a greater variety of types and sizes than those from Gnalić. Additionally to coils of wire similar in size to those from the Gnalić shipwreck, the Drevine shipwreck yielded coils of very fine wire and of flattened wire, transported in small wooden boxes (Fig. 8). These items belong to the category of so-called 'Leonische Waren', which are typical of the seventeenth and eighteenth centuries. Nuremberg was an important manufacturing center for this type of product. The term 'Leonische Waren' alludes to the fact that the method of manufacture was allegedly brought to Nuremberg by a craftsman from Lyon (Rawitzer 1988). Since Nuremberg has been famous for its wire production since the fourteenth century, when Nuremberg craftsmen were credited with the invention of the water–powered wire pulling machine, which greatly increased the quantity and quality of wire which could be produced (von Stromer 1977), this alleged introduction from Lyon has to be treated with skepticism. The wire found in Drevine shows that while the general typology of traded goods remained the same, the products evolved, thanks also to new manufacturing technologies.

The cargo from the Drevine shipwreck indicates that at this time there still existed a demand for Central European copper alloy and other metal products. It is not possible to estimate the importance and amount of this trade based on one partially excavated shipwreck, and other excavated shipwrecks of the same period in the Mediterranean are rare, but as late as the end of the eighteenth century merchant manuals assert that

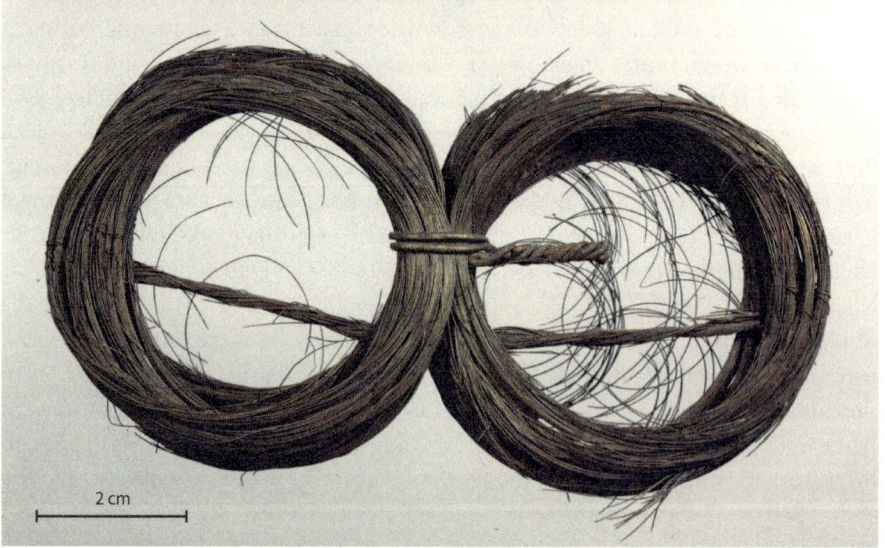

Figure 8: Small wooden box with coils of thin wire from the shipwreck of Drevine in the Maritime Museum of Dubrovnik (top) and one of the coils of fine wire from the same site stored in the International Centre for Underwater Archaeology in Zadar (bottom).

Nuremberg still produced large amounts of objects which were exported, presumably also to Venice and beyond (Metrà 1794, 446). Since the Drevine shipwreck has been only partially excavated, and most of the recovered crates are still unopened, it is not possible to determine the exact composition of the assemblage of 'Nuremberg wares' present on the ship. In addition to the types of wares which we already know from Gnalić and other shipwrecks, the Drevine site yielded sets of knives tightly packed inside wooden crates, which until now have not been recovered from other sites, and shall therefore be presented here in more detail.

The knives are very unelaborate and utilitarian objects with simple, wooden handles. Some of the blades carry a mark in the shape of a '*W*' on the base of the blade, others have a mark which looks like a sun on the wooden handle. It has not been possible to

2 cm

Figure 9: Knives with papier – mâché scabbards from the shipwreck of Drevine, currently stored in the International Centre for Underwater Archaeology in Zadar.

attribute these simple marks to a European production center. The knives were transported in wooden Crates within simple, unadorned sheaths made from papier-mâché (Fig. 9). In many German cities, the manufacture of sheaths and scabbards for knives and other instruments from paper and other materials was an additional income for bookbinders. In Nuremberg, *'Futteralmacher'* (scabbard-makers) are attested since the late sixteenth century.[5] Their guild was united with the guild of the *'Buchbinder'* (bookbinders) in 1621 (Schindler 2016, 15). Papier-mâché scabbards were manufactured out of several layers of scrap paper, shaped with glue around a wooden model of the instrument for which they were being made. The more precious scabbards were then covered with leather, textile or parchment (Prediger 1772, 228-235). This was not the case with the Drevine sheaths, the surface of which was simply painted black and imprinted with a coarse structure in order to imitate leather. Clearly, these are cheap items, which, like the knives, were very likely produced and exported in large numbers, as is typical for Nuremberg wares.

The scrap paper used for the manufacture of the sheaths of the Drevine knives consists of pages from printed books and provides an important clue to the origin of the knives since a number of the paper fragments carries texts which can still be read. At present, it has been possible to identify five books to which some of the fragments belong.[6]

No paper fragment shows signs of binding, and the larger fragments can be clearly identified as print sheets. This was the normal practice at the time. Books were traded and exchanged as printed sheets and then brought to the bookbinder by the customer (Janzin and Güntner 2007, 167). The printed sheets used for the manufacture of the sheaths could have been discarded because of printing errors. However, no such obvious errors can be seen on the surviving fragments. Since these form only a small part of the original print sheets, the errors might simply have been situated on the parts which

---

5   Stephan Braun, Futteralmacher, attested 1582: Grieb 2007, 170.

6   They are, in chronological order: N. Selnecker/L. Messen, Libellvs Brevis Et Vtilis, de Coena Domini editus, Argentinae (Strasbourg) 1561; M. Flacius Illyricus, Clavis scripturae S. seu de Sermone Sacrarum literarum, Basilea (Basel) 1567; P. S. Melanchthon, Confessio Paucis Articulis Complectens Summam Doctrinae de vera praesentia Corporis & Sanguinis Christi in Coena dominica (*etc.*), Vitebergae (Wittenberg) 1574; L. Martini, Der Christlichen Jungfrauen Ehrenkräntzlein, Prag, ca. 1580; H. Müller, Geistliche Seelen–Musik, Frankfurt 1694.

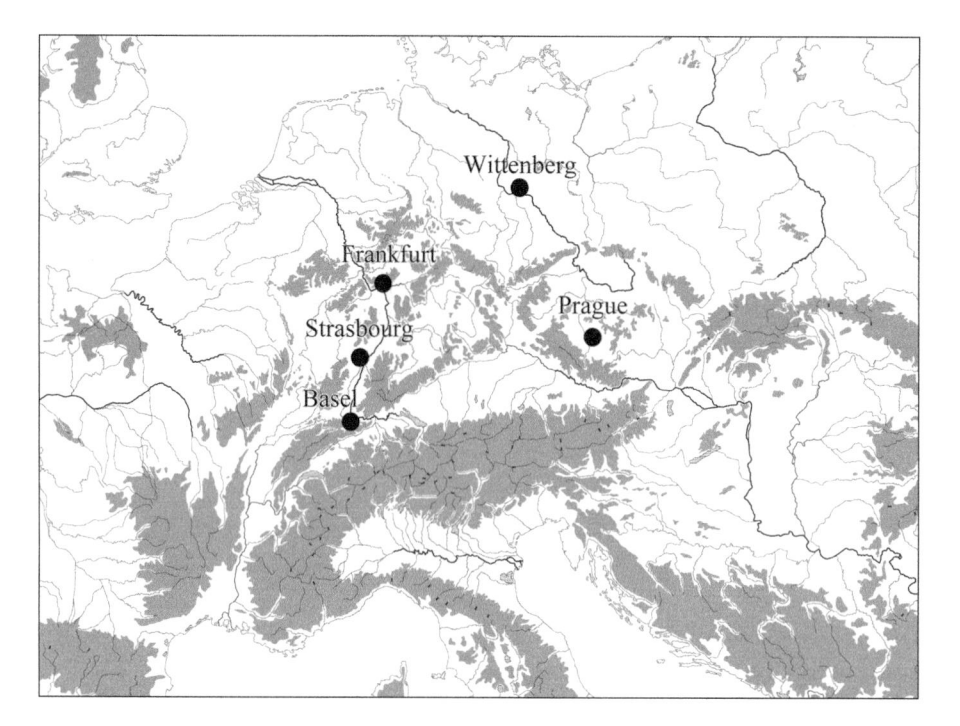

Figure 10: Places of print of the identified printed sheets used for the manufacture of the knife sheaths from the shipwreck of Drevine.

did not survive. However, most of the pages belong to books which were originally published over 100 years prior to the time they were used to manufacture the sheaths. It seems unlikely that waste paper was stored that long. The print sheets could, therefore, have been flawless but been discarded and sold as scrap paper after their owners gave up hope that they would be able to sell them. The fact that the printed sheets were stored for over 100 years gives an interesting insight into the trade and manufacture of books in the early modern period. Printed works could apparently be sold and bound into books decades or even a century after they left the printer's press. The youngest text from the shipwreck of Drevine which could be identified is from a protestant songbook published in 1694, which provides a terminus post quem for the sinking of the ship which is later than the one provided by the brass tokens (1688). In this case, the time between printing and re-use as scrap paper seems to have been relatively short, so maybe the songbook sheets did indeed contain errors and were therefore discarded shortly after printing.

All books are of religious nature and can be attributed to the protestant faith. While in the seventeenth century there were important production centers for knives in Austria which traded extensively with Venice, for example in Steyr (Keller 1981, 27-28), it is unlikely that protestant books circulated there in large quantities after the counter-reformation took hold. Therefore, a German origin of the knives is likely. The places of print are distributed widely across the German-speaking area, ranging from Basel in the west to Prague in the east (Fig. 10). The largest book fairs in Germany took place in Frankfurt and in Leipzig (Janzin and Güntner 2007, 167). The wide distribution of the printing locations of the texts identified in Drevine demonstrates the complexity and wide range of book–trade in Europe during this time. It also gives insights into the circulation and recycling of scrap paper in the late seventeenth century. Given the wide circulation of goods in those times the paper fragments do not allow us to pinpoint the place of production of the knives more precisely than *'protestant, German-speaking Central Europe'*.

The knives, together with the rest of the assemblage from the shipwreck of Drevine, show that there still was an important trade of common, everyday goods from Central Europe to Venice and from here towards the coasts of the Mediterranean in the late seventeenth or early eighteenth century. The composition of the traded copper-alloy goods remained almost unchanged. This contradicts the common assumption that the trade from Nuremberg and other German cities declined greatly during the seventeenth century, and hints at the possibility that trade was still thriving along the old medieval routes, even if its relative importance vaned in comparison with the new trade routes along the West African coast.

Conclusions

The object category termed *'Nürnberger Waren'* in sixteenth to nineteenth-century texts can be observed in post-medieval shipwrecks in the Adriatic. These shipwrecks, together with the written sources, demonstrate an important trade with these objects from their production centers in Central Europe towards the Mediterranean coasts of the Levant and Northern Africa from the sixteenth to the early eighteenth century. The origins of this trade can be traced back to the twelfth century. This shows the high continuity of trade contacts across long periods of time, despite the changing political situations in Europe, Northern Africa, and the Near East. During this time, there seems to have existed a continuous demand for certain goods in markets around the Mediterranean and in sub–Saharan Africa. Trade with these goods, therefore, represented a constant across the centuries. Even though the trade with such everyday goods in the Mediterranean was probably less profitable than the trade which was being carried out via the ports of the Atlantic, the shipwrecks in the Adriatic show that it was probably never interrupted, and possessed a high continuity.

This flow of goods meant that important amounts of copper and other metals left Europe and were thus removed from the recycling cycle from the middle ages onward. The effect this might have had on the European mining industry has yet to be studied in more detail. It must also have had an important effect on the manufacturing economy of the production centers which supplied the traded goods, and played an important role in shaping and maintaining cultural contacts in the Mediterranean and beyond. It is likely that the extension of the market for Nuremberg goods was an important factor for the creation of a diversified and highly specialized production in those German cities which maintained close commercial ties to Venice.

In addition to the economic aspects, trade with Central European copper alloy products was also of cultural significance. For one thing, it brought about intensive contacts between merchants and diplomats across the Mediterranean. But, and this is probably even more important, the goods exported to the Ottoman Empire became part of the material culture of the population, just as the goods imported from the east played an important role in European culture. Brass chandeliers from Nuremberg and glass window panes from Venice likely adorned Ottoman palaces and mosques. Ottoman tailors used thimbles made in Nuremberg in their work, and men and women alike might have fastened their dresses and turbans with pins made in Central Europe. Wooden dolls from Germany were sold cheaply in markets in Cairo, and as a consequence children in Egypt and in Nuremberg would play with the same type of toys. Because these are common and everyday objects, interactions and engagement with them were regular and frequent. They, therefore, played a role in shaping the world which people on both sides of the Mediterranean lived in. As Colin Renfrew stated:

> 'For the individual who comes to terms with the realities of existence from the moment of birth, it is the encounters with things – the everyday artifacts in current use within the society in question – which establish the world in which he or she lives, just as much as the encounter with the realities of space, time, and bodily existence (including ingestion and excretion) which form the universal parameters of human existence' (Renfrew 2004, 30).

Little is still known about the value and meaning which the people in the Ottoman Empire attributed to the goods imported from Europe. European research has focused on the reception of Turkish culture in European societies (for example Grothaus 1985; Fleet 1995; Bevilacqua and Pfeifer 2013), and therefore the reception of European material culture in the Ottoman Empire in the early modern era is not well understood. We do not know if European imports were seen as exotic goods, and if the people who purchased them were conscious of the fact that they had been traded over long distances from a culturally very different place. The finds from the Adriatic shipwrecks show an early modern Mediterranean world which appears less divided than we would think by looking at the political and military history of the time. In the Mediterranean, material culture seems to have been a unifying factor which crossed the boundaries of politics and ideology, and its exchange was a constant across changing political landscapes for centuries. The study of everyday objects like Nuremberg Wares has the potential to provide insights into these important networks of material and cultural exchange.

References

Barbon, F.H. 2005. *I segni dei mercanti a Venezia nel Fondaco dei Tedeschi*. Cornuda (Treviso): Antiga.

Bayley, J., Cotton, J., Rehren, T. and Pernicka, E. 2014. A Saxon brass bar ingot cache from Kingsway, London, in: Cotton, J., Hall, J., Keily, J., Sherris, R. and Stephenson, R. (eds.). *Hidden Histories and Records of Antiquity. Essays on Saxon and Medieval London for John Clark, Curator Emeritus, Museum of London*. London: LAMAS (Special Paper 17), 121-128.

Berg, M. 2015 (ed.). *Goods from the East, 1600-1800. Trading Eurasia*. Houndmills: Palgrave Macmillan.

Bevilacqua, A. and Pfeifer, H. 2013. Turquerie: Culture in Motion, 1650-1750. *Past and Present* 221, 75-118.

Braunstein, Ph. 1977. Le marché du cuivre à Venise à la fin du moyen–age, in: Kellenbenz, H. (ed.). *Schwerpunkte der Kupferproduktion und des Kupferhandels in Europa 1500-1650*. Kölner Kolloquien zur internationalen Sozial- und Wirtschaftsgeschichte 3. Köln, Wien: Böhlau, 78-94.

Brusić, Z. 2006. Tre naufragi del XVII o XVIII secolo lungo la costa Adriatica orientale, in: Guštin, M., Gelichi, S. and Spindler, K. (eds.). *The heritage of the Serenissima. The presentation of the architectural and archaeological remains of the Venetian Republic*. Koper: Založba Annales, 77-83.

Darmstaedter, E. 1969. *Die Alchemie des Geber*. Wiesbaden: Sändig.

Diefenbacher, M. and Endres, R. 2000. *Stadtlexikon Nürnberg 2000*. 2nd ed. Nürnberg: Tümmels.

Eser, T. 2002. Unter Tage, unter Wasser. Nürnberger Artefakte als archäologische Funde, in: Maué, H., Eser, T., Hauschke, S. and Stolzenberger, J. (eds.). *Quasi Centrum Europae. Europa kauft in Nürnberg. 1400-1800*. Nürnberg: Verlag des Germanischen Nationalmuseums, 96-115.

Fleet, K. 1995. Italian Perceptions of the Turks in the Fourteenth and Fifteenth Centuries. *Journal of Mediterranean Studies* 5, 159-172.

Gerhard, H.-J., Kaufhold, K.H. and Engel, A. 2001. *Preise im vor- und frühindustriellen Deutschland: Nahrungsmittel, Getränke, Gewürze, Rohstoffe und Gewerbeprodukte*. Stuttgart: Franz Steiner.

Gluščević, S. 2006. Ritrovamenti medievali e postmedievali dalle acque dell'Adriatico orientale croato, in: Guštin, M., Gelichi, S. and Spindler, K. (eds.) 2006. *The heritage of the Serenissima. The presentation of the architectural and archaeological remains of the Venetian Republic*. Koper: Založba Annales, 73-76.

Grieb, M.H. 2007. *Nürnberger Künstlerlexikon: Bildende Künstler, Kunsthandwerker, Gelehrte, Sammler, Kulturschaffende und Mäzene vom 12. bis zur Mitte des 20. Jahrhunderts. Band 1. A–G*. München: K. G. Saur.

Grothaus, M. 1985. Zum Türkenbild in der Kultur der Habsburgermonarchie zwischen dem 15. und 18. Jahrhundert, in: Tietze, A. (ed.). *Habsburgisch–osmanische Beziehungen*. Beiheft zur Wiener Zeitschrift für die Kunde des Morgenlandes 13. Wien: Verlag des Verbandes der wissenschaftlichen Gesellschaften Österreichs, 67-89.

Heberer, M. 1610. *Aegyptiaca servitus*. Heidelberg: Gotthard Vöglin.

Herbert, E.W. 1984. *Red Gold of Africa. Copper in Precolonial History and Culture*. Madison: University of Wisconsin Press.

Homeyer, C.G. 1870. *Die Haus- und Hofmarken*. Berlin: Königliche Geheime Ober–Hofbuchdruckerei.

Janzin, M. and Güntner, J. 2007. *Das Buch vom Buch: 5000 Jahre Buchgeschichte*. Hannover: Schlütersche.

Kellenbenz, H. 1960. Nürnberger Handel um 1540. *Mitteilungen des Vereins für Geschichte der Stadt Nürnberg* 50, 299-324.

Kellenbenz, H. 1977. Europäisches Kupfer, Ende 15. bis Mitte 17. Jahrhundert. Ergebnisse eines Kolloquiums, in: Kellenbenz, H. (ed.). *Schwerpunkte der Kupferproduktion und des Kupferhandels in Europa 1500-1650*. Kölner Kolloquien zur internationalen Sozial- und Wirtschaftsgeschichte 3. Köln, Wien: Böhlau, 290-351.

Keller, K. 1981. *Das messer- und schwertherstellende Gewerbe in Nürnberg von den Anfängen bis zum Ende der reichsstädtischen Zeit*. Schriftenreihe des Stadtarchivs Nürnberg 31. Nürnberg: Stadtarchiv Nürnberg.

Knabe, W. and Noli, D. 2012. Die versunkenen Schätze der Bom Jesus: Sensationsfund eines Indienseglers aus der Frühzeit des Welthandels. Berlin: Nicolai.

Lazar, I. and Willmott, H. 2006. *The Glass from the Gnalić Shipwreck*. Koper: Univerza na Primorskem.

Lux, S. and Althoff, R. 1995 (eds.). *Kissipenny und Manilla. Geld und Handel im alten Afrika*. Duisburg: Kultur- und Stadthistorisches Museum.

de Mas Latrie, L. 1866. *Traités de paix et de commerce et documents divers concernant les relations des chrétiens avec les Arabes de l'Afrique septentrionale au moyen–âge*. Paris: Plon.

McCracken, G. 1988. *Culture and Consumption: New Approaches to the Symbolic Character of Consumer Goods and Activities*. Bloomington: Indiana University Press.

Meder, L. 1562. *Handel–Buch: darin angezeigt wird, welcher gestalt inn den fürnembsten Hendelstetten Europe allerley wahren anfencklich kaufft, dieselbig wider mit nutz verkaufft, wie die Wechsel gemacht, Pfund, Ellen unnd Müntz uberal verglichen und zu welcher zeit die Merckten gewönlich gehalten werden*. Nürnberg: vom Berg/Newber.

Meixner, B. 2010. *Haithabu. Fernhandelszentrum zwischen den Welten*. Schleswig: Archäologisches Landesmuseum.

Metrà, A. 1794. *Il mentore perfetto de' negozianti*. Trieste: Wage, Fleis & Comp.

Mitchiner, M. 1988. *Jetons, Medalets & Tokens. Volume I. The Medieval Period and Nuremberg*. London: Seaby.

Monod, T. 1969. Les 'Macden Ijâfen': une epave caravaniere ancienne dans la Majâbat al–Koubrâ, in: *Actes du 1er Colloque International d'Archéologie africaine. Fort–Lamy (République du Tchad) – 11-16 Décembre 1966*. Etudes et Documents Tchadiens, Memoires I. Fort–Lamy: Institut National Tchadien pour les Sciences Humaines, 286-320.

Peltzer, R.A. 1909. *Geschichte der Messingindustrie und der künstlerischen Arbeiten in Messing (Dinanderies) in Aachen und den Ländern zwischen Maas und Rhein von der Römerzeit bis zur Gegenwart*. Aachen: Cremersche Buchhandlung.

Prechtl, J.J. 1830 (ed.). *Technologische Encyklopäedie: oder, alphabetisches Handbuch der Technologie, der Technischen Chemie und des Maschinenwesens, Band 2*. Stuttgart: J.H. Gotta.

Priesner, C. 1997. *Bayerisches Messing. Franz Matthias Ellmayrs 'Mößing–Werkh AO. 1780'*. Stuttgart: Franz Steiner.

Radić Rossi, I., Bondioli, M., Nicolardi, M., Brusić, Z., Čoralić, L. and Vieira de Castro, F. 2013. Brodolom kod Gnalića – ogledalo renesansne Europe. The Shipwreck of Gnalić – Mirror of Renaissance Europe, in: Filep, A. and Jurdana, E. (eds.) 2013. *Gnalić. Blago potonulog broad iz 16. stoljeća. Gnalić. Treasure of a 16th Century Sunken Ship*. Zagreb: Hrvatski povijesni muzej, 65-95.

Rawitzer, B. 1988. *Leonische Drahtwaren und Gespinste. Studien zu einem Spezialgewerbe in Mittelfranken anhand der Archive des 19. Jahrhunderts*. Veröffentlichungen zur Volkskunde und Kulturgeschichte 29. Würzburg: Verlag der Bayerischen Blätter für Volkskunde.

Renfrew, C. 1975. Trade as Action at a Distance: Questions of Integration and Communication, in: Sabloff, J.A. and Lamberg–Karlovsky, C.C. (eds.). *Ancient civilization and trade*. Albuquerque: University of New Mexico Press, 3-59.

Renfrew, C. 2004. Towards a Theory of Material Engagement, in: De Marrais, E., Gosden, C. and Renfrew, C. (eds.). *Rethinking materiality. The engagement of mind with the material world*. Cambridge: McDonald institute for Archaeological Research, 23-31.

Schama, S. 1988. *The Embarrassment of Riches: An Interpretation of Dutch Culture in the Golden Age*. Berkeley, Los Angeles: University of California Press.

Schindler, T. 2016. Mondförmige Stempel zum Prägen durch Wiegen. Fileten des 19. Jahrhunderts. *Kulturgut aus der Forschung des Germanischen Nationalmuseums* 48/1, 12-15.

Smith, A. 1776. *An Inquiry into the Nature and Causes of the Wealth of Nations*. Reprint 1975, in: Todd, W.B. (ed.). The Glasgow Edition of the Works and Correspondence of Adam Smith, Vol. 2: An Inquiry into the Nature and Causes of the Wealth of Nations, Vol. 1. Oxford: Oxford University Press.

Stadler, H. 2006. The brass candlesticks, sconces and chandeliers from Gnalić wreck, in: Guštin, M., Gelichi, S. and Spindler, K. (eds.). *The heritage of the Serenissima. The presentation of the architectural and archaeological remains of the Venetian Republic*. Koper: Založba Annales, 107-109.

von Stromer, W. 1977. Innovation und Wachstum im Spätmittelalter: Die Erfindung der Drahtmühle als Stimulator. *Technikgeschichte* 44/2, 89-120.

Unknown Author 1559. *Vndterricht eins gantzen Handelbuchs. Darinnen mit Trewhertzigem gemueth die art eines rechten ordentlichen Buchhaltens angezeigt wird.* Frankfurt a. M.: Han/Weigand.

Vierhaus, R. 1984. *Deutschland im Zeitalter des Absolutismus (1648-1763)*. Göttingen: Vandenhoeck & Ruprecht.

de Vries, J. 2008. *The industrious revolution: consumer behavior and the household economy, 1650 to the present*. New York: Cambridge University Press.

Willett, F. and Sayre, E.V. 2006. Lead Isotopes in West African Copper Alloys. *Journal of African Archaeology* 4/1, 55-90.

With the Warship Kronan in the Wake of Paracelsus

Archaeological Finds Reflecting the Conception of Drugs in Seventeenth-Century Sweden

Björn Lindeke & Bo Ohlson

Abstract

On the first of June 1676 Sweden´s man-o´ war Kronan, perished in an explosion while engaged in a battle in the Baltic Sea. Apart from some cannons, retrieved soon after, the knowledge of the wreck´s location sank into oblivion until 1980. The rediscovery of the ship 26 m below the surface marked the start of a marine-archaeological project that to date has produced about 35,000 objects. A closed find like this constitutes a peep-hole straight into a number of aspects of late-seventeenth-century society. Dealing with the discovery of a marked pharmaceutical-medical context, this article raises immediate questions of naval health care and the assortment of drugs used. It focuses on the relations between the retrieved objects and Swedish culture in wider contexts, such as the influx of goods and knowledge from Central Europe, a. o. reflecting a major shift in the medical paradigm around 1650, the proof is given of long-range trade patterns, and demonstrations of social stratification as well as pharmaco-technical procedures, and also proof of the links between professional literature and actual practice.

Keywords: seventeenth century, culture transfer, Galenic medicine, marine archaeology, medicinal artefacts, medicinal chests, medicinal drugs, medicinal paradigm, naval pharmacy, Paracelsian medicine, the Warship Kronan, trade patterns

In the seventeenth century, Sweden became a dominant political and military power in northern Europe. This position was established through the country's intervention in the Thirty Years' War and, later in that century, through victorious battles against Denmark. Nevertheless, on June 1, 1676, during the Scanian War, the Swedish Navy was hit by one of its greatest disasters ever, when its flagship, Kronan ('The Royal Crown'), exploded and sank in the Baltic Sea, off the east coast of Öland.

in: Kahlow, S. (ed.) 2018: *Transfer between sea and land. Maritime vessels for cultural exchanges in the Early Modern Period*, Sidestone Press (Leiden), pp. 63-86.

This mark of disgrace occurred during a skirmish with an allied Danish-Dutch fleet and is attributed to bad seamanship within the Swedish squadron. The Kronan had been designed by the English *shipwright Francis Sheldon the Elder* (1610-1692) and was built at the Stockholm shipyard between 1665 and 1668. At the time she was one of the largest sailing vessels in Europe, carrying 110 to 126 guns and a crew of 850 (Zettersten 1903, 574) with a calculated displacement of 2,200 to 2,300 metric tons (Glete 1999, 18). Eight hundred men went down with the ship. The Kronan constituted a floating society, albeit entirely male, in terms of both crew numbers and social structure, and this was during a period when there was rarely any clear distinction between military and civilian society (Einarsson 1997). The consequences of the tragedy have long been a major source of historical and, since the 1980s, archaeological data.

Marine archaeology

On August 8, 1980, twenty-four years after his discovery of the Vasa, Anders Franzén, together with three associates, located and identified the wreck of the Kronan. Like the Vasa, she was on Franzéns search-list of Swedish warships lost in Swedish Baltic waters during the sixteenth and seventeenth centuries. She lay at a depth of 26 m, at a position 3.4 nautical miles due east of the village of Hulterstad on southeast Öland. In the spring of 1981, Kalmar County Museum was appointed to lead fieldwork along with further marine archaeological investigations. The underwater work on the Kronan that has taken place ever since, three to four weeks every summer has been made possible almost exclusively by the voluntary help of professional divers.

The finds in the wreck had lain untouched for more than 300 years and thus provide a time capsule of life on board. After 34 years of continuous investigations, 85% (680 sq. m.) of the wreck-site has been examined to date, recovering more than 30,000 separate artefacts, grouped into 17,500 catalogue entries, ranging from canons, skeletons, sculptures to coins, buttons, and insects (Einarsson 2015, 14).

Since the late 1990s, a pharmaceutical-medical context has been established for quite an extensive area of the wreck site. The research process has its starting point in the physical finds and then proceeds to the consultation of applicable historical sources, with the results from the two finally being assimilated. This means that the results emanate from two sets of interlinked disciplines, one where archaeology interacts with history and one where the humanities meet the natural sciences. Hitherto, the findings have been highlighted by the recovery in 2001 of a reasonably well-preserved medical chest, followed by medicinal weights in 2003, a wooden bowl (an apothecary's tool) for gilding pills in 2004 (Lindeke *et al.* 2009) and a dental instrument during the 2013 excavation.

When combined with written evidence, the plethora of archaeological finds of pharmaceutical-medical origin turned out to be an excellent source for information, regarding the trans-national approach to and treatment of medicinal drugs in this early modern period. The finds also provide an insight into a pan-European and global circulation of objects, and that of medical substances in particular (Fors 2016).

Historical background – Scholarly medicine reaches Sweden

Interests of the State were a major driving force in the development and modernisation of early modern Swedish society. The mid-1600s saw the birth of many important Swedish state functions, the creation of which predominantly orchestrated by the Royal Chancellor of the Realm *Axel Oxenstierna*. Not only the military hierarchy but also important personalities within the civil administration were successive to become integral members of the governing class (Wetterberg 2003, 273-276). More often than not, these attributes could be combined in one and the same person. It had become realized that skill and knowledge were important driving forces.

Partly as a consequence of the Reformation, when King Gustav Vasa indiscriminately threw out the old with the new, scholarly medicine had been slow to establish itself in the Nordic Countries and more so in Sweden than in Denmark. Very few dynamic university-educated physicians appeared before the middle of the seventeenth century (Hjelt 1891, 6; Lindroth 1975, 375-412). Family connections, contact networks, and international ties were essential in early modern society and when there was a great demand for skilled people in general, immigration presented an opportunity. The warlords, who were active in the European arena, often governing the newly acquired provinces of the Swedish realm, had insight into the wickerwork and could arrange necessary contacts. For their well-being royals and aristocrats, a new class of nobility and burghers insisted on the immigration of a spectrum of medical competences. From1650 onwards notably the Swedish counts *Magnus Gabriel De la Gardie, Carl Gustaf Wrangel* and *Per Brahe the Younger*, all closely related to the Crown, exercised a great influence on society, not least when it came to culture and science. At times all three held positions as chancellors at universities within the Swedish realm, *De la Gardie* in Uppsala, *Wrangel* in Greifswald and *Brahe* in Turku. They established useful foreign contacts having been already enthused in their formative years as peregrinators on the Continent. Later as significant patrons, they attracted learned men from abroad among them medically skilled individuals (Fåhreus 1936, 220-235; Losman 1980, 107-109; Ullgren 2015, 214-248). Thus, with the establishment of medicine in early-modern Sweden, several of the country's physicians and most apothecaries came to be non-ethnic Swedes, belonging notably to the country's Protestant German minority.

From the mid-1600s, we can see a development in the organisation of medical services and the provisions of medicines, originating from the royal court with the nobility and the armed forces as promoters. The Navy was a sizeable organisation during the times of the Swedish Empire. The commencement of the barber-surgeon's guild took place in 1646. The Admiralty got its first university-educated physician in 1654, when the Swedish doctor *Peter Schallerus* (ennobled *Gripenflycht*) was granted the title of the physician of the fleet, and set about organizing the medical service of the Navy (Wendt 1950, 297-298). In 1663 he became one of the four founding members of the Collegium Medicum, which would soon constitute part of the state administration, headed by the Regent's personal physician, *Archiater Grégoire François Du Rietz*. A native of Flanders, born in Arras in 1607, educated in France and called to Sweden in 1642, *Du Rietz* became a naturalized Swedish nobleman in 1651 (Sacklén 1822, 1-3). He also appeared as Schallerus' teacher (Sacklén 1822, 7-8). The pharmaceutical trade was protected by privilege, with each pharmacy being founded through a royal charter, and the Swedish Apothecary's Society was founded in 1675 (Ahlberg 1908).

Historical background – Alterations in the medicinal paradigm

In the mid-1660s, official Swedish guidelines concerning appropriate ingredients and procedures for the preparation of medicines were yet to come. The first Swedish pharmacopoeia, *Pharmacopoeia Holmiensis* did not appear until 1686, when it was released by the Collegium Medicum (1686). Meanwhile, it was recommended that medicines should preferably be prepared according to the Augsburg Pharmacopoeia (*Dispensatorium Augustanum*). When it materialized, *Pharmacopoeia Holmiensis* carried the subtitle *Galeno-Chymica,* which meant that consideration was to be given not only to the old herbals but also to newer chemical remedies based on raw material from the 'mineral kingdom'. The Galenic and the chymical actually reflected two major theories about healing and the body. Galenic medicine, compatible with Aristotelianism, simply meant a continuation of well-heeded and reliable Hellenistic, Roman medical traditions; while chymical medicine, as introduced by *Paracelsus,* constituted part of a neo-platonic and hermetic world-view where one relied on healing through sympathetic magic (Lindroth 1943, 460; Lund 1901, 181-190; Sybelist 1655). Chymical medicine, while often controversial, successively gained ground in Europe during the seventeenth century.

In the 1620s, the court physician (archiater) of the king Gustav II Adolf, *Jacob Robert of Struan,* a Scotsman, set the tone in medical matters. In 1623, in addition to being a court physician, he was also granted a privilege for the second pharmacy in Stockholm, the *Guenon.* Having settled in Sweden, he was made a nobleman (*Robertson*) in 1630 and introduced into the Swedish house of nobles in 1635 (Forsstrand 1925, 37-54). Not too keen on medical novelties, he is described as a *galenic* physician, preferring to prescribe herbs and spices (Lindroth 1943, 448). This was true also for the Swedish doctor *Anders Sparman*, the city physician of Stockholm at the time. In this capacity, *Sparman* was succeeded in 1660 by *Zacharias Wattrang*, also a Swedish-born physician (Sacklén 1822, 4-5). As city physician of Stockholm, *Wattrang* became one of the founding members of the Collegium Medicum (see above). The emergence on the scene of *Du Rietz, Schallerus* and *Wattrang,* who adhered to influences from continental Europe, altered the setup and facilitated the introduction of a medical regimen in favour of chymical remedies. Thus, within almost thirty years, Paracelsian medicine had become the medical school of choice for the Swedish elite (Lindroth 1943, 447-468). Nevertheless, Galenic theory was far from being abandoned as reflected in the sub-title, *Galeno-Chymica,* of the first pharmacopoeia, when issued in the 1680s.

Carl Gustaf Wrangel, the Swedish Lord High Constable, had, like many of his contemporaries, adopted the new theory of healing by use of the chymical or Paracelsian medicine, as practiced by a number of early modern physicians on the European continent. He was instrumental in bringing the medical practice round to this 'novelty' (Losman 1980, 107-109). For example, a German, *Christian Heraeus*, recognized for his learning, came to Sweden under the patronage of *Wrangel.* He was a son of *Johan Heraeus*, who was a physician in the family of *Count Johan Alberecht II of Mecklemburg-Güstrow,* but also the owner of the pharmacy of the city of Güstrov (Ebentraut 2006, 59). *Christian* stood out as a chemist, knowledgeable in mineralogy and skilled in distillation. As a member of *Wrangel's* court he arrived in Sweden in 1669 (Losman 1980, 43), rapidly got a position at the *Ministry of Mining* in Stockholm, and ended up as a court apothecary and eventually as personal physician to the queen dowager, *Hedvig Eleonora*. A pharmacy was operated in conjunction with the *Ministry of Mining*. According to an authorization of 10 March 1671, an important early task for *Hereaus* was to procure pharmaceutical products from minerals (*Medicamenta Chymica*):

> *'Permission is hereby granted to Laboranten* [chemist] *Heraeus to seek out all kinds of Materials that exist here in the Realm and that the Collegium provide him with these and that he then manufactures thereof all sorts of Medicaments, items that of greater Metals are expected to be able to be made.'* [1]

Two years later, on 10 March 1673, *Hereaus* received his privilege as the owner of this pharmacy, later to be named the *Blackamoor* (Nordholm 1973, 35-36).

Provision of medicines for the Navy

From 1660 onwards, Doctor *Peter Schallerus* was responsible for the organisation of the medical service of the Navy. At the time of the provision of the *Kronan* he was assisted by the Navy's apothecary, *Alexander Steckert,* and its barber-surgeon, *Herman Fuchs*, both Germans. A separate pharmacy (*Apotekarstugan*) for the navy was first mentioned in 1650 (Zettersten 1903, 106-116 and Wendt 1950, 298), and boatswains were referred to as collectors of domestic herbals (AKP1658).

> *'Further to Doctor Schalleri's request to obtain some Boatswain who now after 14 days' picking had gathered some useful Herbs and Blooms for the needs of the Admiralty's Pharmacy, it was resolved that he should get an additional 6 to 8 men, who together with the Apothecary travelled out and collected same.'* [2]

However, it is not apparent how much raw material was actually collected, and what was prepared at the *Apotekarstugan*. Medical drugs were indeed supplied by the town pharmacies, and investigations of contemporary historical documents in war archives reveal that the contents of the medicine chests of the Navy were most likely delivered by *Christian Heraeus* (AKP1679).

> *'The Medicaments were discussed, and the High Commissioner informed that all have been ordered from Apothecary Herreus* [!], *whom alone the Admiral allows making Chests and Boxes for them, one of them was sent there to take measure of how large they should be.'* [3]

---

1   *'Förelades laboranten Heraeus fullmakt skolandes han uppsättia allehanda meterialier som här i riket finnas och Collegium skaffa honaom dem tillhandfe och han sedan tillverka därav allehanda medicamenter, persedlar som av större metaller väntas att göras kunna.'*

2   *'§ 3.Uppå Doctor Schalleri anfordran, att få några båtsmän som nu på 14 dagars tid plockande och hopsamlade några nyttiga kryddor och blomster till Amiralitets Apotekets behov, blev resolverat att han, skulle få 6 à 8 man därtill, som jämte Apotekaren utreste och Colligerade sådant.'*

3   *'13. Om medicamenterna blev discurrerat [diskuterat], och berättade överkommissarien att de är alla beställte hos Apothekaren Herreus [!], allenast holm Ammiralen låter göra kistor och lådor åt dem, sändandes en av dem dit till att taga märke [mått] huru stora de skola vara.'*

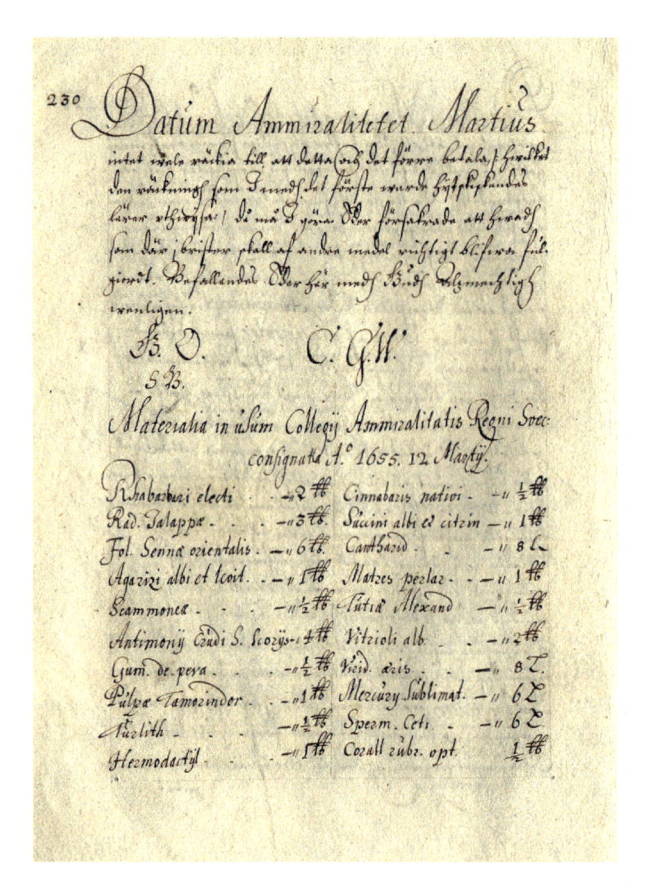

Figure 1: First page of the requisition of Materia Medica from Amsterdam ordered by Carl Gustaf Wrangel in 1655 (AKP1655).

The protocols of the Admiralty show, that on several occasions direct imports from abroad were also undertaken to supply these chests. This mainly involved rare and exotic substances as vital ingredients of *galenic* as well as *chymical* prescriptions.

One such import is worth examining in detail (AKP1655). In 1655 during the Polish War, *Carl Gustaf Wrangel,* at that time Lord Admiral of Sweden, ordered medical supplies from Amsterdam, which was a central hub for almost everything connected with the trade and not least for pharmaceuticals. The order contained 95 different items and was executed by the regularly used Swedish agent, *Peter Trotzig* (Fig. 1). The items in the list were denoted by their Latin names, according to the contemporary pharmacopoeias, and concern simple ingredients *(simplicia)* rather than ready-made pharmaceutical compositions *(composita)*. The list was dominated by herbals and included 12 simple gum resins as well as 21 items constituting *Medicamenta chymica*. Several of the latter comprised inorganic chemical compounds, mainly oxides and salts based on the elements antimony (Sb,) arsenic (As), lead (Pb), iron (Fe), potassium (K), copper (Cu), mercury (Hg), sodium (Na), and zinc (Zn), all belonging to the Paracelsian collection of remedies. The total consignment comprised 80 kg, 13 kg of which was lead oxide, an important ingredient for the preparation of lead plasters and for dressings. A little more than 8 kg of potassium tartrate together with close to 2 kg of antimony sulphide was requested, suitable for the preparation of *Tartarated Antimony* or *Tartar Emetic* to cause vomiting and sweating, and three different mercury formulae, for preparations against vermin and the treatment of syphilitic ulcers. Notable among the herbs were close to 1 kg of *'Fransosen root'* (*Radix sarsaparillae*), a little more than 4 kg of *'Fransosen wood'* (*Lignum guajaci*), again for the treatment of venereal diseases, mainly syphilis. For the treatment of gastrointestinal disturbances, one finds 2.5 kg of Senna leaves *(Folium Sennae)* and slightly less than 1 kg of the root of Chinese rhubarb (*Radix rhabarbarae*), of the best selection. Furthermore, the delivery also contained half a pound each of opium, pearls, red coral and medieval medicinal earth (*Terra sigillata*); all essentially different, but, for a long time to come, typical components of early modern medicine. Several of the items mentioned above reflect trade relations at the time that extended far beyond the borders of Europe.

Aims of the disquisition

The discovery of a pharmaceutical-medical context, at present comprising nearly 180 catalogued entries, raises immediate questions of naval health care and the assortment of drugs used. To what degree does the recovered medical context conform to what was stipulated to be on board a man-of-war, and did the artefacts constitute a closed spatial context that could be regarded as a functional one for medical and pharmaceutical purposes? Is the context likely to reveal a connection with a specific social stratum on board the ship? In a broader context, further questions might include whether the archaeological finds can confirm evidence for cultural exchange from a global historical perspective within the medical-pharmaceutical discipline. Do the artefacts reflect the professional structure of medicine as a science at the time? Do the finds echo the appreciation, the flux of ideas and the influences affecting attitudes towards medical drugs?

The wreck-site

The wreck of the Kronan is a closed find. As a whole, it forms a functional entity that reached a given place at a single moment in time. Before its discovery, it had not been tampered with and it can yield far more information than that gleaned from many separate finds from different places. The remains of the ship mainly comprise the recognisable two-thirds of the port side of her hull; measuring 40 m by 20 m forwards from the stern. It had lain flat on the sand of the seabed ever since the ship sank. At this site, the sea floor is composed of a thin layer of sand over a thick layer of glacial and moraine clays and any object, organic or inorganic that sinks into it is quite well protected.

When retrieved from the wreck-site, the objects are divided into four categories: common articles for everyday use, personal belongings, ordnance and related objects, and ship's equipment. Osteological material constitutes a significant part of the total finds. By the end of 2014, it amounted to 750 kg, about 72 per cent of which was of human origin, with the remaining 28 per cent being bones of animals, originating from food supplies (Einarsson 2014).

About 800 men lost their lives on the Kronan, 183 of whom were retrieved at the time. Thus, about 600 men followed the ship into the Baltic Sea. Those on board comprised a cross-section of the male population of the Swedish realm of the time ranging from those with few personal possessions to exceedingly rich members of the aristocracy. Among the many lives lost when the Kronan sank, three were leaders of the medical professions. The physician of the Navy, *Peter Schallerus,* its chief apothecary,

Figure 2: The medicine chest being excavated at the wreck of the Kronan.

Figure 3: A number of medicinal flasks of various shapes and sizes have been retrieved from the Kronan. Some flasks are square to fit into the wooden casing.

Alexander Steckert, and its chief barber-surgeon, *Herman Fuchs,* were all on duty on board, and perished, to become recorded as missing in action. These individuals represented an exceptionally high and relatively well-established social, as well as professional, stratum of society, and, with their drowning, the Navy lost a considerable amount of its medical knowledge. The rich array of medical-pharmaceutical finds at the site of the wreck bear testimony to the important responsibilities of these men.

The medical-pharmaceutical context – Storage, receptacles, and containers

Within the context of loose objects were partly destroyed small cabinets and chests along with the principle container (Fig. 2), discovered in 2001, altogether making up about 180 entries, according to the excavation log. Awaiting its reconstruction, the framework of the main chest has been taken apart, freeze-dried, and is stored as a 'Lego kit'. The chest contained around 70 receptacles of glass, earthenware or wood, several being undamaged (Fig. 3). The glass jars and bottles vary in size from 4-5 ml up to half a liter, and many are square to fit into the chest framework. In several cases, their openings are corbelled to facilitate being sealed by parchment, leather or bladder. Residues of sealing occasionally still remain. The glass, essentially of two types – either clear and colourless, or green to brownish – is frequently very thin.

While the medical context at large presents a plethora of earthen jars varying in form, colour, and size, the chest contained only a few jars and pots of blue and white tin-glazed pottery. Round turned wooden jars of set sizes were placed in cassettes fitting into the chest. Notably, one such cassette carried 10 jars, each of c.1 liter, originally marked with cartouches. Among the isolated finds salvaged from the wreck-site are a set of artefacts relating to what appears to be smaller wooden boxes fitted with sliding-lids on which written texts can be discerned (Fig. 4).[4] These artefacts have been recovered on five different occasions over a period of nine years (1998-2007), but are believed to be connected to the main chest.

The simplest text to be elucidated (Fig 4a) reads '*Sem Foenicul*', and the text refers to '*Semen foniculi*', or fennel fruit. The second, '*pl: Rhabar Tóst*'. (Fig. 4b) occurs on the lid of a preserved box. The abbreviation '*pl*', is construed as *pulvis* and the whole text as *Pulvis Rhabarbara Tosti*, which means '*the toasted root of medical rhubarb in powder*'. A third text, '*pl fúmal*' (Fig. 4c), to be interpreted as *Pulvis fumalis*, refers to incense. The abbreviation *pl.* also appears on two additional objects, with a faint ensuing word on one of them discerned as *Rhabar*. The text on the other lid is too faint to be legible.

---

4   The objects were cleaned according to standard procedures as applicable, treated with a preservative (Panacide' 0.5 ml/l), PEG 400 (10 %) and freeze dried. During the course of the cleaning procedures written texts could be discerned on the lids. The texts were documented by photography in different lighting conditions. All texts initially noted remained intact after conservation.

Figure 4: Wooden box fragments with denoted texts; 4a, Sem Foenicúl (fennel fruit), 4b, Pl Rharb Tost (toasted root of medical rhubarb), 4c, pl fumal (incense).

2 cm

Figures 5: The clyster pipe designed to be attached to a bladder (5a). The application of a clyster according to the English surgeon John Ardene in 1412 (5b).

The medical-pharmaceutical context – Appliances and accessories

Finds of instruments and tools are proportionately few. Thus, no closed find of, for example, a barber-surgeon's chest, has as yet materialized. However, some isolated highly informative objects did appear: a pestle of green glass presumably belonging to a glass mortar, a wooden nozzle identified as a clyster pipe (Fig. 5), a syringe-tip made of horn and a forged iron forceps for tooth-extraction (Fig. 6). This dental instrument

Figure 6a: The forceps for teeth-extraction found in 2014.

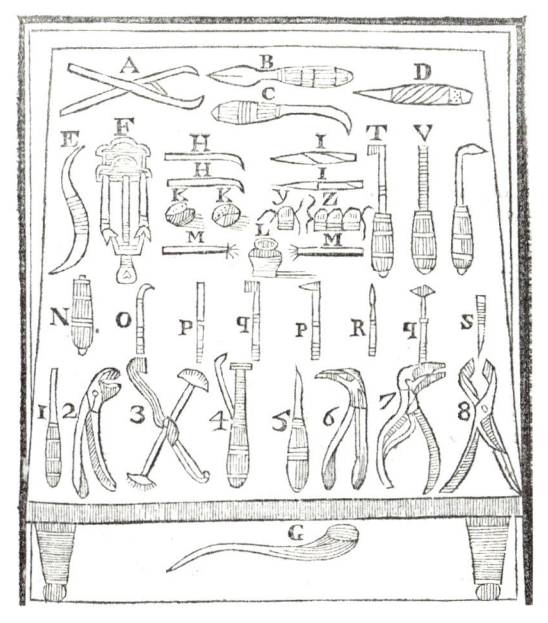

Fig. XL. POUR LES GENCIVES ET LES DENTS.

Figure 6b: Dental instruments depicted in Dionis 1708.

Figure 6c: Saint Appolonia the patroness of dentistry holding a forceps in her left hand. Painting by Albertus Pictor (†1509) in Härnevi Church, north-west of Stockholm.

Figures 7: The scruple weight marked 'CW', ascribable to the weight-maker Christoph Weinmann in Nuremberg, before (7a) and after (7b) conservation.

measures 12.4 cm and does not seem to have an adjusting screw. The clyster pipe is designed to be attached to a bladder (Fig. 5b), and the horn-tip to a pewter syringe.

Moreover, among the large quantities of odds and ends classed as solitary finds, three apothecary's weights were identified. Two of them measure two scruples (nominal weight 2.48 g), recovered in 2003, and the third an ounce (nominal weight 29.69 g), recovered in 1999. The apothecary's (or medical) weight system differs from that in common use and is divided differently. The Swedish medical weight system, which was derived from Nuremberg, Germany, was laid down in the charter of the Collegium Medicum in 1668. One of the scruples is heavily corroded while the other one is in very good condition with a weight of 2.32 g and stamped *'CW'* (Fig.7). The ounce weight, crusts included, weighed 29.76 g (nominally 29,69 g), and measured 18.5 x 18.5 mm at the base, 13 x 13 mm at the top, with a height of 14.5 mm. An elusive solitary find in the pharmaceutical context was a hemispherical wooden bowl, unearthed in 2004, with traces of gold adhering to its concave inner surface. However, this had a perceived connection to finds in previous excavations, two glass jars (one in 2002 and one in 2001) containing organic matter, sprinkled with gold flakes and a bundle of gold foil, (in 1996). This prompted the idea that gilded pills were prepared on board the Kronan.[5]

The medical-pharmaceutical context – medicinal drugs

If now we return to the medicinal drugs, our still on-going macroscopic and microscopic, physical and chemical analytical work has resulted in some rather interesting results. To date, 15 herbals and seven Paracelsian elements ascribable to *Medicamenta chymica,* have been positively identified as isolated substances (*simplicia*) or in mixtures (*composita*), representing at least 20 different remedies.

Hitherto identified herbs (Appendix 1) are: anise (*Semen anisi*), fennel (*Semen foeniculi*), galangal (*Radix galangae*), ginger (*Radix zingiberis*), pine resin (*Resina*

---

5   For further details see Lindeke *et al.* 2009.

Figures 8: Two small wooden boxes (8a) containing externally well-preserved seeds (8b) of bottle gourd, squash and watermelon.

Figure 9: The ivory capsule with its loose base-plate containing a salve moulded directly into the cylinder. The exclusive material and exquisite craftsmanship reveal a luxury object.

abietis), horse-chestnut (*Aesculus hippocastanum*), calabash (*Lagenaria sicerari*), clove (*Cariophylli aromatici*), long pepper (*Piper longum*), nutmeg (*Nucis moschatae*), watermelon (*Citrullus lanatus*), pumpkin (*Cucurbitae pepo*), rhubarb (*Radix rhabarbari*), senna leaves (*Folium sennae*) and black pepper (*Piper nigrum*). They have been identified as such or in mixtures. For example, senna leaves together with clove and some other non-positively identified ingredients, supposedly a tea for the stomach, was contained in one round wooden jar. Mixtures of wonderfully preserved cucurbit seeds were deposited in two small wooden boxes (Fig. 8). For the final identification of

Figures 10: Thin glass jars from the medicine chest containing: 10a, elemental sulphur (Flores sulphuris) and 10b, mixtures of antimony sulphide and antimony oxide (Antimonum crudum).

the seeds, we were assisted by the USA-based Cucurbit Network (2003).[6] According to the deciphered texts (see above) there were two variants of rhubarb in the medicine chest, the dried root (*Radix rhabarbari*) and the roasted root (*Radix rhabarbari tosti*). Similarly, the presence of fennel (*Semen foniculi*) and incense *(Pulvis fumalis)* can be deduced from texts applied on fragments of broken boxes (see above).

A most noteworthy solitary find is a salve, encased in a screw-topped capsule of turned ivory with a push-through base. The stick is composed of a mixture of lard and wax (Fig. 9).

The chymical preparations are represented by the presence of formulations containing the elements antimony (Sb), lead (Pb), gold (Au), iron (Fe,) copper (Cu), mercury (Hg) and sulphur (S).[7]

Mercury is present in a formulation composed of the elemental metal and pine resin (*Resina abietis*) in a simple ointment (*Unguentum hydrargyri*), contained in a small stoneware jug. This was actually the first find subjected to chemical analysis. Elemental sulfur (*Flores sulphuris*) was found in a broken glass jar in the major medicinal chest (Fig. 10a).[8] Among the finds in the chest, three glass receptacles turned out to contain antimony, as a mixture of its oxide and sulfide (partly oxidized, *Antimonum crudum*) (Fig.10b) but also in formulations with this mixture together with different

---

6   Thomas Andreas Editor, The Cucurbit Network, P. O. Box 560483, Miami, FL 33256, USA.

7   Scanning microscope analysis (SEM) was performed at the Glass Research Institute (Glafo) at Växjö, Sweden. Details on the analyses can be obtained upon request (bjorn.lindeke@telia.com).

8   The SEM analysis clearly showed that sulphur (S) and oxygen (O) were the only elements present in the samples, with the former accounting for 95 per cent of the total weight and the atomic ratio S:O being 10,2:1.

herbal constituents.[9] All three jars were remarkably heavy and the contents exhibited yellow-orange-reddish colours and had densities ranging from 3.6 to 4.6 g per ml. The gold has been previously dealt with (see above). One drawer in the chest contained yellow amber (*Succinum citrinum*) in the form of granules. Formulations containing lead, iron, and copper remain to be further analyzed.

So far, no fewer than nine plasters, more or less in the form of sausage-shaped rolls, have been retrieved from the wreck-site. They were spread over the area and we can here talk about three different sub-contexts, one central, one about 3 m to the NW and one about 4 m SE of the central one. The plasters have been salvaged over a time span of ten diving seasons: three in 2003, one in 2004, three in 2005 and two in 2013. They have as yet not undergone any detailed analysis, but presumably, all of them are among those listed in the *Pharmacopoeia Holmiensis* of 1686 (see above). Ocular inspection reveals a predominance of herbal constituents and the texture of natural resin (*Styrax balsam*?) is discernable. Spot tests show that at least one or two of the plasters contain lead.

Finds of wine and spirits are rather extensive at the wreck-site, and due to contextual factors, it is likely that some of these were intended for medical use. The *Pharmacopoeia Holmiensis* lists some alcohols for this purpose: *Spiritus Vini simplex, Spiritus Vini Gallici* and *Spiritus Vini rectficatus* (Collegium Medicum 1686, 7). These have been identified among the contents 28 analyzed bottles.

Discussion

In early modern times, Sweden had to rely on import of many ingredients for the formulation of medicines. Raw materials could originate from southern Europe or various parts of the Old and New Worlds. Amsterdam, Antwerp and Hamburg/Altona were prominent places at that time in Europe for the purchase of constituents of medicinal drugs. From a Swedish' perspective, trade connections, developed since the Middle Ages, were well in place (Dalhede 2001). Baltic and North Sea ports, Stockholm included, were linked through trade and family networks. In 1650, the Dutch purchased about 40 per cent of all Swedish iron and Sweden acquired about one-half of its imports from Amsterdam (Lindblad 1990). Thus, the Dutch Republic was Sweden's foremost trading partner. Contacts were already established with several trading houses and agents, such as Peter Trotzig (see above), were on location (Losman 1980, 197-209; Lindblad 1990, 205-228).

Not only was the material of the drugs and equipment imported, it was also necessary to rely on foreign recognized prescriptions and instructions for the formulation of medicines. It would be *c.* 40 years before Sweden produced its first pharmacopoeia, *Pharmacopoeia Holmiensis,* in 1686. In the meantime, drugs were prepared primarily according to the Augsburg Pharmacopoeia (*Dispensatorium Augustanum*), and later also to the Danish system (*Dispensatorium Hafniensae*) edited in 1658. All the same, the leading circles in the Swedish realm were quite well informed about the state of the art, and phenomena from the medical arena in Europe were rapidly adopted. To a great

---

9   The densities of the sampled materials were determined at 20°C using a 5 ml flask pycnometer. The substances were dried to constant weights. Drying was done *in vacuo* <1 kPa over P_2O_5 for 65 min. at 60.0°C. Corrections were made for an estimated seawater salt content of 0.8 per cent.

extent, this depended on actions catalysed by individuals belonging to the country's German minority.

The full and varied medical-pharmaceutical context on the wreck-site shows that the *Kronan* was well equipped, at least qualitatively, in this respect. In addition, the best medical support was accessible in the form of the Navy's own physician, *Peter Schallerus,* its chief apothecary, *Alexander Steckert,* and its chief barber-surgeon, *Herman Fuchs.*

Of the drugs found on the Kronan, the five 'Paracelsian' elements ascribable to *Medicamenta chymica* are conspicuous, most notably antimony. These have been positively identified as such or present in mixtures, representing at least twenty different remedies. Antimony was the leading element in Paracelsian medicine and medical formulations containing this element had become quite common in Europe in the late seventeenth century. In the literature, they are known as *'Antimonials'* (Leméry 1707). These drugs have been credited with mainly emetic properties, but antimony-containing compounds were also used as purgative and diaphoretic curatives. The source of the element is mainly the mineral stibnite, consisting of raw, blue-grey antimony-trisulphide (*Stibii trisulfidum crudum*). This can be converted to antimony-trioxide (*Oxidum stibiosum*) or the orange-red antimony-pentasulphide (*Stibii pentasulfidum*), but most common are more or less unspecified mixtures of the various sulphides and oxides. Stibnite had a very central role within alchemy, as one marvelled at the array of coloured substances that could be procured from the element. Accordingly, alchemists considered antimony to be one of the best starting materials for making gold (Leméry 1707). Elemental sulphur (*Flores sulphuris*), a common and typical curative, belonging to the *Medicamentis chymica,* is listed in *Pharmacopoea Holmiensis* together with some composed preparations in which it is an ingredient (Collegium Medicum 1686). Contrary to what we found for antimony, sulphur is not among the compounds in the requisition from 1655 ordered by the Admiralty (AKP1655), but this is not unexpected since, from the Middle Ages, sulphur had been produced domestically, and from time to time even exported. This also goes for alum, another important Paracelsian remedy, of which there were vast resources within Sweden, often together with sulphur. Alum neither is on the requisition nor is it found in the medical context at the wreck-site. The latter is not to be expected since alum comprises a readily water-soluble salt. This also goes for other water-soluble compounds such as tartaric acid.

As previously stated, Paracelsian medicine began to make strong inroads into the Swedish realm in the early 1600s, later to become the medical speciality of choice of the elite (Lindroth 1943, 452). In line with this, evidence is that the contents of the medicine chests intended for the Admiralty were supplied by *Christian Heraeus* at the Blackamoor pharmacy (AKP16790517), a provider of *Medicamenta chymica.* Ten years later, in 1686, the *Pharmacopoea Holmiensis* lists no less than 17 antimonial preparations (Collegium Medicum 1686). To sum up, the antimonial finds from the Kronan in particular, confirm that through influences from Protestant Europe, Paracelsian medicine had become well established in Sweden by the mid-1600s.

Regarding the herbs, many seeds, at first glance looked quite well-preserved, as for example the horse chestnuts and the cucurbits (Fig. 8). However, although the seeds coats appeared completely intact, the embryos inside had long since deteriorated. However, why were cucurbit seeds brought along? The *Pharmacopoea Holmiensis* comprises three formulae containing various cucurbit seeds, albeit in all three cases combined with a number of other ingredients (Collegium Medicum 1686). One of these would have been used in cases of bladder stones and related ailments as recorded by Johannes (1684, 287):

> '*The kernels of these herbs pounded and drunk with warm Wine or sweet Milk that mitigates the burning when letting one's Water, cleanses the Kidneys, Thighs and the Bladder; However one should more often take this medicament when the cause of Stone is in the Bladder, than when in the Kidneys.*'

In fact, similar claims are made even to-day for some herbal formulations containing cucurbit seed on the Swedish market.

Another interesting discovery involved two formulations of medical rhubarb, *Rhadix rabarbarae* and *Radix rabarbarae tosti* (Fig. 4b). The best quality medicinal rhubarb, the root of *Rheum palmatum,* comes from China, where it has been regarded as an important medicinal remedy ever since 2,700 B.C. Knowledge about the drug probably did not reach Europe until the first century A.D., with interest culminating in early modern times.

The Englishman *Roger Bacon* commented in the 1260s on the use of the root: '*Likewise the Latins say that Rhubarb purges bile, but the Greeks and Aristotle that it purges phlegm*' (McVaugh 2009). Four different formulae containing rhubarb are described in the *Pharmacopoeia Holmensis* of 1686, but no roasted (*rabarbarae tosti*) variant is mentioned. Neither is it mentioned in the *Swedish Medical* tariff of 1687 or in that of 1739. The earliest source mentioning the use of the roasted root in Europe is by *Ryff* (1602, 182). At about the time of the Kronan, the Swede *Herman Nicolai Grim* clearly used the drug in his practice when employed as a physician by the Dutch VOC (Verenigde Oostindische Companie) in East India (Grim 1684, 185-186). Grim was a remarkably well-travelled person, who through his contacts was instrumental in a cross-cultural exchange of medical manners and customs (Fors in press). Born on Gotland, Grim received his education as a barber-surgeon in Copenhagen. He visited Greenland, and after spending years in Ceylon, on the coasts of Coromandel and Malabar, he became employed as chief barber-surgeon in Batavia. He returned to Sweden via Gotland and in 1698 turned up in Stockholm. His work *Compendium Medico-Chymicum*, its first edition published in Batavia and a second in 1684 in Augsburg (Grim 1684), was the most extensive pharmaceutical work of its time to be written by a practicing Swedish doctor. We know from documents found in the Swedish War Archives that *Carl Linneaus*, when physician of the Admiralty, included the roasted variant of the rhubarb root (Fig. 11) among Navy supplies on the eve of the war against Russia in 1741 (Lindeke 2009: RA, 1741). So far, the year 1741 has been regarded as the oldest documented date for the use of roasted rhubarb in Swedish medicine. With respect to the finds from the Kronan, this date can now be moved back by at least 65 years.

Why then all this fuss about the *roasted* root of rhubarb? Medicinal rhubarb exhibits two types of pharmacological effects, one astringent and one purgative. Depending on the dose, one or the other will dominate. It had been learnt by experience that when roasted the root loses nearly all of its purgative properties and becomes more of a tonic. This information, which through cultural exchanges can probably be traced back to China, eventually reached users together with the drug

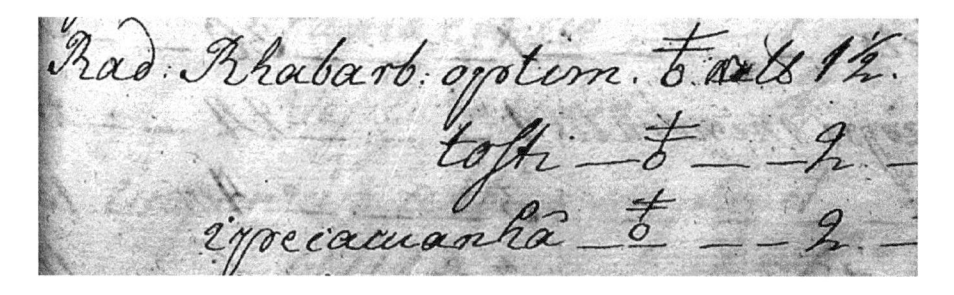

Figure 11: The reference to powdered Radix Rhabarbara Tosti in Linneaus' memorandum to the Collegium Medicum in 1741.

(see for example Grim). It should be noted that the sources for our roasted roots – the Kronan, Grim and the VOC, Linnéaus and the Swedish Navy – all involve activities on board ships at sea, that is, in situations that one would be far better off without any purgative effects.

Before discussing tools and instruments, it might be fitting to mention the incense, *Pulvis fumalis*. Incense has been, and still is, used in almost every society with cultural exchange going back to Neolithic times. Incense is not really a medical ingredient but rather an aromatic biotic material that releases fragrant smoke when burned, and as with ink and sealing wax, it was prepared by apothecaries in early modern times. Two related formulas for incense are listed in the *Pharmacopoeia Holmensis*, one is *Candela pro fumo*, and the other *Pulvis pro fumo communis*. Incense can be composed of a variety of ingredients. One of the Swedish formulae contained the resins amber, copal, styrax, and virak, together with lavender and rose-petals. Amber is endemic to the southern parts of the Baltic Sea. Copal could come from several sources, but in the actual case probably from *Hymenaea verrucosa* in East Africa. Styrax was harvested from *Styrax tonkinensis,* an East Asian tree, and virak (also called olibanum) from *Boswellia Carteri* native to Somaliland and neighbouring countries.

Few tools were recovered from the medical-pharmaceutical context, and, as stated earlier, a rather well-preserved barber-surgeon chest (if such existed) still awaits discovery. Nevertheless, some of the finds found separately can be regarded as unique. This includes the hemispherical wooden bowl for gilding pills, the scruple weight and, last but not least, the forged-iron tooth-extraction forceps (Fig. 6a), unearthed in 2014; that is, in the 34th season of excavations. Details of the discovery of the wooden bowl and evidence of the medical use of gold on board have been discussed elsewhere (Lindeke *et al.* 2009). Nevertheless, as regards cultural exchange, the practice of coating pills with precious metals goes back to Avicenna (AD 980-1037) and appears to have come of age in the 17th century (Bela 2006). The Swedish National Archives contain a record of the use of gilded pills for headache *'förgyllte hufvudpiller för 3 mark'*. This dates to 1584, when the itinerant German apothecary *Abraham Gutschimtz* presented a bill amounting to three marks, to the Duke at the Swedish castle of Gripsholm (RA 1584).

Regarding the scruple weights (Fig. 7), consultation of historical sources reveals that the mark *'CW'* belonged to Christoph Weinmann, a weight-maker in Nuremberg, who used these initials, arranged vertically inside an oval, as his maker's

TRANSFER BETWEEN SEA AND LAND

mark from 1667 onwards (Lockner 1981, 825).[10] He became a master craftsman in 1657 and a sworn master craftsman ('Geschworener') in 1669, which means that he supervised the quality of production in Nuremberg. This proves that not only the Swedish medical weight system but also the necessary equipment, as laid down in the charter of the Collegium Medicum in 1668, derived from Nuremberg. According to its stamp, the scruple could not have been cast by Weinmann earlier than 1667 and it must have arrived on board the Kronan no later than early 1676. This specimen is considered to be the oldest so far found in Sweden.

The discovery of the forceps for extracting teeth has attracted some attention among dental historians. This find takes us back to Alexandria in 249 A.D. and the death of *Saint Appolonia*, the patroness of dentistry (Fig. 6c). Instruments of this kind (Fig. 6b) were known and used in Europe at the time of the Kronan (Dionis 1708, 49). Here too, the ship's specimen is considered to be the oldest so far retrieved in Sweden. Finally, for treatment of the opposite end of the body, there is the cluster pipe for insertion into the rectum (Fig. 5a). An illustration from 1412 describes the procedure (Fig. 5b), where a barber-surgeon (?) holds a pig's bladder attached to the pipe to perform the operation. Here it illustrates an enema cure for gout, as described by the English surgeon John Arderne in his *De Arte Phisicaliu et de Chirurgia* (Svenberg and Jones 2015).

The wreck of the Kronan is often compared to that of the Mary Rose, the famous flagship of Henry VIII, which went down just outside Portsmouth in 1545, 131 years earlier (Rule 1982). This shipwreck also produced a rich, albeit somewhat different, medical-pharmaceutical context, namely a barber-surgeon's cabin on the starboard side of the main gun-deck, which contained not only medicines but also a wealth of tools and instruments. An undamaged medicinal chest was recovered in 1980 (Castle and Derham 2005). Forty out of 44 analysed formulae contained herbal and/or animal constituents, particularly in formulations based on fats, waxes or oils. Of the remaining four formulae, one showed the presence of copper and sulphur, one of lead, one of mercury, and one of zinc and sulphur. There were also plasters, along with dressings. Taken as a whole, the medicinal context on the wreck-site of the Mary Rose reflects Galenic rather than Paracelsian medicine. This is not unexpected since Paracelsus died in 1544 and his theories had as yet not come of age (Lindroth 1943). In this respect, the Mary Rose differs from the Kronan.

While the closed finds on the Kronan produced by the medicine chests point to a strikingly homogeneous medicinal context for professional use, a few discoveries stand apart from this. Gilded pills and a cerate encased in a capsule of turned ivory must reflect personal belongings. The law of 1667, signed by Charles XI, clearly stated that the ships of the royal fleet should be provided with an ample selection of applicable medicinal drugs (Carl XI, 1667), but this was hardly meant to include gilded pills or ivory capsules. However, these items fit in well with the luxurious context that is so conspicuous in the functional entity presented by the wreck of the Kronan. This in turn reflects the almost mandatory need for exuberance among the up-and-coming nobility of the period (Lappalainen 2007, 250-256). Formulae ordered by the nobility frequently

---

10   We are very much indebted to Dr. Patrick Cassitti, University of Bamberg, who was of great help in tracking down the provenance of the scruple.

involved luxury items. While the order for the Navy made by *Wrangel* in 1655 included just a few such articles – two balms, pearls, and red coral – his private orders could be of quite a different kind. For example, while he was staying at his castle Spyker in Rügen in May 1676, one of his private requisitions was directed to the physician *Wedelin Sybelist* in Hamburg. It contained 55 items, 21 of which were distilled ethereal oils and *Confectio alchermes comp.* (RA 1676). The latter was a composition containing musk, ambergris, carmine and, indeed, even gold. Here we are talking about medical remedies of a sort that were typically in fashion for the royalty and nobility. Ethereal oils and such types of *Confectios* were among the most expensive remedies that money could buy.

While focussing on cultural exchange, it would be inappropriate not to expand somewhat on the contribution of *Wedelin Sybelist* (Wacker 2013, 453). Just like Grim, he was an experienced and well-travelled individual who may have influenced Swedish medical practices. Born in Halle, *Sybelist* became a doctor of medicine in Wittenberg in 1625. From 1634 to 1642, he was personal physician to Mikhail Fedorovich, the Tsar of Russia. After some years in Northern Germany, among other occupations, he attended *Fredrik III*, the Duke of Holstein-Gottorp, who happened to be the father of the Swedish queen dowager, *Hedvig Eleonora*. In 1652, *Sybelist* then turned up at Wolfenbütteler Hof (court) as personal physician to Duke *August the Younger of Brunswick-Lüneburg*. In the 1660s *Sybelist* came under the patronage of the Swedish count *Magnus Gabriel De la Gardie*, who was then governor in Riga. After spending some time with the Swedish army, he moved to Stockholm to work as a director at the laboratory of the *Ministry of Mining,* from whence he returned to Hamburg in 1670. This was when *Heraeus* took over responsibility for the laboratory. *Sybelist* was a devoted Paracelsian physician and instrumental in disseminating the theories of chymical medicine (see above). This interest matured during his stay with Duke *August* at Wolfenbütteler Hof. The two of them had a common interest in alchemy and while at Wolfenbütteler Hof, *Sybelist* published his *Manuale Hermeticum* (1655). In these early modern times, Wolfenbüttel was an important cultural hub in Central Europe that was visited by hordes of peregrinating noblemen. Notably, Duke *August* was one of the acquaintances of *Carl Gustav Wrangel,* and the Swedish National Archives contains correspondence between the two from the period 1647-1666. Both had a common interest in chymical medicine and according to Losman (1980, 163), Duke *August* was in many ways normative for *Wrangel.* With this, *Sybelist* will be the final osier that we entwine into the wickerwork of royalties, aristocrats, noblemen, physicians, apothecaries and barber-surgeons who were instrumental in getting Paracelsian medicine recognized in Sweden.

Conclusions

The discovery of a pharmaceutical-medical context on the wreck-site of the Kronan initiated a research process in which archaeology joined forces with medicine and pharmacy. A systematic analysis of each physical find spurred the consultation of applicable historical sources whereby many forgotten and dormant documents could be revitalized. What can the physical finds associated with a given date in maritime and medical history tell us about the reliability of what was set down in the historical documents? Can they shed further light on facts and occurrences? We found that the combined information from artefacts and documents does give answers, is confirmative and generates new information. As opposed to other closed finds such as the officer's chest with its rich contents, the medicine chests offer a strikingly homogeneous context. They point exclusively to substances of a medicinal nature. The archaeological finds are in good accord with contemporary historical source material. Circumstances and statements that appear in written sources are convincingly confirmed by the artefacts that survived from the medical-pharmaceutical archaeological context. We see items that are relevant to Wrangel's requisition from Amsterdam in 1655 and, with few exceptions most of the finds from the *Kronan* can be connected with drugs listed in the *Pharmacopoeia Holmiensis,* when it materialized ten years later.

When consulting the Swedish War-Archives it was possible in fact to come across several requisitions of *Materia Medica* from Amsterdam dating to the 1650s and onwards. All concern the ingredients of different kinds of medicaments that should be of the best possible quality. Thus, through an extensive exchange of knowledge, those in leading positions in Stockholm were already well-informed and up-to-date, fifty years prior to the distribution of the *Pharmacopoeia Holmiensis.* Not unexpectedly, these requisitions followed the common European pattern for *Materia Medica*, based on the various more or less identical pharmacopeias of the time: *Dispensatorium Nürnbergiensis 1546* (Germany), *Dispensatorium Augustanum 1564* (Germany), *Dispensatorium Hafniensae 1658* (Denmark) and *Collectanea Chymica Leydensia 1684* (Holland). Since contacts with trading houses were already well-established and commissionaires were in place, pertinent information could be transmitted together with products and commodities. With Amsterdam as an intermediary hub for the trade in pharmaceuticals, exotic influences spread, albeit indirectly. A trend for exotica took hold during the seventeenth century as European traders and aristocrats realized what lay beyond the oceans. The constituents of the incense, *Pulvis fumalis,* found in the Kronan was dependent on trade with the Arab world, and the medicinal rhubarb, *Rhadix rabarbarae,* depended on trade with China. This was a century of a colonial concurrence, in which Sweden *per se* was not very successful. However, some adventurous individuals travelled widely and the discovery of *Pulvis rabarbara tosti* on board the Kronan has led us to Grim. Here was a man who knew how to exploit the opportunities offered by the VOC, make records of his experiences, and bring them back to Europe, and, ultimately, to Sweden (Fors in press).

These goods transported the influences and exotic features that became quite the fashion among the Swedish nobility and royalty in the mid-1600s, and festivities on Moorish themes were not uncommon (Ullgren 2015, 165). The name *Blackamoor* given to the pharmacy owned by *Hereaus*, is a further example of such cultural exchange.

Two of the discoveries with a medicinal context – equipment for the gilding of pills and a salve encased in a capsule of turned ivory – yield a further dimension than data on shape and function. Such objects often had a symbolic value and fit into the material culture of the *Kronan* at large, which reveals the strident ambition of the time, on the part of the social elite to constantly manifest its social and material superiority (Englund 1989, 70). Such an ambition is accentuated in the private requisition made by *Wrangel* in May 1676, reflecting a new material culture which revolved around the consumption of expensive imported medical substances (Fors 2016).

Finally, the scruple is *one* explicit example that illustrates and confirms cultural exchange between Nuremberg and Stockholm during the time of the Swedish Empire.

Sweden not only adapted the medical weight system of Nuremberg, but Stockholm also became a market for 'Nuremberg Ware'.

The content of the medicine chest found on the Kronan clearly reflects the attitude to medicinal drugs current throughout the Swedish realm and confirms the on-going change in the European paradigm with respect to *Materia medica,* of which Sweden in 1676 was an integral part.

Acknowledgements

The authors would like to express their thanks to Lars Einarsson and Max Jahrehorn at Kalmar County Museum for pleasant cooperation and creative discussions in the evaluation of the archaeological finds and to Hjalmar Fors Uppsala University for fruitful discussions with respect to the cultural exchange in the development of early modern medicine in Sweden. Thanks also to Gertie Johansson at the Hagstömer library, the Karolinska Institute for here never-ending support in supplying applicable illustrations. The work was supported by grants from Apoteket AB, Activa Science Work AB and the Swedish Academy of Pharmaceutical Sciences, which are gratefully acknowledged.

References: archives

Riksarkivet (RA), Swedish National Archives

RA. 1584, Kammarkollegiet 1584. Medicinalväsendet 4:3 *Apotekens register 1581-1584*

RA, Skoklostersamlingen E:8183

RA 1676, Skoklostersamlingen. E:8201 letter, 26th May

RA 1741, Collegium Medicum, *Inkomna handlingar, allmänna serien 1741-1750*, p.44 ff. 284 (E2-7).

Krigsarkivet (KA), Swedish War Archives

Protocols of the Admiralty (AKP)

Year-month-date

AKP1655-03-12

AKP1658-05-25

AKP1679-01-17

References

Ahlberg, K. 1908. *Den svenska farmaciens historia*. Stockholm: Wilhelm Billes Bokförlags Aktiebolag.

Bela, Z. 2006. Who invented Avicenna's gilded pills? *Early Science and Medicine*11. Leiden: Koninklikje Brill NV, 1-10.

Carl then Elfft, 1668. *Sveriges Rijkes Siö-Lagh*. Göteborg.

Castle, J. and Derham, B. 2005. The contents of the Barber-Surgeon's cabin, in: Gardiner, J. and Allen, M.J. (eds.). *Before the mast – Life and death aboard the Mary Rose*. Portsmouth: The Mary Rose Trust, 189-225.

Collegium Medicum 1686. *Pharmacopoeja Holmiensis, Galeno-Chymica*. Facsimile1979. Stockholm: Rediviva.

Dahlhede, Ch. 2001. *Handelsfamiljer på Stormakttidens Europamarknad.* Partille: Warne förlag.

Dionis, M. 1708. *Cours d'Operations de Chirurgie, demonstrées au Jardain Royal.* Bruxelles: Les Frères t'Srerstevens et Antoine Claudinot.

Ebentraut, R. 2006. Das virtuelle Schloss – Die Sprache der Inventare unter Johan Albrecht II. *Schoss Güstrow. Prestige und Kunst 1556-1636*, (Ausstellungskatalog). Güstrow.

Einarsson, L. 1997. Artefacts from the Kronan (1676): categories, preservation and social structure, in: Mark, R. (ed.) 1997. *Artefacts from Wrecks. Oxbow Monograph* 84. Exeter, 209-218.

Einarsson, L. 2015. *Rapport om 2014 års marinarkeologiska undersökningarna av regalskeppet Kronan.* Kalmar: Kalmar County Museum.

Englund, P. 1989. *Det hotade huset. Adliga föreställningar om samhället under stormaktstiden.* Stockholm: Atlantis.

Fors, H. 2016. Medicine and the Making of a City. *ISIS* 107.3, 473-494.

Fors, H. (in press). Extracting the exotic. Global chymical medicine in the seventeenth century. Routledge.

Forsstrand, C. 1925. En Stockholmsläkare under förra hälften av 1600-talet. *St. Eriks Årsbok.* Stockholm, 37-54.

Fåhraeus, R. 1936. *Magnus Gabriel De la Gardie.* Stockholm: Hugo Gebers Förlag.

Glete, J. 1999. Hur stor var Kronan? Något om stora örlogsskepp i Europa under 1600-talets senare hälft. *Forum Navale* 55. Karlskrona, 17-25.

Grim, H.N. 1684. *Comp. Medico-Chymicum.* Augsburg: Theophili Göbelii, 2nd ed. Augsburg.

Hjelt, O.E.A. 1891. *Svenska och finska medicinalverkets historia 1663-1812, Vol I.* Helsingfors.

Lappalainen, M. 2007. *Släkten, makten, staten – Familjen Creutz i 1600-talets Sverige och Finland.* Stockholm: Norstets.

Leméry, N. 1707. *Traité de l'Antimoine.* Paris: Jean Boudot.

Lindblad, J. Th. 1990. Evidence of Dutch-Swedish trade in the 17th century, in: Lemmic, J.Ph.S. and van Konningsbrugge, J.S.A.M. 1990 (eds.). *Baltic affair. Relations between the Netherlands and North-Eastern Europe 1500-1800.* Nijmegen, 205-228.

Lindeke, B. 2006. Linné rustar för krig. *Hippokrates* 23. Helsingfors, 97-121.

Lindeke, B., Ohlson, B., Einarsson, L. and Jahrehorn, M. 2009. Gilded pills in the medical chest on board the warship Kronan. *Journal of Nordic Archaeological Science* 16. Uppsala, 25-31.

Lindroth, S. 1943. Paracelsismen i Sverige till 1600-talets mitt. *Lychnos-Bibliotek 7.* Uppsala: Almqvist & Wiksell.

Lindroth, S. 1975. *Svensk Lärdomshistoria.* Stockholm: Norstedts.

Lockner, P. 1981. *Die Merkzeichen der Nürnberger Rotschmiede.* Munich: Bayerisches Nationalmuseum.

Losman, A. 1980. *Carl Gustaf Wrangel och Europa.* Stockholm: Almqvist & Wiksell.

Lund, T. 1901. *Hälsobegrepp i Norden under sextonde århundradet.* Stockholm: Hugo Gebers Förlag.

McVaugh, M. 2009. The 'Experience-Based Medicine' of the Thirteenth Century, in: Sylla, E.D. and Newman, W.R. (eds.). *Evidence and Interpretation in Studies on Early Science and Medicine.* Leiden, 114.

Nordholm, U. 1973. Några data om Morianens apotekare under de första hundra åren. *Farmacihistoriska sällskapets årsskrift*. Stockholm; Apotekarsocieteten, 35-47.

Palmberg, J. 1684. *Serta Florea Svecana el. Den Swänske Örtekrantz, Gudi den aldra högste til åhra, den naturälskarom til lust och behag, 2nd ed.* Stregnäs.

Rule, M. 1982. *The Mary Rose -The excavation and Rising of Henry VIII's Flagship*. London: Conway Maritime Press Ltd.

Ryff, M.G. 1602. *Neuwe außgerüste deutsche Apotheck*. Straßburg: Lazari Zetzners.

Sacklén, J.F. 1822. *Sveriges läkarehistoria ifrån konung Gustaf I:s till Närvarande tid*. Nyköping: P.E. Winge.

Svenberg, T. and Jones, P.M. 2014 (eds.). *De Arte Phisicaliu et de Chirurgia by John Ardene*, (English edition). Stockholm; Fri Tanke.

Sybelist, W. 1655. *Manuale Hermeticum, sive Introitus Quadrifolis in magnum Philosophorum opus*. Wolfenbüttel.

Uddenberg, N. 2015. *Lidande och läkedom I – Medicinens historia fram till 1800*. Stockholm: Fri tanke.

Ullgren, P. 2015. *En makalös historia – Magnus Gabriel De la Gardies uppgång och fall*. Stockholm: Norstedts.

Wacker, G. 2013. *Arznei und Confect – Medikale Kultur am Wolfenbütteler Hof im 16. und 17. Jahrhundert*. Wiesbaden: Harrassowitz Verlag.

Wendt, E. 1950. *Amiralitetskollegiets historia 1634-1695*. Stockholm: Lindbergs.

Wetterberg, G. 2003. *Levande 1600-tal*. Stockholm: Atlantis.

Zettersten, A. 1903. *Svenska Flottans Historia. Åren 1635-1680*. Norrtelje: Norrtelje tidning.

Appendix
Pharmaceutical versus related modern botanical names on the identified herbs

Senna leaves *(Folium Sennae; ex Cassia senna, C. angustifolia)*
Chinese rhubarb *(Radix rhabarbarae; ex Rheum palmatum)*
anise *(Semen anisi; ex Pimpinella anisum)*
fennel *(Semen foeniculi; ex Foeniculum vulgare)*
galangal *(Radix galangae; ex Alpinia officinarum)*
ginger *(Radix zingiberis; ex Zingiber oficinale))*,
pine resin *(Resina abietis; ex Pinus & Abies sp.)*
horse-chestnut *(Aesculus hippocastanum)*
calabash *(Lagenaria sicerari)*
clove *(Syzygium aromaticum)*
long pepper *(Piper longum)*
nutmeg *(Nucis moschatae; ex Myristica fragrans)*
watermelon *(Citrullus lanatus)*
pumpkin *(Cucurbitae pepo)*
rhubarb *(Radix rhabarbari; ex Rheum palmatum)*
black pepper *(Piper nigrum)*

Exotic Animals

Thoughts about Supply and Demand Based on Archaeological Finds

Simone Kahlow

Abstract

From Antiquity onwards, the demand for exotic animals has been met demonstrably on a large scale. Rulers especially regarded the possession of these animals as a means to demonstrate their influence on and superiority over third parties. As it were, gifting exotic animals was considered a diplomatic means. This intention continued through the Middle Ages and the Early Modern Period. However, was the selection of these rarities changed over time. Access to foreign goods increased especially with the discovery of new sea routes. As it were, the interest in owning such items increased at the same time. Rulers built menageries and organised animal fights, scholars studied exotic animals and attempted to impose a systematic order on them. Private individuals came into the possession of apes or monkeys, parrots, parakeets or turtles and tortoises, and thereby increased their reputation. Agents acted as procurers, intermediaries and collectors, and at the same time boosted demand through their supply. Countless exotic animals were brought to Europe, dead or alive. The journey by ship was unbearable for humans and animals alike, and ended in high mortality rates for the majority of animals.

Written sources provide a comprehensive insight into the need for exotic goods, they also allow concrete statements on procurement and placement. The transport of so-called exotica, however, has so far received little attention. Especially in archaeology, the subject of supply and demand of exotic animals seemingly leaves much to be desired, something that will be addressed by the following contribution, with special consideration given to apes and monkeys.

Keywords: exotica, exotic animals, trade patterns, apes and monkeys, Early Modern Period, curiosity, maritime vessels, shipwreck, underwater archaeology, seafaring, menagerie, medical institutions, routes, agency, actors, shops

in: Kahlow, S. (ed.) 2018: *Transfer between sea and land. Maritime vessels for cultural exchanges in the Early Modern Period*, Sidestone Press (Leiden), pp. 87-118.

Preoccupying oneself with medical institutions of the Early Modern Period can harbour surprises and provide a novel turning point for one's own research. More specifically, when within those institutions one repeatedly encounters exotic animals such as primates, dating to the period between the sixteenth and nineteenth century. Inevitably, this observation leads to an array of questions:

How did those animals enter those institutions? What purpose did they serve? Were they regarded, for example, as research objects?[1] Did they enter the institutions dead or alive? Since when do we have evidence for the import of exotic animals to Europe? What animals are they specifically? Who were the customers and who were the executing agents? How were live animals transported, and what were their chances of survival?

Answering these questions widens the view on the relationship between cultural transfer, trade goods, actors and distribution, as will be seen in the following.

Source criticism

The analysis of available written and material sources as well as archaeological remains in order to investigate the above-mentioned questions involves a number of methodological problems. Two essential factors are the identification and location of foreign animals.[2]

1. Identification: False statements or descriptions in primary sources as well as poorly preserved bone fragments make it difficult to identify foreign species. For example, in their so-called travel journals authors may occasionally describe animals that they have never seen themselves, but only know from hearsay, or they may have even copied descriptions from other texts. Illustrations, too, are thus a source of the strangest depictions of exotic animals. The archaeological preservation of bone depends on many different factors. For example, after being shipwrecked, animals may have been flushed overboard in varying circumstances, or washed overboard after decomposition, or other marine animals removed parts of the carcass. Archaeologists very rarely find complete skeletons. Especially small bones are thus lost easily. Philippe Migaud (2011, 287) points out:

> 'Furthermore, bones may not always be preserved in the sea for two basic reasons: They are a source of calcium that aquatic life readily absorbs, and sea currents and tides significantly erode the characteristic bone markings and tuberosities of each species, making identification harder. Finally, underwater excavations are sometimes carried out in extremely difficult conditions, where visibility is poor, making the collection of bone material rather haphazard (micro-fauna bones for example).'

2. Location: Finds of exotic animals on land but also in shipwrecks often offer no clue as to whether the animal had ever left its native land alive. Instead, transport of

---

1   Regarding the approaches of historical actors to natural history see Förschler and Mariss (2017).
2   A similar compilation for Antiquity can be found in Hornig 2000, 178.

Figure 1: Elephant boarding a ship. Villa Romana del Casale, AD third to fourth century.

trophies, study objects or clothing is conceivable, as is assumed in the case of a leopard skull (*Panthera pardus*) that was brought to Hungary in the fourteenth century, possibly with the fur still attached (Bartosiewicz 2001). Furthermore, many of the archaeologically investigated merchant ships had been found near the shore or near ports. Recovering the cargo would have been of the highest priority, as long as the crewmembers had been able to save themselves and the ship was still within reach. It has to be assumed that exotic animals had therefore been taken to safety too, as they were considered valuable goods.

Animal rarities wanted: Dead or alive

Antiquity

Already in Antiquity there was an established system of importing exotic animals.[3] In Classical Antiquity, for example, foreign dogs, horses, silkworms, lions, camels and elephants were imported alive. They served economic, military, diplomatic and representative purposes (Hornig 2000, 178). So-called *venationes* (animal baiting) in Roman amphitheatres are, amongst others, archaeologically verifiable. The cruel habit of bringing together different animals for a fight served the amusement of the people. Countless animals died. Bones of lions, panthers, tigers and bears, unearthed at the excavations at the Colosseum in Rome, afford an insight into the diversity of animals (Mocchegiani Carpano 1974). How these animals came to Europe already in Antiquity can be gleaned especially from pictorial sources (Fig. 1). Most impressive is a mosaic depicting an elephant in the port of Ostia at the 'Piazelle delle Corporazioni' in front of the office of the representatives from Sabratha / Libya. This mosaic acted as an advertising board and was supposed to point out that the shipping company was specialised

---

3   For example, there were monkeys in the Minoan-Mycenaean pictorial world, bones of camels in the Bronze Age (Early Cypriot I) in Cyprus (Hornig 2000, 180-181) and the skull of an Iron Age Barbary macaque in Ireland (Waterman *et al.* 1997, 122-123). According to Waterman (1997, 123), monkeys were given as diplomatic gifts among rulers and were popular pets in the Mediterranean, already during this period. See also Miziur (2012-2013).

in *'large animal transports'* (Hornig 2000, 181). Elephants were representational as well as pack animals and therefore versatile. The same applies to the mainly Asian camels and African dromedaries, which is evident in the archaeological records of the Roman Empire and the Early Modern Period in Germany, Austria and Hungary.[4]

Middle Ages

With the demise of the Roman Empire and up to the Middle Ages, there is decreasing evidence for the transport of foreign animals. The available sources relate to the exchange of impressive animals such as the elephant Abul-Abbas, which was given to Charlemagne as a present in AD 802 (Hack 2011, 22). Abul-Abbas was a typical diplomatic gift[5] of the Abbasid-Carolingian alliance that had been maintained over three generations from the second half of the eighth to the first half of the ninth century (*ibid.,* 28). It took the animal about a year and a half to travel to Aachen from Baghdad. His journey covered more than 5,000 kilometres, on foot and by sea.[6] Charlemagne himself arranged for the transport and *'recruited* [...] *the maritime know-how of the northern Italian coastal cities'.* In order to have the animal brought to Aachen, he had a means of transport and several accompanying ships readied in Liguria. Hack (2011, 25; translation by the author) pointed out the problems that came with transporting an elephant across the sea:

> *'A fully grown elephant weighs between 3.5 and 6.5 tonnes and requires daily about 200 kg of food and 100 litres of water. The vessel must be constructed in such a way that the inevitable movements of the animal cannot lead to it capsizing. In Antiquity, elephantagoi (elephant transporters) were use for this purpose, but these special purpose-built ships had long been out of use in AD 800.'*

Abul-Abbas probably spent the last eight years of his life partly in an animal park in Aachen. Rulers used such institutions to demonstrate their wealth, power and reputation. The elephant died, possibly of foot-and-mouth disease, in AD 810 at Lippeham, a journey of several days from Aachen (Hack 2011, 38-40). So far, elephants are rare in the European archaeological record. A medieval rubbish pit in Chester (Great Britain) yielded the ulna of a fully-grown animal. It is dated between 1290-1410 AD (Smith 2008, 354). As no other bones of the individual have been recovered, it remains unclear whether the entire animal ever resided in Chester or died there. The bone may possibly have been kept as a keepsake or a curiosity.

---

4   For archaeological evidence from Hungary see Bartosiewicz 1995, 119; Bökönyi 1969 and Bökönyi 1974, 227. For corresponding evidence from German-speaking areas see Benecke 1994, 328 and Galik *et al.* 2015.

5   Diplomatic gifts had an economical as well as a political purpose. On the one hand, the recipient acquired luxury goods that were otherwise difficult to get by. On the other hand, the exchange of such goods constituted an expression of mutual appreciation and was therefore beneficial for a peaceful coexistence. Exchanging gifts among rulers had usually a long-standing tradition. It was a *'strategy to impress but not to humiliate the recipient, on the contrary to increase their prestige'* (Hack 2011, 30; translation by the author).

6   Obviously, the animal's accompanying keepers decided in favour of a long detour to avoid crossing hostile territory. Therefore the journey became considerably longer and thus also more arduous (Hack 2011, 23).

The above-mentioned manorial animal parks changed substantially in the way they were equipped during the Middle Ages. Initially they contained a collection of game animals for the hunt, but increasingly there was a presence of exotic animals. The latter comprised during the Middle Ages predominantly of '*monkeys and apes, antelopes, leopards, camels, giraffes, elephants, onagers, parrots, panthers, ostriches or tigers*' (Paravicini 2003, 577; translation by the author). There are notable geographical differences in the procurement of foreign animals. For the Marienburger Tresslerbuch of 1399-1409 can be stated:

> '[…] *that around 1400 in these remote areas the move from game reserve to exotic menagerie has not been made conclusively: no lion, leopard, lynx or camel, as they were stated to be in the animal park of the English King Henry I in Woodstock during the first half of the 12th century. But monkeys that once were able to break free and subsequently went on to damage the images of the saints in the chapel of St. Anne, those had been in the Grand Master's possession already since 1406. And in 1408 he received from Lübeck the henceforth indispensable lion*' (Paravicini 2003, 75; translation by the author).

Especially great apes (such as chimpanzees or orangutans) and monkeys (such as guenons, Barbary macaques or baboons) left their traces in written sources, in pictorial representations and in the archaeological record alike. For this reason, amongst others, they feature especially prominently in this contribution. Guenons and their relatives from northern and western Africa were known in the Occident even before the so-called 'European Expansion' and thus before the discovery of the sea routes to the Americas and to India. This is shown exemplary in the skull of a '*small monkey*' that had been recovered together with a gold coin of the Byzantine emperor Romanus III Argyros (1028-1034) from a rubbish pit at the Flachsmarkt (flax market) in Mayence, Germany (Lindenschmit 1904, 354). It is near impossible to date rubbish pits stratigraphically (Schütte 1986). This makes it difficult to determine whether skull and coin had been disposed of at the same time, and we need not even discuss the longevity of coins at this point. Nevertheless, it is tantalising to mention that the pit was dug on the premises of the so-called Stadionerhof or Bickenbau, where, during the Middle Ages, two houses were located bearing the name '*Zum großen und kleinen Affen*' ('The big and the little monkey').[7] There are three possiblities here: 1. The find and the property's name belong together, and the skull is rather more late medieval. 2. The find and the property's name belong together, and the keeping of monkeys in this area had a longstanding tradition or was historically important. 3. The find and the name of

---

7   Thanks to Daniel Schneider for this information (written communication dated on 5 November 2017). Schneider points out that there were several buildings bearing the names of monkeys or apes in this area over the course of two centuries, possibly due to the old street name '*Affengasse*' ('monkey/ape lane') (Schneider 2016).

the building are unrelated. It could be assumed the animal's characteristics led to the naming of the street or the property.[8]

Sadly the exact species of the medieval monkey from Mayence cannot be determined anymore. As mentioned above, it was predominantly guenons and their relatives that were brought to central Europe before the fifteenth century, especially Barbary macaques, hamadryas baboons and *chlorocebus* monkeys from northern Africa (Dittrich 2002, 16). Upon reaching sexual maturity these animals can become ferociously aggressive. However, as we will see, most of these monkeys that were forcefully moved to Europe never even lived to their second year. An example is the skull of a *chlorocebus* recovered from a rubbish pit at 11 Pieterskerkgracht in Leiden.[9] This was a young animal that, according to Suurmond-van Leeuwen, was brought from Africa to Europe aboard a ship returning from India (Suurmond-van Leeuwen 1981, 7). In my opinion, the skull could well date to the 15th century. Two points speak in favour of this: The skull was found with an assemblage of pottery from that time. However, there are obvious difficulties with dating non-existent 'rubbish layers' in pits, as mentioned above. Secondly, there is the assumption that demand for the aggressive *chlorocebus* species could have decreased with the onset of the 'European Expansion'. This assumption is backed by archaeological sources. Buyers had access to tamer guenons or capuchin monkeys. Finally, there are questions whether the specimen from Leiden ever came to Europe alive. Finding a single skull elicits the assumption that it served as a study object, or was kept as a curiosity in the household, as has been assumed for the elephant bone from Chester.

A Barbary macaque (*Macaca sylvanus*), archaeologically recovered from Hitzacker Castle (Germany), also died at a young age. The animals's remains date to the fifteenth century too. Older individuals of this species, namely juvenile and adult animals, have been recovered from Cuckoo Lane in Southampton (Great Britain), dating to 1290, and from Joymount near Carickfergus Castle in Northern Ireland, dating to 1400.[10] Barbary macaques are clever animals and can easily be taught to perform tricks. They were therefore often kept as pets in medieval well-to-do households (Jansen 1952).

Reviewing the accumulated medieval archaeological sources about monkeys and apes appears to reveal – to the current state of knowledge – that up to the fifteenth century no apes but only monkeys from northern Africa were brought to Europe. Amongst these the Barbary macaques are dominant. This observation is notable for the simple reason that historical and archaeological sources come together at this point. Written sources show that during the Middle Ages monkeys came as diplomatic gifts into the homes of sovereigns. However, information on the type of monkey in general and their origin is often lacking. With the help of archaeology, the state of sources

---

8   Hans Blesken, for example, investigated the origin of prison names. Monkeys or apes frequently appear in this context too. The author relates this to the *'unpleasant characteristics'* of those animals, such as *'lewdness, vanity and malice'* (Blesken 1963, 367). In the case of the Mayence Flachsmarkt one should note that the properties were of Jewish heritage. Whether the property or street name relates to the Jewish population should be investigated more closely by the historians.

9   Thanks to Ralf Mulsow for information on this find (written communication dated on 18 December 2017).

10   There are only two arm bones from Hitzacker (Kocks 1978, 179). In Southampton, a skull and collarbone were recovered (Noodle 1975, 334). The juvenile animal from Southampton was allegedly in the possession of one Richard Southwick who died in 1292 (Waterman *et al.* 1997, 121). From Joymount a skull and skeleton are known (Armitage 1983, 268).

on the medieval period improves significantly. Thus, archaeology complements the historical, written disciplines. The primates referred to were obviously monkeys, preferentially Barbary macaques. Another notable observation is that the monkeys did not originate in Asia, which at the time was connected to Europe through an extensive trade network, the terrestrial and maritime Silk Road.[11] However, compared to the Silk Road the distances from northern Africa via the Street of Gibraltar to Portugal and Spain, and further north of the Alps were relatively short. The animals stood a much higher chance of surviving the journey and went on to delight their recipients while still young.[12]

Early Modern Period

The fifteenth century provided the initial boost for the mass transportation of humans, animals and goods across even further distances than was the case in the Middle Ages. During this time the search for a sea route to India was met with success and not one but two continents, America and Asia, brought riches to the Europeans, thereby increasing the demand for foreign animals, plants and other objects.

Princely courts, scholars and better-off families developed a rapidly increasing demand for exotic animals that were mainly landed by ship in Lisbon in this early phase of expansion (de Tudela and Gschwend 2001, 8.). Regarding the passion for collecting at the courts, Gschwend (2015, 31) states: *'Collections of live animals became an extension of the Kunstkammer outdoors, set in gardens planted with newly imported flora'*. Nearly every European sovereign participated in the giving, receiving and collecting of exotic animals to a smaller or larger extend. The Habsburg Rudolf II (1552-1612) kept at the time at Ambras Castle a guinea pig chamber, two monkey houses, and a lion enclosure.[13] Archduke Ferdinand I (1503-1564) owned a lion house at Prague Castle. In 1548 he ordered a lioness from a merchant in Gdánsk, but she died on the journey to Prague (Dobalová 2015, 46).[14] Between 1552 and 1571 Katharina of Austria (1533-1572) gave away lap dogs from China, parrots, an elephant and a civet cat to her relatives and other persons important to her.[15] *'In 1583 a guenon chamber is mentioned*

---

11 Regarding trade between Europe and Africa from the twelfth to the fifteenth century, see Graham-Campbell and Carver 2007; 2011, 361-364.

12 The journey may possibly have been even shorter for the animals. It is assumed that Barbary macaques already lived in Gibraltar during the Middle Ages (Waterman *et al.* 1997, 122): *'The earliest reference to the apes there [in Gibraltar] dates from AD 711, when they were observed by the Moorish invader Tarik Ibn Sijad, and it seems likely that they were brought there from North Africa either by the Moors themselves or by one of the many groups of seafarers – Phoenicians, Greeks or Romans – who over the centuries linked southern Spain with north Africa.'*

13 http://www.wienerzeitung.at/themen_channel/wissen/natur/767509_Tierischer-Hofstaat.html? (13 December 2017). Guinea pigs (*Cavia porcellus*) are known in the archaeological record from the sixteenth to nineteenth century, for example from Hill Hall Manor in Essex in 1574-1575 (Hamilton-Dyer 2009), from a Belgian plot that is attributed to be middle class and dates to the beginning of the seventeenth century (Pigière *et al.* 2012) and from the Royal London Hospital in the nineteenth century (Morris 2014).

14 The names of buildings are not always indicators for the animals kept there. The so-called *'lions' court-yard'* at Prague Castle thus served as a keep for exotic predators in general, including lions (Dobalová 2015, 45). Birds were kept in the *'Pheasant House'* (*ibid.,* 46). How luxurious these installations were is evident from the records from Ambras Castle: The aviaries were masoned and equipped with running water and heaters (Kuster 2015, 57).

15 de Tudela and Gschwend 2001, 15.

at the castle of Arnstadt; there was also a box with a guenon pup in the closet' (Lange 2014, 7). In addition, at the princely court of Güstrow (Mecklenburg) there was a building exclusively for guenons in 1576 (Mulsow 2007, 60).

Foreign animals were in high demand at the courts, dead or alive. Deceased animals went into the cabinet of curiosities. Especially sought after were birds-of-paradise from Guinea with their colourfully fluorescent feathers. Birds-of-paradise probably rarely survived the journey to Europe. Therefore, it appears to have been customary for a long period of time to kill and mount them before loading them on board.[16] This preparatory work was done on occasion by local people who sold the ready mounted animals to the foreigners, mostly without feet or wings and sometimes even without head (George 1980, 93). The clipping and drying of the birds led to negative consequences in the knowledge of animals. For a long time, European naturalists mistakenly believed that birds-of-paradise had no feet at all. For example, the French naturalist and botanist Pierre Belon (1517-1564) described the animals as *'balls of feathers without head or feet'* *and thought that 'they hung from the branches of trees by the long tail feathers'* (George 1980, 94). Wilma George, researching the discovery of new animal species in the sixteenth and seventeenth century, states that *'No one had seen a live bird of paradise until some specimens were brought back successfully at the end of the eighteenth century' (ibid.)*.

Living exotica were displayed in menageries or served their time in travelling menageries.[17] The latter were mobile playhouses with an extensive entertainment programme. Latest in fifteenth century the general audience were, for a fee, presented with bears, monkeys and apes, as well as humans with deformities, amongst others, who in the best case performed tricks or were supposed to evoke a chill in the onlookers.[18] The courtly menageries were on the other hand stationary establishments in gardens near mansions and for a long time only accessible to a select audience. There is also archaeological evidence for exotic animals from courtly menageries. The menagerie in the Tower of London existed for more than 600 years. Excavations in the Tower grounds in 1937 yielded remains of 19 dogs (of different breeds) as well as the skulls of a leopard and two lions that had lived and died in the Tower of London between the thirteenth and seventeenth century.[19] While the leopard skull (AD 1440-1625) was so poorly preserved that it did not offer much information, the remains of the lions lead to the assumption that they were buried whole after death. It is unlikely that they were skinned in order to preserve their fur. An adult age is established at least for Lion 1 (NHM C.1952.10.20.15), AD 1280-1385. The dating of Lion 2 with AD 1420-1480

---

16 The relationship between exotic mounts such as birds-of-paradise, warehouses of the Indian Companies and experimental scholars was the topic of an article by Cook (2002).

17 *'The term menagerie derives from the French word ménage and means household and husbandry and originally described livestock farming. The term war primarily used to describe the vivaria of Ebersdorf Castle. Finally in the middle of the 17th century, the word was established as part of the language, which resulted from the influence of the Palace of Versailles and its zoological park'* (Kuster 2015, 55).

18 Irsigler and Lassotta 1996, 126-131; see also Rieke-Müller and Dittrich 1999.

19 The big cats' remains were handed over to the Natural History Museum of London and can be viewed in their image database: https://nhmimages.com/en/search/do_quick_search.html?q=TOWER+OF+LONDON (16 January 2018). The comprehensive compilation of research results that have been used for this contribution can be found in O'Regan *et al.*, 2006. Regarding the menagerie at the Tower of London in general see Parnell 1999.

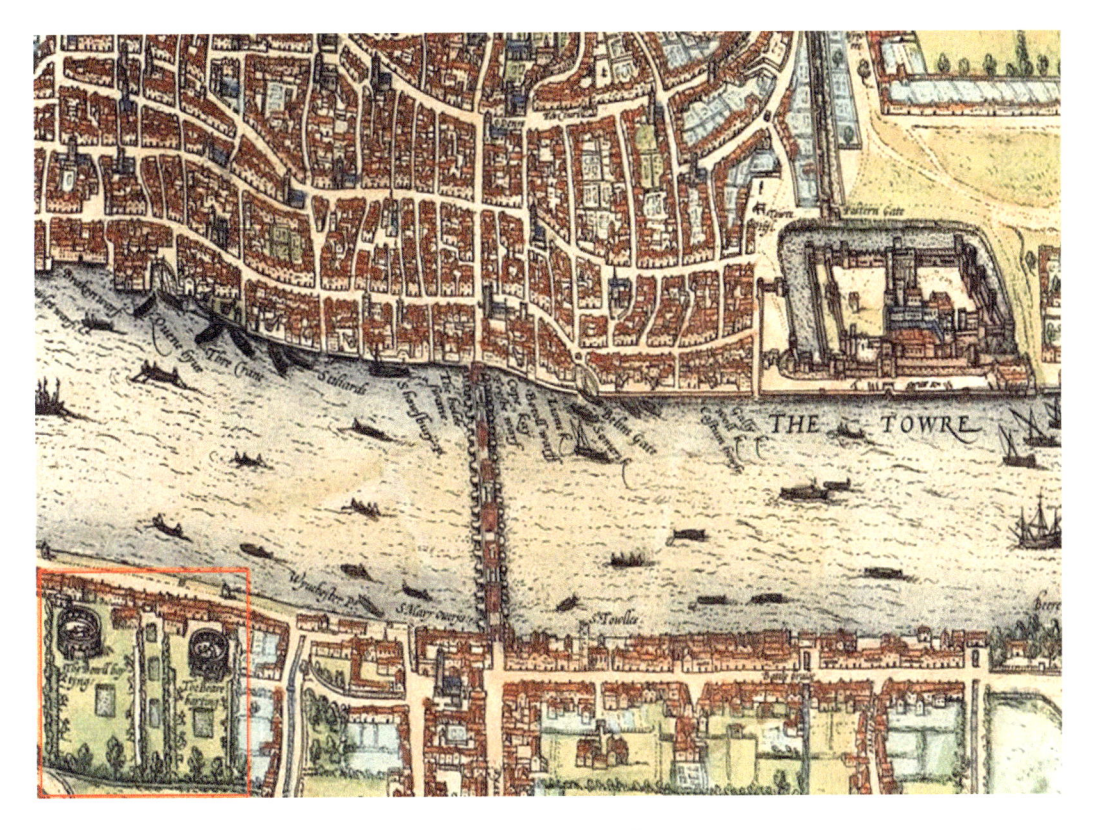

Figure 2: Detail of the map of London by Georg Braun.

(NHM C.1952.10.20.16) is especially interesting as it coincides with an event noted in the *Chonicle of London*, in 1436 *'deyde all the lyons that were in the Tour of London, the whiche was nought sen in no mannys tyme before out of mynde'* (Nicolas and Tyrrell 1827, 123). This event could be connected to the outbreak of a highly contagious disease among the animals, as was assumed earlier on to be the case with the elephant Abul-Abbas who had died in AD 802 together with many other artiodactyls (cloven hoofed animals).

Animal fighting – during which, amongst others, exotic large animals fought dogs – was as popular in the Middle Ages and in the Early Modern Period as *venationes* were in the Roman Empire. Again, archaeological evidence for this is known from London. About 1.5 km west of the Tower of London, during excavations in Bankside, Southwark, between 1999 and 2000, a dual purpose building was unearthed serving as the *'Hope playhouse'* and the *'animal baiting area'* (Mackinder 2013). Since the second half of the 16th century animal baiting has taken place in the baiting area. The amphitheatres erected for this purpose can be found on the maps of *'Agas'* (about 1562) and *'Braun and Hogenberg'* (1572), with the designations *'The bolle bayting'* and *'The bear bayting'* (Fig. 2). In the immediate vicinity of the theatres were kennels for dogs and bears (young and white bears) as well as two ponds.[20] One pond was used to wash the bears, the other to dispose of dead dogs (Mackinder 2013, 11). The historial sources are supplemented by archaeological investigations. The remains of several dogs, one brown bear, but also of horses were brought to light. The animals date mainly into the sixteenth and seventeenth century.[21]

Apes and monkeys are, to the best of my knowledge, not mentioned in connection with animal fights. However, their presence in the Tower of London up until the nineteenth century is evident in written and pictorial sources, although there is no archaeological evidence to date. Indeed, during the Early Modern Period, owning a monkey was no longer the privilege of the sovereigns but popular with nobles and merchants too. From the fifteenth century onwards, enabled by new sea routes and advances in seafaring, mona monkeys, tantalus monkeys and collared mangabeys from Westafrica and south of the Sahara as well as capuchins from South America came to Europe. These cute animals can be found repeatedly in numerous portraits. The Renaissance depictions of these animals contain *'in Christian imagery a symbol of sinfulness, in a profane imagery a symbol of depravity through sensual pleasures, in princely portraits a symbol of power or the claim to it'*.[22] There is also archaeological evidence for monkeys during the Early Modern Period up until the nineteenth century. To my knowledge, they are exclusively mona monkeys (Africa) or capuchins (South America). It is no surprise that capuchins only came to Europe as part of the European Expansion; the archaeological evidence starts no sooner than the seventeenth/nineteenth century.[23] However, the area of the mona monkeys was already known to the Europeans in the Middle Ages. Why have they not been found earlier in the archaeological record? Either the lack of medieval examples on European territory is due to the fact that such evidence has not yet been uncovered or archaeozoologically recognised or due to only transporting monkeys over short distances, meaning those that came from North Africa or Gibraltar. Dittrich (2002) also describes the absence of monkeys from East Africa and Asia in European paintings, even though these species would have been easier to keep. In her opinion difficult transportation, spoiled food and lack of clean water aboard merchant ships were responsible for this (Dittrich 2002, 16).

Of monkeys and scholars
The oldest archaeological evidence for a monkey from the Early Modern Period was the initial starting point for this contribution. They were the remains of a guenon from

---

20 It is likely that the white bears were polar bears. White animals were especially high on the regents' wishlist (Paravicini 2003, 588). Animals from the North were usually less sought after by the courts, apart from falcons (Mehler *et al.* in press), than those from the South or East (Paravicini 2003, 590). On the other hand, Henry III received a polar bear from King Hakon III of Norway. The animal was supposed to fish for its own food from the Thames and was taken there on a lead for this purpose (*ibid.*, 579).

21 The dog bones showed traces of blunt force and skinning. It is assumed that their meat served as food for their conspecifics (Mackinder 2013, 15).

22 Translation by the author after Dittrich 2002, 18, footnote 32, with further paintings depicting apes and monkeys.

23 To my knowledge, there are to date two capuchins known from the archaeological record, one in Dordrecht (Suurmond-van Leeuwen 1981) and one in London (Armitage 1983, 268).

TRANSFER BETWEEN SEA AND LAND

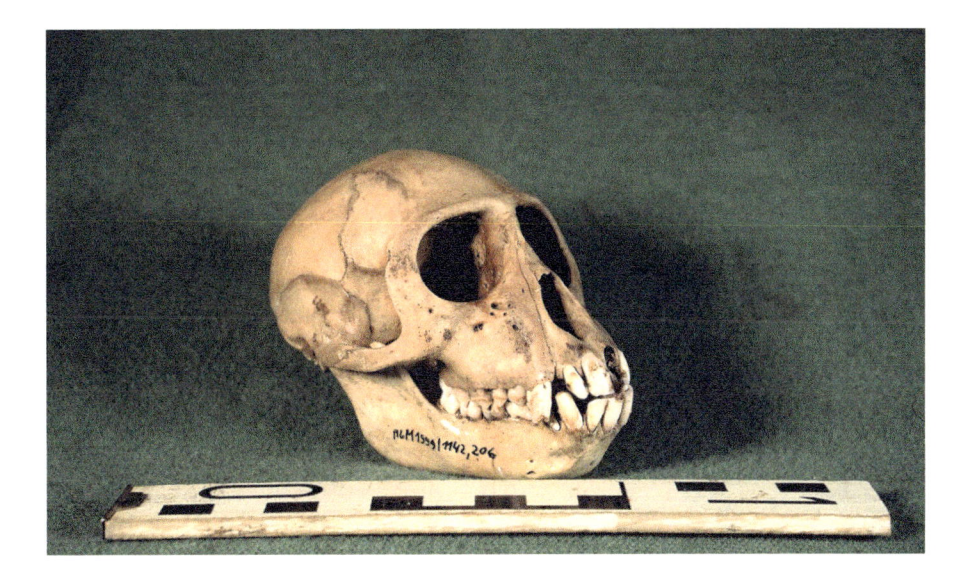

Figure 3: Skull of a cercopithecus, domus medicorum in Rostock (Germany), seventeenth century.

the *domus medicorum* in Rostock (Fig. 3).[24] The find originates from a brick cesspit and dates to the period between the second half of the sixteenth and the first half of the seventeenth century. During this time, Rostock was an important trans-shipment centre where goods from around the world were loaded and unloaded. It is to be assumed that among those goods were exotic animals too.

The animal's front teeth had been shortened slightly during its lifetime, either through an accident or through human agency. This caused the root canal to lie open, leading to persistent pain for the animal.[25] If indeed the teeth had been shortened through human agency, one has to question the motivation for such an operation.[26] Was it to minimise danger from those pointy teeth? In fact, the animal's bite was still dangerous; the teeth were still pointy. It is therefore questionable whether shortening the teeth made the adult animal less dangerous. Such an operation would however lead to the compelling assumption that the animal lived in a human household.[27] The owner could have lived or worked in the '*domus medicorum*' or had access to exotic animals via direct contacts. Here, the notes of the surgeon Nicolaes Tulp (1593-1674) are noteworthy, who, in 1654, wrote in his *Observationes Medicae*, the medical observations, an

---

24   Mulsow 2005, 434. Among the remains were a skull and some bones of the extremities (Mulsow 2007, 60). Among the remains of the postcranial skeleton were two bones of the upper arm, a left pelvis, a right heel bone, a rib bone and a right radius (written communication by Ralf Mulsow dated on 22 May 2015). Many thanks to Ralf Mulsow for his support with the photo of the monkey from the *domus medicorum* in Rostock.

25   Assessment by the veterinary surgeon Susanne Glodde in Schöneiche near Berlin (written communication dated on 22 January 2018).

26   Assumption by Mulsow (2005, 434).

27   It seems to be an adult animal, as the cranial sutures are nearly closed. Monkeys become increasingly aggressive with age, but can also become dangerous in situations they regard as distressing. Thus, *The Daily Post-Boy* reported on 14 December 1728: '*A Monkey kept by a Person at Chapham in Surrey, being much provoked, broke loose from his Chain, and running eagerly to a child of 2 years old, put it in such a Fright that it died soon after.*'

account of a female great ape and its behaviour, completed by an artistic impression. It is unknown when he studied the animal. However, it is known that the stadtholder of Holland, Frederick Henry, Prince of Orange (1584-1647) had been given the ape as a diplomatic gift together with *'several big cats, an Indian elephant, various types of deer and other exotica'* by the Dutch East India Company (Haikal 2016, 31-32). Apart from studying live or dead apes and monkeys, medical professionals had another reason for wanting to get hold of them. The sixteenth-century naturalist and physician Conrad Gessner (1516-1565), who described guenons for the first time in detail, stated that the monkey's heart was used as a medicine, it was deemed to strengthen the heart and potency in humans.[28]

The specimen from Rostock could well have come to the *domus medicorum* as a study object, after it had died somewhere else. This notion is supported by written sources from and about physicians of the Early Modern Period. According to such sources, the English physician and sergeant surgeon Sir Astley Paston Cooper (1768-1841) acquired dead exotic animals from the above-mentioned menagerie in the Tower of London and was thus able to dissect rare specimens. The examination of an elephant was fraught with problems of a special nature (Cooper 1843, 336-337):

> '[…] *he* [Cooper] *had entered into terms with the persons connected with the Menagerie at the Tower, to send to his house all the animals which died in that Institution. It would seem that the keepers acted fully up to the letter of my uncle's wishes, so that this Menagerie became one great source of his supply in this department.*
>
> *In the course of the year 1801, an Elephant, which had been one of the principal features of the exhibition, died. Immediate notice of the circumstance was, as usual, sent to Mr. Cooper, and, notwithstanding the unwieldy bulk and enormous weight of the animal, he determined to have it brought to his house in St. Mary Axe, where he was still living, and to dissect it. He accordingly hired a cart, in which, after a considerable degree of exertion, the Elephant was deposited, being afterwards covered with a large cloth, in order that it might attract as little notice as possible on its way. In this manner it arrived at St. Mary Axe, and the cart having been driven into the court-yard before Mr. Cooper's house, the outer iron gates where closed, and they set about attempting to get it into an outhouse, devoted to purposes of dissection. All their efforts, however, to effect this proved unavailing, and after a vast deal of trouble, they found themselves obliged to leave it lying exposed in front of the building.'*

Cooper also conducted animal experiments and to this effect kept a large number of dogs. Animal experiments and animals as demonstration or study objects have a longstanding tradition with scholars such as surgeons and naturalists (Hart *et al.* 2008, 18-28).[29] That such experiments should be conducted on live exotica seems

---

28 'Was man von dem Affen in der Arzney brauche' (https://bildsuche.digitale-sammlungen.de/index.html?c=viewer&l=de&bandnummer=bsb00086947&pimage=00020&v=100&nav=, 17 October 2017).

29 The same applies to experiments on humans (Stollberg 2014).

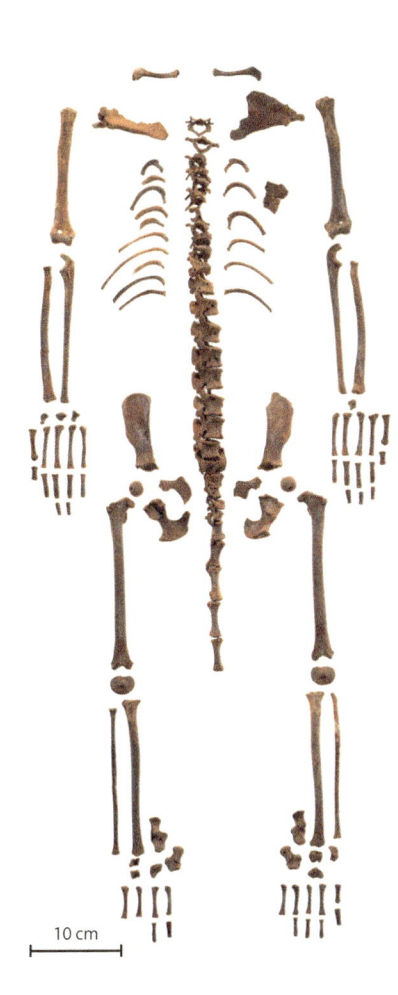

Figure 4: Possible mona monkey, Royal London Hospital, grave 251.

rather unlikely to me, up until the eighteenth-nineteenth century. Contrary to native, fast-breeding animals, they were hard to come by and their acquisition was not cheap. Still, the archaeological material from medical institutions often shows a mix of exotic and native animals. The latter often in large numbers. Material recovered from the premises of the Royal London Hospital and other medical institutions of the eighteenth-nineteenth century contains bones of foreign animals as well as dogs, cats and rabbits.[30] The animals served an educational purpose, as is evident by cut marks, drill holes and wires on the bones.

Excavations on the premises of the Royal London Hospital also yielded remains of guenons (Fig. 4). One specimen, *Cercopithecus mona*, was placed in a grave together with a cow skull and human remains showing postmortal damage. The guenon's skeleton is almost complete, only the skull is missing. The animal died between the first and second year of life. As guenons are weaned at about twelve months, this animal was taken from its mother much too young and was still growing.[31] This is supported by evidence of a so-called *'healed greenstick fracture'* on the fifth digit of the left hand, a fracture that usually only occurs during growth of the long bones. According to Morris *et al.* (2011, 371), the young animal could have been injured while it was caught or during transport. Another pathology constitutes an infection of the right collarbone (*clavicula*) (Morris 2014, 108-109). The humerus of a further guenon (*Cercopithecus sp.*) from the investigated area showed fine cut marks on the distal epiphyseal end. They are distinct evidence for a postmortem dismemeberment of the animal (*ibid.*). Weter the animal had come to Europe dead or alive cannot be determined any more. The question is unavoidable though, when dealing with the transfer of exotica. For example, capuchin monkeys had to cover a rather long journey by ship. The trip from South America to London took about three to four months on a sailing ship. During this time, the ani-

---

30 Regarding the Royal London Hospital compare Fowler and Powers 2012, 163-165; Morris 2014, 108-110. Further medical-archaeological evidence of animals comes from the Royal Infirmary, Edinburgh Henderson *et al.* 1996, 940; the Anatomy School, Craven Street, London (Hillson *et al.* 1998/1999, 15); and the Old Ashmolean Museum, Oxford (Mitchell *et al.* 2011, 94).

31 Information on the origin and behaviour of guenons: http://eol.org/pages/1010637/details (16 October 2017).

mals had to be protected from illness, food shortages and accidents. No easy task and, indeed, the existence of written records of successful transports of exotica increases only from the 19th century onwards, that is, at the time of steamboat shipping, which shortened the travel time considerably. Therefore, if the find situation is not enough to establish that the animals were kept in captivity and therefore alive in Europe, as in the case of the menagerie, other methods must be used to clarify this question. Of particular interest in this context is the work of the much-quoted zoologist Philip Armitage. He examined the jawbone of a capuchin monkey, which appeared on the banks of the Thames, at Brooks Wharf, in London. Based on further finds, the bone is dated to the period between 1610-1710 (Armitage 1983, 262). Armitage noted that capuchin monkeys are highly susceptible to calcium-deficient bone diseases such as rickets and osteomalacia. In the wild, the animals feed on *'leaves, fruit, butterflies, spiders, grubs of various beetles and birds'* eggs, which prevent calcium deficiency (*ibid.*). Captive animals, on the other hand, received a rather one-sided diet consisting of fruits and vegetables. A lack of calcium in archaeologically recovered capuchin monkeys could therefore prove that the animals were kept in captivity. In fact, Armitage found such a deficiency in the jawbone from Brooks Wharf and two comparative objects of captive capuchin monkeys.[32] Such studies thus have great potential for a number of questions that also arise in the branch of established animal studies (see Kalof 2017).

Keep on running: From inquiry to agency

Agency

As previously stated, exotica have been in demand since Antiquity. With their help, one could gain prestige and influence, forge bonds, make money and expand knowledge. So far, however, those who regulated the offers, set up large networks and even went looking for exotic animals to meet, or even increase, the demand have hardly been heard. The first priority was the contact with middlemen, the mediators within the indigenous population. They were eyes, ears and hands in the endeavor to satisfy the Europeans' needs for curiosities and exotica. This was noted in many travel reports. The Swedish physician and naturalist Clas Fredrik Hornstedt (1758-1809) reported in 1785 from his journey and his stay in and around Batavia (now Jakarta) that, after only a few months, he had procured animals for shipment to Europe: *'three species of sharks, sixteen species of birds, one albatross and a big octopus in a bottle'* as well as *'numerous mammal crania'*. He had acquired them by trade and purchase. However, he also shot and mounted birds himself. This again provides clear evidence that birds were deliberately killed before the crossing. The same applies to insects (*ibid.*, 183). Hornstedt's reports are also exciting against the background that they provide an insight into the communication with the foreign population. His mediator, for example, was a slave who apparently also saved him from death when Hornstedt set foot on an island and was there threatened by locals.[33] His slave rescued him with the words (Skott 2013, 184):

---

32   *Ibid.*, 266.
33   Kumar 1989, 248-249.

'This man is my master. He is a Tuhan Sackit (doctor) who has come a long way, from the other side of Mecca. He never harms a human being. Every day he collects roses, which he puts in between sheets of paper. He shoots birds and puts cotton wool inside them after removing the meat. He skewers flies on needles, he buys snakes and fish which he puts in arrak [alcohol] and sends them home to his king. He has now arrived here to your island to seek shelter from the sweltering midday sun.'

Travel reports provide information on how traders, naturalists and sailors got hold of exotica. For example, the Frenchman Jean de Lèry, who lived in Brazil from 1557 to 1558, reports how the locals shot capuchin monkeys down from the trees with arrows, after which they were cared for until they recovered and then sold to dealers (Armitage 1983, 266).

Written documents from the seventeenth century, especially from princely courts, record the importance of exotica as diplomatic gifts. They testify to clients and agents and offer insights into the most important European transit centres of the time: Lisbon, Seville and Antwerp, dealing with goods from America, Asia and the Far East. In addition, these papers reveal the difficulty of bringing exotic animals to Europe alive. Almudena Pérez de Tudela and Annemarie Jordan Gschwend (2001) studied the trade in exotic animals between the Iberian courts and Central Europe in the Renaissance. The analysis of the documents, *cédulas* = licences, from Spain, Portugal, Austria, Belgium, Italy and the Czech Republic not only reveals a ranking among luxury goods and exotica coveted at the courts, but also documents the importance of the agents / buyers, who were essential in regulating supply and demand.[34] They were sent to European trans-shipment centres as well as into distant lands in order to fulfil the wishes of the princely courts. These agents were, for example, *'couriers, diplomats, servants, sea captains, soldiers, Fugger agents and merchants'* (*ibid.*, 2). In this sense, the imperial envoy Hans Khevenhüller (1538-1606) worked for almost 30 years for the Habsburgs, especially for Rudolf II (1552-1612), who was probably one of the most important art collectors of his time. His records include *'precise details regarding ships, cargoes and sea captains, many of whom he knew personally'* (Gschwend 2015, 32).

'Khevenhüller acted as an important bridge between northern and southern Europe, imprinting the kunstkammers he helped form and enlarge for the Austrian Habsburgs his own distinctive tastes and connoisseurship' (*ibid.*).

'His network of merchants in Lisbon, Seville and Goa proved invaluable, and he depended upon reliable informants in Iberia, America and India. […] Khevenhüller built up an extensive network, rewarding well those who helped him with his shopping. His scouts in Seville and Lisbon had standing orders to buy at these ports anything rare or unusal' (Gschwend 2015, 31).

'Everything from seeds to a rhinoceros passed Khevenhüller's personal inspection, receiving his stamp of approval before acquisition and shipment to Central European courts. The logistics involved in shipping these exotic creatures, either by

---

34   Regarding the agents, see especially de Tudela and Gschwend 2001, 13.

land or by sea, involved incredible planning and organization on Khevenhüller's part. Without his loyal servant and Master of the Horse, Pedro Fuerte, none of these wild animals would have made the journey alive to their imperial menageries in Austria and Bohemia' (Gschwend 2015, 32).

Shops

Curiosity sellers and shops are, in addition to the agents, an important aspect in the distribution of exotic goods into the hinterland (Fig. 5). At the beginning of European Expansion, exotic goods were, once safely arrived in Europe by ship, first sold at the Spanish transhipment ports. The exact details of this procedure have, to my knowledge, so far been only inadequately researched. However, it is well known that, for example, since the second half of the sixteenth century, Lisbon had been specialising mainly in luxury Asian goods and that these have all been sold on the same street (van der Veen 2015, 137). Agents / middlemen were also usually aware of the goods that were to enter the port by ship (see Geissler in this book, 122 as well as de Tudela and Gschwend 2001, 9). Therefore, they were quickly on site, negotiated prices with the right contact persons and thus received the coveted goods. In Italy, it is known that dealers sometimes specialised in certain curiosities. For example, Leone Tartaglini, who lived in Venice, focused on natural curiosities in the second half of the sixteenth century (Welch 2009, 60). He had his own curiosity cabinet and a sales shop. Both businesses privileged one another both in purchase and in sales. Tartaglini's special

Figure 5: The Curiosity Seller by Cornelis de Man (1621-1706).

focus was on *'sort of extravagant fish'*. For the sale of his dried specimens he owned an illustrated book, a catalogue (Findlen 2002, 304-305). His best clients included pharmacists who also sold curiosities and considered them at the same time to be a feature of their stores. They *'must have seen the fabrication of natural objects as a demonstration of professional skills – the ability to manipulate nature. They filled their shops with those marvels, real and imaginary, that help to sell their medicines […]'* (*ibid.*, 306-307).

The Vereenigde Oostindische Compagnie (VOC) was founded at the beginning of the seventeenth century. It was based in Amsterdam, Middleburg and Batavia (now Jakarta). As a result, the port city of Amsterdam played an important role in the distribution of goods, and for this city there exist written sources that provide an insight into the so-called East Indies shops. Jaap van der Veen examined various documents mentioning shops with East Indies wares and East Indies shopkeepers. He found a veritable shopping arcade right in the city center, similar to Lisbon (van der Veen 2015, 137): *'At least fourteen East Indies shops were to be found on the Warmoesstraat and in the Pijlsteeg, the alley that opened onto that street. Another shop had a particularly strategic location, directly opposite the Oost-Indisch Huis (East Indies House).'*

Van der Veen argued that those who dealt in foreign goods eventually gained some sort of expertise in valuing exotica and curiosities. They may also have gained their knowledge from other shopkeepers and traders trading in '*East Indies wares*'. Due to their expertise, they had a good reputation and were sometimes called in to estimate

Figure 6: Dutch seaman with exotic animals by Pieter van den Berge (1659-1737).

the value of an estate. So far it is unclear whether there were any *shopkeeper in East Indies wares (winckelier van Oost-Indise waren)'* before 1652. This is the date of the first reference to this particular occupational title. Previously, sellers may have been referred to simply as traders or named after the goods they preferred to trade, such as *'porcelain seller (porceleynvercoper)'.*[35] The merchant Andries Marcusz appears as a porcelain seller until 1634 and is finally referred to as the *'shopkeeper in East Indies wares'* in 1652 (van der Veen 2015, 137). Marcusz runs the business together with his wife. And women also repeatedly appear as *'saleswoman in indies wares'* (*ibid.*, 139) and as 'jack of all trades' in these shops: *'A contract drawn up with one woman states that she was to keep the shop clean and tidy; furthermore, when something was purchased in the shop, she was to deliver the goods to the customer's house.'*[36]

Written sources prove beyond a doubt that shopkeepers not only commissioned orders but, depending on the occasion, bought luxury goods and exotica from seamen (Fig. 6). The sale of these goods in their stores earned them a profit that sometimes exceeded the actual purchase value threefold (van der Veen 2015, 138-139). Van der Veen made the exciting observation that the shops remaines always up-to-date. Demand determined supply. Thus, in the middle of the seventeenth century, the interest turned from Chinese to Japanese goods. This is reflected above all in the increase in tea and tea sets (van der Veen 2015, 139-140).

Shops such as in Lisbon and Amsterdam offered all the exotic goods that could satisfy the demand. This included animals, although the evidence for those is significantly poorer in the written sources compared to Chinese dishes or tea. According to the sources, Barend Jansz. van Kippen sold birds-of-paradise (*ibid.*, 137) at the beginning of the seventeenth century. François Evens, who along with his partner wished to trade with foreign goods *'from and to people ranging from the greatest to the least, including apprentices and sailors'* sold a cockatoo to a customer in 1655. This bird came off the ship half dead already, *'dat de kacatou bij de ketting neer hing, wesende bijcans doot'* and indeed died shortly after the sale.[37]

Curiosity sellers and their shops were also prominent in London and Paris. Scientists and traders deliberately travelled to those cities with the intention of visiting these stores and connecting with people who shared their interests. These include, for example, the British horticulturist and architect John Evelyn (1620-1706), who visited in February 1644 a curiosity shop called Noah's Ark in Paris. There *'are sold all curiosities naturall of artificial, Indien or European, for luxury or use, as cabinets, shells, ivory, porselan, dried fishes, insects, birds, pictures, and a thousand exotic extravagances'* (Findlen 2002, 299).

---

35   The nickname *'Porceleyn'* of the merchant Barend Jansz. van Kippen, trading at the beginning of the seventeenth century, refers back to the wares that he sold preferentially (van der Veen 2015, 137).

36   Van der Veen 2015, 138; Stadsarchief Amsterdam, notary C. Tou, noatrial archives 1457, April 28, 1667.

37   Van der Veen 2015, 140; footnote 30; Stadsarchiv Amsterdam, notary J. Weer, notarial archives 2126:699-700, 20 September 1655.

Figure 7: Ways of transport in the eigtheenth century by Daniel Chodowiecki (1774).

Failure

In the general pattern of supply and demand of exotic animals, the agents were often unsuccessful. Problems could already arise at the point of communication. The *Ipswich Journal* reported on the fourth of January 1729:

> 'The following Mistake or Blunder has been lately discovered to the great Diversion of People in genereal: A Merchand of this city trading to the West-Indics, hav ing wrote to his correspondent to send him two Monkeys, which word he spelled too, the Correspondent took it for Number 100, upon which he bought up 56 Monkeys, the Fright where of by Agreement came to 56 Guineas, beside the prime Cost. They all arrived safe with a Bill of Landing, to the great Surprise of the Merchant here, who has been given to understand, that the other 44 [?] shall be shipped off assoon as they can be procured.'

Newspaper reports from the Early Modern Period are generally to be taken with a pinch of salt regarding their truthfulness; however, such misunderstandings not at all inconceivable.[38]

---

38 Newspapers have been used as a political tool, with a variety of metaphors, and as an entertainment tool (Harris and Lee 1986; Black 2001). It is therefore appropriate to exert caution regarding the truth of these messages. Thanks to Patrick Schmidt, University of Rostock, Department of History for support in interpreting this subject (written communication dated 24 January 2018).

A significant factor for the agents was the survival chances of the animals during their journey to the recipient. In contrast to the partly harsh climate in Europe, many animals came from warm, almost tropical regions. Thus, the onward journey into the European inland with carts, barges or on foot was exhausting for the animals (Fig. 7). For example, the Frenchman Frédéric Cuvier (1773-1838) described a young female orangutan that had been shipped from Borneo via Mauritius to Spain in 1807 and was finally transported to the Seine across the snow-covered Pyrenées. The journey took eight months in total. Due to the cold, the animal lost several fingers, refused to eat and suffered from fever. The orangutan was looked after intensively in the house of the advocate Godard and even medically treated:

> *The means which most contributed to reconstituting this animal are good food, suitable temperature and, above all, loving care. At first it was attempted to fight the disease with tonic drugs, and since quinine could not be given by ordinary means, it was given to enemas.'* [39]

The animal died within a few weeks of being handed over to its intended owner, Joséphine Bonaparte, from a *'throat infection'* (Cuvier 1810).[40]

In transit: Goods crossing bridges

Ships were indispensible in transporing animals, especially in large numbers, from one continent to the next as well as from harbour cities to the hinterland. The transport of exotica was a critical operation, especially during the time of sailing ships, as the duration of the journey depended on many different factors such as the weather, navigational abilities and crew size. The longer and stormier the crossing, the rarer the occasion that the 'live' cargo reached Europe 'alive'. The losses were immense. The animals starved, died in accidents or due to negligence and climatic conditions. Diet especially became a problem with increasing travel time, for the crew as well as for the exotica.[41] Often, the crew had no idea what the animals needed for survival. Contrary to large animals that came to Europe as diplomatic gifts, those exotica that were transported *en masse* aboard sailing ships had no indigenous carers. There were consequences attached. The German soldier Georg Franz Müller returned from abroad in 1669 aboard a ship together with parrots, cockatoos, cassowaries and monkeys / apes as well as a porcupine. He reports: *'All animals perished during the journey, with the exception of Javanese apes / monkeys, who had grown all lopsided in their cages and couldn't walk anymore.'* [42] The above-mentioned Hornstedt again notes that he had kept two chameleons in a glass bottle, which died after his slave had left it lying in the

---

39 Translated from German: Haikal 2006, 89, after the French original: Cuvier 1810.
40 Regarding the menagerie of Josephine Bonaparte see Belozerskaya 2006, 292-293.
41 Regarding the handling of disease aboard ships during the Early Modern Period according to the archaeological record see Kahlow 2013.
42 van Gelder and Sauer 2004, 171; Stiftsbibliothek Sankt Gallen, Ms 1278: manuscript by Georg Franz Müller, Ausführliche Denckhwürdige beschreibung der reisen zu wasser und landt ('Notable description of the journeys on water and land'); Ms 1311: manuscript by Georg Franz Müller, Reise nach Batavia und Java ('Journey to Batavia and Java').

TRANSFER BETWEEN SEA AND LAND

sun (Skott 2013, 184). The French sales agent Jean Barbot (1655-1712) lost on his journey to Europe more than 50 parakeets and more than 100 apes / monkeys which he had bought on Principe Island in the Gulf of Guinea (Robbins 2002, 29). Especially cannon shots and rats are thought to be responsible for the death of many birds (*ibid.*). Apes and monkeys were not always locked away, and their short-lived freedom could lead to significan injuries or even being washed over board. Being shipwrecked, then, spelled on occasion the end for crew and live cargo. A case in point is the death of a rhinoceros that came from India to Portugal as a diplomatic gift in 1515. The journey took four months. The animal had an indigenous carer and was fed with straw, hay and rice. After a few months in Portugal, King Manuel decided to gift the rhinoceros to Pope Leo X (1513-1521) in Rome. A relatively small ship was loaded with the really quite large animal and other gifts such as exotic spices. The ship sank in a storm at the Ligurian coast shortly before reaching its destination. Crew and rhinoceros went down. The rhinoceros could have easily swam ashore, had it not been chained. A few days after the shipwreck, the goods and the drowned animal were washed ashore. The Portuguese king subsequently decided that the rhinoceros be mounted and taken to Rome (Bedini 2006, 142-165). To this intent the carcass was shipped back to Lisbon, treated there and again shipped to Rome. The crossing was successful, but subsequently the trail of the stuffed rhinoceros was lost.[43]

The small incident recounted here is but an example for all those large merchant ships that sailed the seas between the fifteenth and nineteenth century and brought whole shiploads of exotica to Europe in order to satisfy demand. The loss of whole ships belonging to the big trading companies is evident in written sources. Between 1602 and 1795 the VOC, for example, sent around 4700 ships to Asia alone, of which only 3500 returned to Texel.[44] As a rule, the return journey always played out differently from the outward journey. Instead of the seven to nine months that the ships needed to get from Texel to Batavia, the return fleet needed now 'seven weeks less due to favourable winds' (Haikal 2015, 119). The 200-strong crew was also cut down to make space for transporting the high volume of goods that had been bought. Here exotic birds counted – next to monkeys and apes – among the most important 'live cargo' from overseas (*ibid.*, 51). Although the shorter travel time was beneficial for the exotica, reducing the crew while simultaneously overloading the ship with cargo could have potentially tragic results for ship, crew and cargo.

The high number of losses that the companies had to suffer is met by a relatively small proportion of archaeologically salvaged ships. There are several reasons for this. A significant factor in relation to this article, however, is above all the shipwreck on the open seas. There must be funds and necessities to find a ship in the open sea, and then be able to investigate it archaeologically. Instead, many scientifically investigated shipwrecks come from coastal areas. As will be seen in the following, some wrecks have yielded exotic animals, but without any indication for 'mass transportation'. The rea-

---

43 Around the same time another exotic large animal belonging to the pope, the elephant Hanno, was mounted for posterity. This animal, too, had been a gift of the Portuguese king and died in 1516 at about seven years of age. The skin was removed and mounted on a wooden elephant (Dittrich 2001, 12).

44 Pelzer-Reith 2011, 50. According to Gelder around 4 % shipwrecked (van Gelder and Sauer 2004, 163). Texel was an important stopover for ships of the VOC. In Texel, the vessels waited for favourable weather condition and were loaded with supplies.

sons for this were outlined in the source criticism above. In order to return to the starting point of this article, the next section will demonstrate a cycle in which shipping, exotica, cultural transfer and medicine in the Early Modern Period can be viewed.

Up to now, apes have hardly been mentioned in this contribution. This is due to firstly, to the fact that they have, to date, not appeared in the archaeological record of the stated investigation period. Secondly, they seem to have come to Europe as live specimens only from the seventeenth-eighteenth century onwards. However, they then appear in increasing numbers – in bars, menageries and on dissection tables.

The eponym for the chimpanzee species was a female. It was a young animal that came to London in September 1738 with the ship Speaker and its owner, Captain Henry Flower. The animal was originally from Guinea. There, the locals called it in the Bantu language Chiluba *'Chimpanze'* – a name that the Europeans took over and that eventually established itself (Haikal 2006, 46). The about 18-months-old female lived under the name *'Madame Chimpanzee'* in Bars (Randall's Coffee-House and the White Peruke) on the banks of the Thames. Dressed up like a child, she performed a rehearsed show (Haikal 2016, 46-47). After about half a year in captivity, she died of *'periodic fever'* in February 1739. Incidentally, it was quite common that ships' captains owned chimpanzees – who died within a few months. The latter was partly due to the fact that the sociable, group living animals had to live without peers and received an inadequate diet. For example, Daniel Beeckman, captain of an English merchant ship of the EIC (*East India Company*), reports that he had bought an orangutan in Borneo. It lived with Beeckman for seven months and finally died of *'dysentery'* (Beeckman 1718, 37-38). The Dutch naturalist Arnout Vosmaer (1720-1799) was also in possession of a young orangutan female that he had received as a gift from the VOC in 1776. Up to this time, the animal had first been shipped from Borneo to Batavia and finally to Cape Town and Europe over a period of about seven months. Vorsmaer studied the creature in detail and attributed human traits to it. This animal also died after six months in captivity (Haikal 2006, 60-62).

Since archaeological evidence for the import of great apes is missing, a specimen is to be cited in the following, that is still in the Natural History Museum in London and is dated a good half century before *'Madame Chimpanzee'*. It is the skeleton of a chimpanzee whose journey, death and postmortem examination are well documented. The male juvenile animal had arrived in England in 1698 together with a female on a ship from Angola, Africa (Haikal 2016, 45). While at sea, the male, who was allowed to move relatively freely on the ship, had broken his left jawbone through a fall onto the ship's cannons (Tyson 1699, 16). The resulting abscess probably led to blood poisoning. The animal died shortly after arriving in London. In the seventeenth century, one was aware of the curiosity of naturalists and doctors. Therefore, dead exotica were frequently advertised or passed on through contacts. This may be one of the reasons why their remains are not more frequently found in urban excavations dating to the Early Modern Period. The physician and anatomist Edward Tyson (1650-1708), one of the luminaries of his time, received the carcass of this particular chimpanzee. He was familiar with the dissection of animals, even exotic animals. In his book on the chimpanzee, which he described as *'orang-outang'* and *'pygmie'*, he compared it to humans and other primates (Tyson 1699). He was fascinated by the similarity between the anatomy of the animal and that of humans. However, Tyson also made notes on the

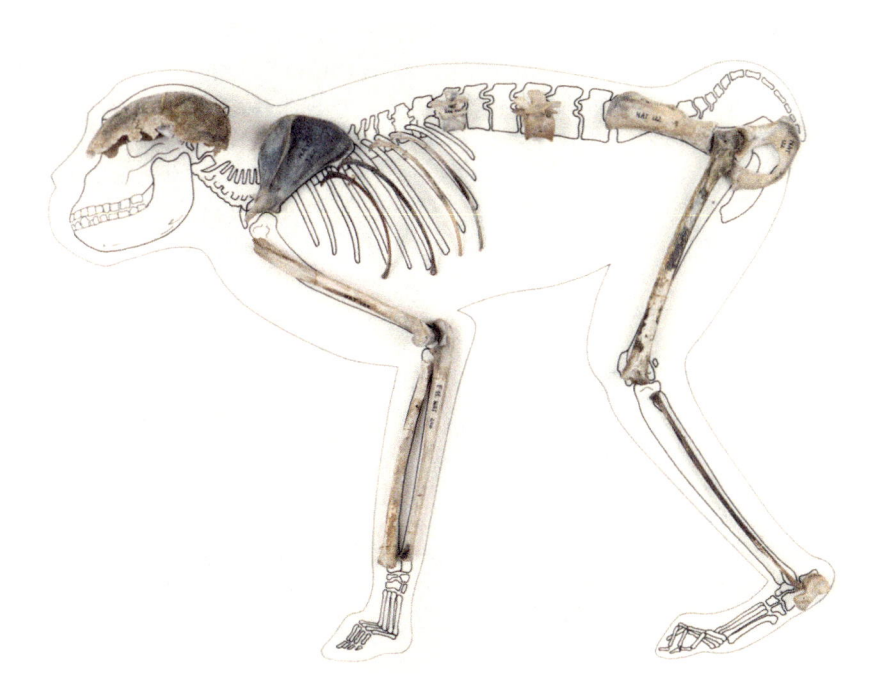

Figure 8: Remains of the Barbary macaque, wreck of the Dauphine, 1704.

behavior of the animal on board, information he must have received from the captain or a crewmember. According to this, the animal had always been friendly, hugged the crew, slept in a bed with his head on the pillow and wore clothes (Tyson 1699, 7-8).

Although it has to be assumed, due to written sources, that apes and monkeys were brought to Europe by ship in large numbers, it cannot be proven archaeologically. To my knowledge there has only been one monkey recovered from a shipreck to date. It is the skeleton of a Barbary macacque from the French merchant ship Dauphine, which had sunk in 1704 at the port of Saint Malo in France (Fig. 8).[45] Migaud believes that the animal *'was on board ship as a companion rather than as dinner'* (Migaud 2011, 289). He justified his assessment with the observation that the animal was almost completely preserved and showed no signs of dismemberment. Animals brought variety into everyday life at sea. Although exotica were taken on board primarily as a commodity, the crewmembers increasingly grew attached to them in the course of the journey. However, special circumstances may have led to the animals being left to their fate. The *Mid Sussex Times* of 30 March 1897 printed a note on an event several years previously that had occurred in the *'Chinese Sea'*. A ship had encountered a wreck with a monkey sitting on its rail. Not a living soul was on board. With the order *'Hands, chase monkey!'* the animal was rescued.[46]

Parrots were also among the exotica that were in great demand in Europe and shipped in large numbers across the seas. Those sailors particularly who wanted to sell their goods

---

[45] Many thanks to Élisabeth Veyrat for her support with the picture of the macaque.

[46] In the case of *'Hands, chase moneky'*, there is a clear parallel to the much-used phrase *'All hands on deck'*, which suggests that this report could be a didactic metaphor.

at home, interacted with their birds, trained them and taught them to speak. However, not always did the birds arrive in Europe. The Frenchman Jean de Léry (1536-1613) reported that the sailors of the Le Jacques on their way back from South America were starving and ate their monkeys and parrots (Stemm *et al.* 2013, 105).

The remains of a single parrot have so far been recovered from a shipwreck. It is the Spanish ship Buen Jesús y Nuestra Señora del Rosario of the Tierra Firme fleet *navio*, which sank at the Florida coast in 1622. Two bones were recovered from the wreck (tarsometatarsus and femur) and identified by Armitage as remains of a '*blue-headed parrot (Pionus menstruus)*' (Armitage 2013, 161). The *Pionus* species are native to Central America and the northern parts of South America. Armitage thus assumes, that the animal came into Spanish ownership through trade with the mainland (*ibid.*, 163):

> '*Opportunities for such trade would have been possible when the Spanish Tierra Firme fleet of galleons galled at the important ports/way stations of Portobello (Panama) and Cartagena (Columbia) to load gold and silver from the mines of Peru, Ecuador, Venezuela and Columbia before sailing to join the convoy a Havana and the trans-Atlantic crossing to Seville, Spain.*'

From European soil, a single archaeological find of a parrot is known so far, which, however, could not be specified. The remains come from Castle Mall in Norwich, Norfolk and date into the second half of the seventeenth century (Albarella *et al.* 1997, 51-52).

Parrots not only belonged to the menageries of influential rulers, but are also found in private households of the nobility. From the sixteenth century onwards, they are often pictured with women. Marcy Norton noted that parrots are not just about the transfer of goods, but also the transfer of knowledge and habits (Norton 2012). Thus South American parrots were already kept as pets, even parts of the family, before Columbus came to America. Norton states (*ibid.*, 77): '*Europeans, conditioned through their direct and indirect relationships with persons in the New World learned not only how to train and teach parrots, but perhaps also to follow Amerindians in seeing birds as kin.*' Repeatedly one finds evidence in written sources about this kind of fondness and familial connection that especially female owners who were constrained by their position and domesticity felt for their companions.[47]

Other exotic animals known from ships and excvations on land alike are turtles but mainly tortoises. Armitage, for example, examined the remains of a yellow-footed tortoise recovered from a Dutch shipwreck that sank on the Bermuda coast between 1620 and 1640 (Armitage 1989). Whether the animal has been on board as a commodity or as food for the sailors remains unclear. Overall, tortoises are more commonly known as museum objects and from archaeological excavations on land. However, the use and the exoticism of these animals can only be detected through close examination. Tortoiseshell, from the shell of sea turtles, for example, was an expensive commercial product that could be shaped through heating (Rijkelijkhuizen 2010, 97). The VOC and the WIC in particular traded in tortoises shells during the seventeenth-eighteenth century. Interestingly, these were not so much imports for the Netherlands, but rather

---

47   See also Robbins 2002 and Boehrer 2004.

more for the inner-Asian trade. Marloes Rijkelijkhuizen suspects that the latter was financially more lucrative (Rijkelijkhuizen 2010, 99). The few shells that arrived mainly in the port of Amsterdam amounted to about 100 pieces per year and came mainly from the Caribbean (*ibid.*). Customers of both the natural and the processed shells were exclusively from the social upper classes. The archaeological record includes fans, combs and knife handles from tortoiseshell. Whole shell or the remains of the entire animal can be found, for example, in church graves. Thus, the skeleton of a newly hatched sea turtle was found in a bishop's grave in Bremen Cathedral. It had been kept in a chipwood box (Reichstein 1989). Also of interest is the find of a marsh turtle from London's 'mercantile centre' on Narrow Street, probably dating back to the seventeenth century. Goods from overseas should also have been on offer in the shops located there. Maxine Berg (2007, 264-265) conveys an impression of these sales streets:

> '*The stock and display of these shops were perceived not only as a 'theatre of the streets', but as pavement education. The tourist saw the shops as part of their cosmopolitan education. […] The shops also drew on long tradition of selling exotic, oriental, and especially china ware in the china shops, showrooms, the East India Company sales, and London's auction houses which were fashionable rendezvous for nobility and gentry.*'

The animal from Narrow Street was well preserved. It '*comprised 33 bones representing approximately half of the skeleton of a juvenile including the bony shell […]*' (Killock and Meddens 2005, 81-82). In addition to the possibility that the turtle was offered for sale here or possibly represented a food item, the already-mentioned possibility of animals as pets is not to be underestimated (Thomas 2014). And to return full circle to scientific interest: Even in educational institutions there are turtles and tortoises, which sometimes have holes that suggest that the animals were hung up (Thomas 2010; Fowler and Powers 2013, 164-165).

In addition to finds from ships, finds from transhipment ports should be given more attention upon the appearance of exotic animals. An example of this kind comes from Deptford. Among the bones coming from a brick-built waste pit near the shore at Borthwick & Payne's wharf, Armitage identified sporadic remains of walrus and brown pelican (Armitage 2008/2009). They date back to the period between 1810-1820. This is significant against the background that Deptford was in the early nineteenth century the '*fitting out port and return destination of some of the British Admiralty's most important epic voyages of exploration, resulting in significant advances in navigation, geophysics, geology, botany and zoology*' (*ibid.*). The walrus may have come to Deptford from one of the many Artic explorations. Armitage points out that the walrus had been known in Europe since the 10th century, but the anatomy of the animal had been described only in the 1820s '*when Captain Douglas Clavering's Artic Expedition of 1821-1823 returned with parts of walruses (including flippers), requested by Sir Everard Home (First President of the Royal College of Surgeons) who […] subsequently published a scientific paper on them*' (Armitage 2008/2009). It is very likely that sailors brought parts of this foreign animal to Europe as curiosities or study objects even earlier, as Europe was hungry for knowledge.

Conclusions

As we have seen, the exchange and transfer of exotic animals is a phenomenon that has a long tradition but dramatically increased in the Early Modern Period. The turn from individual, diplomatic gifts in the form of large animals and big cats to mass transportation of especially smaller animals is mainly due to the discovery of new sea routes, improved shipbuilding and navigation. The acquisition of the exotic became tangibly close, more controlled and more lucrative. However, the acquisition and exchange of wares in the form of live goods also led to a transfer of knowledge and traditions. Scholars, merchants and sailors brought these exotic 'living compendia' to Europe. Thus, they increased the demand even further. The desire for exotica was widespread in all walks of life, whether in the form of menageries, as pets or at fairs and in pubs. While the population enjoyed, the animals suffered and usually died within a short time.

As the juxtaposition of exotic animals in the written and archaeological sources shows, these complement each other in a particularly fruitful way. Although archaeological evidence is scarce and may not reflect historical reality, there are indications that exotic species such as monkeys, parrots, guinea pigs as well as turtles and tortoises have been particularly prevalent. Those animals were not just placed in mansions, but were also kept by wealthy families (merchants who purchased them) or even poorer people (sailors who brought them along). Among the archaeological finds, monkeys represent the largest share of exotica. Simultaneously, the observation can be made, that up to the fifteenth century they were essentially monkeys from North Africa and Gibraltar, from the seventeenth century onwards New World monkeys, such as capuchin monkeys, but that Asian specimens are basically missing. Therefore, the current research situation can be stated as follows: Until the fifteenth century, the shorter routes determined the choice of monkeys (as opposed to large animals, such as elephants). However, this conclusion is no longer holds with the European Expansion, and at least written sources now also document the transport of monkeys and great apes from India and Asia.

Physicians and naturalists benefited from the transfer of exotic animals to Europe. However, it seems that they either received the animals as a living gifts or waited for the exotica to die in order to examine their bodies. According to current knowledge, it can be assumed that the many animal experiments that have killed thousands of dogs, cats and rabbits did not include exotica. This may be due to the rarity and luxury these animals represented.

The study of exotica in Europe is an important part of *Animal Studies* and has been increasingly and interdisciplinarily pushed, especially by the British side in recent years. However, research into the cycle of supply and demand of exotic animals in the context of cultural exchanges through shipping is still a desideratum. This contribution could provide an initial approach to meet this need within a larger project.

References

Albarella, U., Beech, M. and Mulville, J. 1997. *The Saxon, Medieval and Post-Medieval mammal and bird bones excavated 1989-91 from Castle Mall, Norwich, Norfolk.* English Heritage Ancient Monument Laboratory Report 72.

Armitage, P.L. 1983. Jawbone of a South American monkey from Brooks Wharf, City of London. *London Archaeologist* 4, 262-270.

Armitage, P.L. 1989. Ship rats, salted meat and tortoises: Selected aspects of maritime life in the 'Great Age of Sail' (1500-1800s). *Bermuda Journal of Archaeology and Maritime History* 1, 143-159.

Armitage, P.L. 2008/2009. Exotic Deptford. *London Archaeologist*, 85.

Armitage, P.L. 2013. 'The deep-sea Tortugas shipwreck, Florida: the animal bones', in: Stemm, G. and Kingsley, S.A. (eds.). *Oceans Odyssey 3: The deep-sea Tortugas shipwreck, Straits of Florida: a merchant vessel from Spain's 1622 Tierra Firme fleet.* Oxford: Oxbow Books, 151-169.

Bartosiewicz, L. 1995. Camel remains from Hungary, in: Buitenhuis, H. and Uerpmann, H.-P. (eds.). *Archaeozoology of the Near East II: Proceedings of the second international symposium on the archaeozoology of southwestern Asia and adjacent areas.* Leiden: Backhuys Publishers, 119-125.

Bartosiewicz, L. 2001. A leopard (Panthera Pardus L 1758) find from the Late Middle Ages in Hungary, in: Clason, A.T., Buitenhuis, H. and Prummel, W. (eds.). *Animals and man in the past: Essays in honour of Dr. A.T. Clason, emeritus professor of archaeozoology, Rijksuniversiteit Groningen, the Netherlands.* Groningen: Archeological Research and Consultancy, 151-160.

Bedini, S.A. 2006. *Der Elefant des Papstes.* Stuttgart: Klett-Cotta.

Beeckman, D. 1718. *A voyage to and from the Island of Borno.* London.

Belozerskaya, M., 2006. *The Medici giraffe: And other tales of exotic animals and power.* New York: Little, Brown and Co.

Benecke, N. 1994. *Archäozoologische Studien zur Entwicklung der Haustierhaltung in Mitteleuropa und Südskandinavien von den Anfängen bis zum ausgehenden Mittelalter.* Berlin: Akademie Verlag.

Berg, M. 2007. *Luxury and pleasure in eighteenth-century Britain.* Oxford: Oxford University Press.

Black, J. 2001. *The English press, 1621-1861.* Stroud: Sutton.

Blesken, H. 1963. Ältere deutsche Gefängnisnamen. *Zeitschrift der Savigny-Stiftung für Rechtsgeschichte. Germanische Abteilung* 80, 357-378.

Boehrer, B.T. 2004. *Parrot culture: Our 2,500-year-long fascination with the world's most talkative bird.* Philadelphia: University of Pennsylvania Press.

Bökönyi, S. 1969. Representations of camels in a Hungarian Medieval chronicle. *Acta Agronomica Academiaie Scientiarum Hungaricae* 18, 247-251.

Bökönyi, S. 1974. *History of domestic mammals in Central und Eastern Europe.* Budapest: Akadémiai Kiadó.

Cook, H.J. 2002. Time's bodies: Crafting the preparation and preservation of naturalia, in Smith, P.H. and Findlen, P. (eds.). *Merchants & marvels: Commerce, science and art in early modern Europe.* New York: Routledge, 223-247.

Cooper, B.B. 1843. *The life of Sir Astley Cooper, bart., interspersed with sketches from his note-books of distinguished contemporary characters.* London: J.W. Parker. Available at https://archive.org/details/lifesirastleyco00unkngoog (Accessed 9 January 2018).

Corrigan, K., van Campen, J., Diercks, F. and Blyberg, J.C. 2015 (eds.). *Asia in Amsterdam: The culture of luxury in the Golden Age.* New Haven, London: Yale Univ. Press.

Cuvier, F. 1810. Description d'un orang-outang et observations sur ses facultés intellectuelles. *Annales du Muséum d'Histoire natuerelle*, 16, 46-65.

de Tudela, A.P. and Gschwend, A.J. 2001. Luxury goods for royal collectors: Exotica, princely gifts and rare animals exchanged between the Iberian Courts and Central Europe in the Renaissance (1560-1612), in: Trenek, H. (ed.). *Exotica: Portugals Entdeckungen im Spiegel fürstlicher Kunst- und Wunderkammern der Renaissance ; die Beiträge des am 19. und 20. Mai 2000 vom Kunsthistorischen Museum Wien veranstalteten Symposiums.* Mainz: Philipp von Zabern, 1-127.

Dittrich, S. 2002. Exoten an den Höfen von Renaissancefürsten und ihre Darstellung in der Malerei, in. Dittrich, L., von Engelhardt, D. and Riecke-Müller, A. (eds.). *Die Kulturgeschichte des Zoos.* Ernst-Haeckelhaus-Studien 3. Berlin: VWB-Verlag, 9-29.

Dobalová, S. 2015. Indigenous and exotic animals in Reniassance Prague, in: Haag, S. (ed.). *An exhibition of the Kunsthistorisches Museum Vienna; Ambras Castle Innsbruck: 18.6.-4.10.2015.* Wien: KHM-Museumsverband, 43-47.

Findlen, P. 2002. Inventing nature: Commerce, art, and science in the Early Modern Cabinet of curiostities, in: Smith, P.H. and Findlen, P. (eds.). *Merchants & marvels: Commerce, science and art in early modern Europe.* New York: Routledge, 297-323.

Förschler, S. and Mariss, A. 2017 (eds.). *Akteure, Tiere, Dinge: Verfahrensweisen der Naturgeschichte in der Frühen Neuzeit.* Böhlau: Böhlau Verlag.

Fowler, L. and Powers, N. 2012 (eds.). *Doctors, dissection and resurrection men: Excavations at the Royal London Hospital 2006.* London: Museum of London Archaeology Service.

Galik, A., Mohandesan, E., Forstenpointner, G., Scholz, U.M., Ruiz, E., Krenn, M. and Burger, P. 2015. A Sunken ship of the desert at the River Danube in Tulln, Austria. *Plos one*, 10.4. Available at http://journals.plos.org/plosone/article?id=10.1371/journal.pone.0121235 (Accessed 6 July 2016).

George, W. 1980. Sources and background to discoveries of new animals in the sixteenth and seventeenth centuries. *History of Science* 18, 79-104.

Graham Campbell, J. and Carver, M. 2007, 2011. *The archaeology of medieval Europe.* Aarhus: Aarhus University Press.

Gschwend, A.J. 2015. '[…] underlasse auch nit mich in Portugal vnnd ander orten umb frömbde sachen zu bewerben': Hans Khevenhüller and Habsburg Menageries in Vienna and Prague, in: Haag, S. (ed.). *An exhibition of the Kunsthistorisches Museum Vienna : Ambras Castle Innsbruck : 18.6.-4.10.2015.* Wien: KHM-Museumsverband, 31-35.

Hack, A.T. 2011. *Abul Abaz: Zur Biographie eines Elefanten.* Badenweiler: Wissenschaftlicher Verlag Bachmann.

Haikal, M. 2015. Affe an Bord. *Mare. Die Zeitschrift der Meere* 110 (6/7), 118-122.

Haikal, M. 2016. *Unheimliche Nähe: Menschenaffen als europäische Sensation*, Leipzig: Passage-Verlag.

Hamilton-Dyer, S. 2009. Animal Bones, in: Dury, P. and Simnson, R. (eds.). *Hill Hall: a singular house devised by a Tudor intellectual.* London: Society of Antiquaries and English Heritage Monograph, 345-351.

Harris, M. and Lee, A.J. 1986. *The press in English society from the seventeenth to nineteenth centuries.* Rutherford, London, Toronto: Fairleich Dickinson University Press.

Hart, L.A., Wood, M.W. and Hart, B.L. 2008. *Why dissection? Animal use in education.* Westport, Connecticut, London: Greenwood Press.

Henderson, D., Collard, M. and Johnston, D.A. 1996. Archaeological evidence for 18th-century medical practice in the Old Town of Edinburgh: excavations at 13 Infirmary Street and Surgeons'Square. *Proceedings of the Society of Antiquaries of Scotland* 126, 929-941.

Hillson, S., Waldron, T., Owen-Smith, B. and Martin, L. 1998/1999. Benjamin Franklin, William Hewson and the Craven Street bones. *Archaeology international* 2, 12-14.

Hornig, K. 2000. Großtiertransporte nach und innerhalb Europas in der Antike – methodische Probleme, Fallbeispiele und kulturelle Rezeption, in: von Schmettow, H. (ed.). *Schutz des Kulturerbes unter Wasser: Veränderungen europäischer Lebenskultur durch Fluß- und Seehandel: Beiträge zum Internationalen Kongreß für Unterwasserarchäologie (IKUWA '99), 18.-21. Februar 1999 in Sassnitz auf Rügen.* Lübstorf: Archäologisches Landesmuseum Mecklenburg-Vorpommern, 177-185.

Irsigler, F. and Lassotta, A. 1996. *Bettler und Gaukler, Dirnen und Henker Außenseiter in einer mittelalterlichen Stadt, Köln 1300-1600.* München: Deutscher Taschenbuch-Verlag.

Jansen, H.W. 1952. *Apes and Ape Lore in the Middle Ages and the Renaissance.* Studies of the Warburg Institute 20. London.

Kahlow, S. 2013. Archäologische Erkenntnisse zu medizinischen Tätigkeiten auf Schiffen der Frühen Neuzeit, in: Nolte, C. (ed.). *Phänomene der 'Behinderung' im Alltag: Bausteine zu einer Disability History der Vormoderne.* Affalterbach: Didymos-Verlag, 125-148.

Kalof, L. 2017. *The Oxford handbook of animal studies.* New York: Oxford University Press.

Killock, D. and Meddens, F. 2005. Pottery as plunder: a 17th-century maritime site in Limehouse, London. *Post-Medieval Archaeology* 39, 1-97.

Kocks, B.-M. 1978. *Die Tierknochenfunde aus den Burgen auf dem Weinberg in Hitzacker/ Elbe und in Dannenberg (Mittelalter): I. Die Nichtwiederkäuer.* Dissertation. München: Ludwig-Maximillians-Universität.

Kumar, A. 1989. A Swedish View on Batavia in 1783-4: Hornstedt's Letters. *Archipel* 37, 247-262. Available at http://www.persee.fr/doc/arch_0044-8613_1989_num_37_1_2574 (Accessed 11 October 2017).

Kuster, T. 2015. 'Zu der Pracht eines Herren gehören Pferde, Hunde […], Vögel […] und fremde Thiere': The Menageries of Arcduke Ferdinand II in Innsbruck, in: Haag, S. (ed.). *An exhibition of the Kunsthistorisches Museum Vienna: Ambras Castle Innsbruck: 18.6.-4.10.2015.* Wien: KHM-Museumsverband, 55-61.

Lange, J. 2014. Affe, Hund, Papagai – Was sagen uns Tiere über Menschen?, in: *Tier im Bild – die menschliche Perspektive. Publikation zum interdisziplinären Symposium 13.-14.11.2014.* Kassel, 7-9. Available at https://www.uni-kassel.de/projekte/fileadmin/datas/…/tier…/Tagungsdokumentation.pdf (Accessed 14 December 2017).

Lindenschmit, L. 1904. Mainz. Sammlung des Vereins zur Erforschung der rheinischen Geschichte und Altertümer. *Westdeutsche Zeitschrift für Geschichte und Kunst* 23, 351-371. Available at https://archive.org/stream/westdeutschezei22unkngoog#page/n380/mode/2up (Accessed 15 November 2017).

Mackinder, A. 2013. *The Hope playhouse, animal baiting and later industrial activity at Bear Gardens on Bankside: Excavations at Riverside House and New Globe Walk, Southwark, 1999-2000.* London: Museum of London Archaeology Service.

Mehler, N., Küchelmann, H.C. and Holtermann, B. (in press). The export of gyrfalcons from Iceland during the 16th century. A boundless business in a proto-globalized world, in: Gersmann, K.-H. and Grimm, O. (eds.). *Bird Symbolism and Falconry through five millennia on a global scale. Centre of Baltic and Scandinavian Archaeology Monographs.*

Migaud, P. 2011. A First Approach to Links between Animals and Life on Board Sailing Vessels (1500-1800). *The International Journal of Nautical Archaeology* 40.2, 283-292.

Mitchell, P.D., Boston, C., Chamberlain, A.T., Chaplin, S., Chauhan, V., Evans, J., Fowler, L., Powers, N., Walker, D., Webb, H. and Witkin, A. 2011. The study of anatomy in England from 1700 to the early 20th century. *Journal of Anatomy* 219, 91-99.

Miziur, M., 2012-2013. Exotic animals as a manifestation of royal *luxuria*. Rulers and their menageries: From the Pompe of Ptolemy II Philadelphus to Aurelian. *Phasis* 15-16, 451-465.

Mocchegiani Carpano, C., 1974. Funde aus dem Kolosseum. *Antike Welt* 5.1, 54.

Morris, J., Fowler, L. and Powers, N. 2011. A hospital with connections: 19th-century exotic animal remains at the Royal London Hospital. *Post-Medieval Archaeology* 45.2, 367-373.

Morris, J. 2014. Explorations in anatomy: the remains from Royal London Hospital. *Anthropozoologica* 49.1, 101-112.

Mulsow, R., 2005. Fakultätsgebäude und Professorenhäuser, in: Jöns, H., Lüth, F. and Schäfer, H. (eds.). *Archäologie unter dem Straßenpflaster. 15 Jahre Stadtkernarchäologie in Mecklenburg-Vorpommern.* Schwerin: Archäologisches Landesmuseum und Landesamt für Bodendenkmalpflege Mecklenburg-Vorpommern, 433-438.

Mulsow, R. 2007. Von der mittelalterlichen Universitas zur reformierten humanistischen Hochschule: Archäologische Funde des späten 16. Jahrhunderts aus der Blütezeit der Rostocker Universität. *Mitteilungen der Deutschen Gesellschaft für Archäologie des Mittelalters und der Neuzeit* 18, 59-70.

Nicolas, N.H. and Tyrrell, E. 1827. *A Chronicle of London from 1089 to 1483 Written in the Fifteenth Century, and for the First Time Printed from MSS. in the British Museum.* London. Available at http://www.gutenberg.org/files/27027/27027-h/27027-h.htm (Accessed 19 January 2018).

Noodle, B. 1975. The animal bones, in: Platt, C., Coleman-Smith, R. and Burn, A.S. (eds.). *Excavations in medieval Southampton, 1953-1969.* Leicester: Leicester University Press, 332-340.

Norton, M. 2012. Going to the birds: Animals, things and beings in early modernity, in: Findlen, P. (ed.). *Early modern things.* New York: Routledge, 53-83.

O'Regan, H.O., Turner, A. and Sabin, R. 2006. Medieval Big Cat remains from the Royal Menagerie at the Tower of London. *International Journal of Osteoarchaelogy* 16, 385-394.

Paravicini, W. 2003. Tiere aus dem Norden. *Deutsches Archiv für Erforschung des Mittelalters* 59.2, 559-591.

Parnell, G. 1999. *The royal menagerie at the Tower of London*. Leeds: Royal Armouries Museum.

Pelzer-Reith, B. 2011. *Tiger an Deck: Die unglaublichen Fahrten von Tieren und Pflanzen quer übers Meer*. Hamburg: Mare.

Pigière, F., van Neer, M., Ansieau, C., Denis, M. 2012. New archaeozoological evidence for the introduction of the guinea pig to Europe. *Journal of Archaeological Science* 39, 1020-1024.

Reichstein, H. 1989. Schildkrötenskelett in einem Bischofsgrab im Bremer Dom. *Tier und Museum* 1.4, 107.

Rieke-Müller, A. and Dittrich, L. 1999. *Unterwegs mit wilden Tieren: Wandermenagerien zwischen Belehrung und Kommerz, 1750-1850*. Marburg/Lahn: Basilisken-Presse.

Rijkelijkhuizen, M. 2010. Tortoiseshell in the 17th and 18th Century Dutch Republic, in: Legrand-Pineau, A. and Campana, D.V. (eds.). *Ancient and modern bone artefacts from America to Russia: Cultural, technological and functional signature*. Oxford: Archaeopress, 97-106.

Robbins, L.E. 2002. *Elephant slaves and pampered parrots: Exotic animals in eighteenth-century Paris*. Baltimore: Johns Hopkins University Press.

Schneider, D. 2016. *Magenza. Topografie der jüdischen Siedlung während des Mittelalters*. Master of Arts. Trier: Universität Trier.

Schütte, S. 1986. Brunnen und Kloaken auf innerstädtischen Grundstücken im ausgehenden Hoch- und Spätmittelalter. *Zeitschrift für Archäologie des Mittelalters* 4, 237-255.

Skott, C. 2013. 'Ask about everything!' Clas Fredrik Hornstedt in Java, 1783-4, in: Alberts, T. and Irving, D.R.M. (eds.). *Intercultural exchange in Southeast Asia: History and society in the early modern world*. London, New York: I.B. Tauris, 161-202.

Smith, I. 2008. Mammal, bird and amphibian bones, in: Garner, D.J., Backhouse, D. and Higgins, D.A. (eds.). *Excavations at Chester, 25 Bridge Street, 2001: Two thousand years or urban life in microcosm*. Chester: Chester City Council, 332-380.

Stemm, G., Gerth, E., Flow, J., Guerra-Librero, C.L. and Kingsley, S.A. 2013. The deep-sea Tortugas Shipwreck, Florida: A Spanish-operatied navio of the 1622 Tierra Firme fleet: Part 2: the artifacts, in: Stemm, G. and Kingsley, S.A. (eds.). *Oceans Odyssey 3: The deep-sea Tortugas shipwreck, Straits of Florida: a merchant vessel from Spain's 1622 Tierra Firme fleet*. Oxford: Oxbow Books, 55-121.

Stollberg, M. 2014. Medizingeschichte: Tödliche Menschenversuche im 16. Jahrhundert. *Deutsches Ärzteblatt*, 111(47), A 2060-2. Available at https://www.aerzteblatt.de/archiv/163779/Medizingeschichte-Toedliche-Menschenversuche-im-16-Jahrhundert (Accessed 13 December 2017).

Suurmond-van Leeuwen, H. 1981. Verslag over het Jaar 1980. *Bodemonderzoek in Leiden* 3, 7-27.

Thomas, R. 2010. Translocated testudinidae: the earliest archaeological evidence for tortoises in Britain. *Post-Medieval Archaeology* 44.1, 165-171.

Thomas, R. 2014. Tortoises and the Exotic Animal Trade in Britain from Medieval to 'Modern'. *Testudo* 8.1, 56-68.

Tyson, E. 1699. *Orang-Outang, sive Homo Sylvestris: or, the Anatomy of a Pygmie compared with that of a Monkey, an Ape, and a Man.* London. Available at https://archive.org/stream/orangoutangsiveh00tyso#page/n9/mode/2up (Accessed 14 December 2017).

van der Veen, Jaap 2015. East Indies shops in Amsterdam, in: Corrigan, K., van Campen, J., Diercks, F. and Blyberg, J.C. (eds.). *Asia in Amsterdam: The culture of luxury in the Golden Age.* New Haven, London: Yale University Press, 134-141.

van Gelder, R. and Sauer, A. 2004. *Das ostindische Abenteuer: Deutsche in Diensten der Vereinigten Ostindischen Kompanie der Niederlande (VOC) 1600-1800.* Univ., Dissertation. Amsterdam, 1997. Hamburg: Convent.

Waterman, D.M., Hamlin, A. and Lynn, C. 1997 (eds.). *Excavations at Navan Fort, 1961-71.* Belfast: Stationery Office.

Welch, E.S. 2009. *Shopping in the Renaissance: Consumer cultures in Italy, 1400-1600.* New Haven, Connecticut, London: Yale University Press.

The Lloyd´s List
A Global Intelligence Unit?

Stefan Geissler

Abstract

The Lloyd´s List, a London-based global business newspaper, was established in the beginning of the eighteenth century. Its main focus were global shipping movements, other maritime news, and reports about wrecks and casualties. With such news, ship-owners, merchants and insurance companies back in London achieved a better understanding of the location of both their ships and goods. The precise information about the location, route, and load of a ship were the most vital parts of the List. As one of the oldest newspapers (some say it is the oldest) the Lloyd´s List provides a unique insight into maritime history in general and also provides us with links to other source material. This article will give a short overview of the history, the different parts of the Lloyd's List and especially the role of information.

Keywords: marine insurance, risk, Lloyd's, maritime trade, global trade network, London, subscriber, agents, underwriter, shipwreck

> '*With the practice of insuring ships and their cargoes against sea risk there would naturally arise the necessity of adopting means to ascertain whether the vessels were seaworthy, and to have the relative qualities of ships in this respect classified and recorded in some manner convenient to persons interested in shipping.*' Lloyd's Register of Shipping 1884, 3.

Edward Lloyd invented the highly specialized business newspaper '*Lloyd's List*' in the beginning of the eighteenth century from the sphere of the '*Lloyd's Coffee House*'. It is still in use as an aggregator of information and knowledge for the needs of the maritime industry and most of the merchants in this business.

Both terms, information and knowledge, are widely used without differentiation. Within my work, a more specific definition is needed and for this I will use the works

in: Kahlow, S. (ed.) 2018: *Transfer between sea and land. Maritime vessels for cultural exchanges in the Early Modern Period*, Sidestone Press (Leiden), pp. 119-130.

from Peter Burke (Burke 2014) and in particular Ikujiro Nonaka (Nonaka 1994, 15): *'In short, information is a flow of messages, while knowledge is created and organized by the very flow of information, anchored on the commitment and beliefs of its holder.'*

Since 1691, businesspersons and private insurers met inside the well-known coffee house in London to negotiate about risk insurances for the global maritime trade. Some years later, the newly established *'Society of Lloyd's'* (the future *'Lloyd's of London'*) institutionalized this interconnection and marked the start of an historically important insurance company.[1] Eventually, London became the 'global centre of maritime insurance business' (Borscheid 2012, 39) till the nineteenth century. Detailed information containing location, route, and cargo of ships were very important. They were collected by the Lloyd's Lists and published weekly, alongside with other maritime news and advertisements. In the early days they provided purely information about the global ship movements, later (then published daily), the contents were tailored to the needs of the maritime merchant of the time.

This article aims to introduce the Lloyd's List (together with both the processing and the gathering of information) as a global source of maritime history. The information collected within the List reveals various nodes of a global maritime trade network, which may point to several areas for further studies. In addition, reasonably accurate temporal and local coordinates about individual wrecks give us the ability to search for new sources in nearby port cities. Therefore, its significance for the maritime archaeology and the cultural and mercantile exchange in the early modern period will be an additional topic. Damaged, wrecked and sunken ships were reported via Sightings or from the different Port authorities. These may be interesting for some archaeologist because the casualties happened worldwide. Such events are the 'worst case' for every ship owner and are well documented. So on the one hand, if a ship sunk near a port, there may lay some additional sources about it in the local archive. On the other hand, a report about a sunken ship on the ocean may give us a hint where it is still located on the ocean floor.

The maritime insurance sector during the early modern period

The Lloyd's List was and still is a specialized Business Newspaper established 1734 in London. The origin was the *'Lloyd's Coffee House'*, an important trading point for maritime merchants and insurers. In addition to the already existing Coffee Houses in this area, the establishment of this new House in the Lombard Street around 1692 marks the beginning of a new hotspot for all people interested in shipping and maritime trade (see Davis 1972, 163).

This was also the birth of the well-known Lloyd's of London, which further improved the Lloyd's List in the following centuries. Britain was by far the largest insurance market in the eighteenth and nineteenth century, but Lloyd's was not exactly an insurance company. The (still) so-called *'insurance marketplace'* Lloyd's provided a

---

1   In contrast to the research about fire insurance, the second pillar of private insurance in Britain, there are no deep source-based studies about the (European) maritime insurance history. See for a summary the book of Zwierlein (2011).

more or less secured space for interested businesspersons who wanted to insure a ship or sign an insurance policy. The trades were run in the Subscriber-Room, a backroom of the coffee house. In this room, underwriters, their agents, ship-owners, and merchants met and made their businesses, ergo, insured ships, their cargoes and their passage. In organizing a trade via the sea, lays a risk of failure. If you or your agent found enough underwriter who will sign an insurance policy, your passage is insured against such risks. In the pre-steam early modern period, a ship passage could take anywhere from weeks to months.

Centuries ago, the first marine insurance was established in London around 1426. Over time, merchants from Venice and the Lombardy developed a way to reduce the effects of omnipresent threats on sea (see Leonard 2014, 2-3). Marine Insurances have existed for a very long time, in the case of London, a police can be dated back to the year 1426. Lombard and Venetian merchants developed over time a way to reduce the effects of omnipresent threats of the oceans. The cost to repair the damage or even the complete refund of a ship were as far as possible distributed in order to minimize the burden on the individual. It became a business through the increase of the available capital of a merchant to provide 'guarantees' against potential 'risks'.

> *'Risks consequently have to be understood as permanent companions of everyday life. As long as people value certain things or conditions and as long as they take decisions in the presence of uncertainty, they will face risks. Risks are hence a basic constituent of life'* (Aven and Renn 2010, 1).

Dealing with risk is part of the everyday business of an early modern merchant. If he regarded them as too threatening, the security of insurance could be an option. Broken down, the transport of goods across the oceans was now a more or less complicated mathematical equation. Risks and potential dangers were offset by the costs of insurance and anticipated profits, and if the result was acceptable for the merchant, the transport was arranged.

Knowledge of risks, including the calculation based on statistics and other data was fundamental to these equations and was therefore provided by Lloyd's and the Lloyd's List. This is not common for an insurance company. Of course, such data and informa-

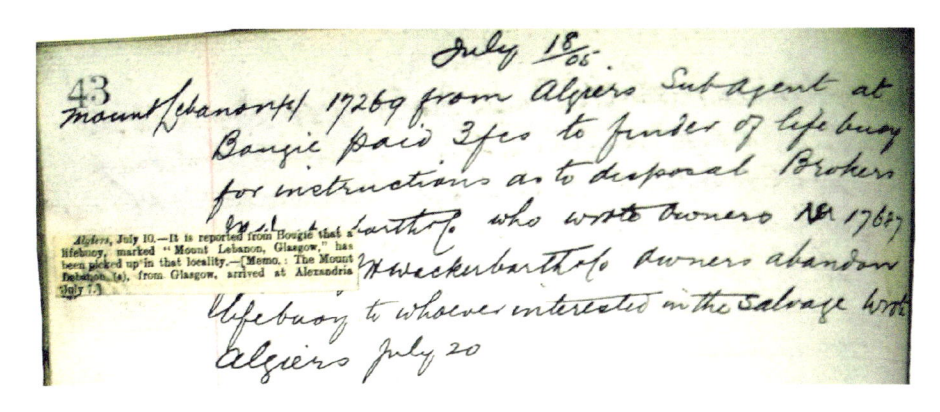

Figure 1: Handwritten report about a wrecked ship and the entry in a Lloyd's List, Minutes 1805. Courtesy of The Corporation of Lloyd's.

tion were more than useful for their own employees, however, granting customers (and potential competitors) this level of insight was a whole different level. The emergence of the Lloyd's List would be incomprehensible without the special position of this company: Lloyds of London is still a well-known brand within the maritime insurers, but it sees itself however not even as an insurance company in the strict sense, but as an internationally unique 'insurance market' (see Kyriakou 2002, 158). Lloyd's has always been provided only its rooms and other services for paid members, and received a commission upon a successful transaction. In addition to a business environment, the persons responsible succeeded to provide their 'marketplace' with other assets to the 'underwriter', support them in their operations and offer good terms so they continue their membership.[2]

The origin of the 'Lloyd's List'

An important, maybe the most valued, element was the 'Lloyd's List'. It was created by systematically collecting, compiling and publishing of departure and arrival messages from ships in English and continental ports:

> 'On the front page appeared the rates of exchange, the microscopic Stock Exchange List of the time, and a few other items of general business interest. The back page was given over to the "Marine List" – arrivals, and occasionally sailings, reported from the principal English and Irish ports … a few paragraphs relating to casualties, speakings, missing vessels, and other items of interest to merchants, ship-owners, and underwriters' (Lloyd's of London, 1934, 7).

Whenever needed the procedure was adapted to the needs of the underwriters, one can speak of a first 'professionalization' of the newspaper from the late eighteenth century. In 1796, the 'Committee of Lloyd's' decided to use a Secretary with special tasks:

> 'The Committee taking into their serious consideration the Arrangement necessary to be made at Lloyds [...] and that the nature and extent of the Business of the Subscribers of Lloyds requires that there should be a Secretary … and to whom through the Master all Articles of Intelligence shall be conveyed and under whose Authority subject to the control of the Committee all information should be regulated for Publication and that in the frequent occasions of intercourse between Lloyds and the different Offices under Government such an Establishment would have peculiar advantages [...].' (Lloyd's of London, 1805, 124).

Here, the foundation of the later information network of Lloyd's is already presented. The Secretary, later the corresponding 'Sub-Committee of Intelligence', supervised the receipt of all 'intelligence' and bits of information, and decided what should happen with it in the best interests of its subscribers. The 'control' of access to this information deserves special attention, as this represented a decisive advantage over potential competitors. Underwriters are willing to take the risk from you, if they calculate your

---

2   See Kyriakou (Kyriakou 2002, 165) for a modern definition of the term 'underwriter'.

passage (and your ship of course) so safe, that they could expect a pay-out. To calculate such risk around oversea-trades, they needed a lot of information. What information now arrived in London as this system was built and who ultimately had access to it, is described below.

Information as a commodity

In the Broad, the later information network of Lloyd's is here already present. The Secretary, later the corresponding *'Sub-Committee of Intelligence'*, supervised the receipt of all 'intelligence' and additional bits of information. Then he decided in the best interests of the subscribers what should happen with it.[3] Lloyds purchased all available sound-lists to allow the underwriters a selection of *'reliable'* Ships for their specific trades: *'That it be recommended to the Committee to procure Lists of all Convoys together with the Sound*[s] *Lists, and that whatever Expenses attend procuring the same […]'* (Lloyd's 1805, 66). The value for information to the economy is obvious, and Lloyd's begun to gather the information.

Collecting the conditions of ocean or coastal vessels was institutionalized early, Lloyd's created the *'Lloyd's Register'*, whose first surviving versions date back to 1764 and 1786. Subsequent statistical data provided a very accurate picture of the current state of the British Merchant Navy and those foreign ships, which made regular business with them to the merchants.[4] The early register books, only available if you paid a high fee, contain some important details about a ship. Its type, size, weight is included as well as the name of the captain, often the owner and the condition of the ship. These registers work well in combination with the List and provide us today with additional sources for our different projects and a unique view on the global early modern trade.

During these early years, the second part was the so-called *'Marine Lists'*. The committee of Lloyds first purchased these different lists, which includes a collection of departures and arrivals of commercial ships, which were collected by harbour registries, subscriber or 'friends' in the appropriate ports and were then usually shipped to London via mail.

These information were printed in London and placed in the subscriber room of the Lloyd's coffee house. Later a customer of Lloyd's could order it to his home or bureau. Such Information turned into a valuable commodity and was exclusively for the special community of the coffee house. The information was private, and so become even more valuable. To understand the value of this information for a subscriber at Lloyd's, one has to clarify his two possible roles. First, he had to have one of the 'permitted' occupations: *'Only Merchants, Bankers, Underwriters, and Insurance Brokers, shall be permitted to become Subscribers on being recommended to the Committee'* (Lloyd's of London 1805, 196).

If someone wanted to consume and use this information, he had to pay a fee to the master of the coffee house. No other people should benefit from it, as you can see based on a note from 1781 in the Minutes of the Committee of Lloyd's. Mr. Tayler, the master of the Coffee House,

---

3   For a deeper, historical view Llorca-Jaña (Llorca-Jaña 2010, 32).
4   Additional information about the content of the annual Lloyd's Register can be found at the Merseyside Maritime Museum (Centre for Port & Maritime History 2004, 2-3).

'having produced a list of Gentlemen frequenting this Coffee House who have not yet paid their Subscription. The committee- ordered that Mr. Tayler write them a letter that the Committee have given him orders to refuse their admittance and their Names to be posted up in the Rooms unless they pay forthwith their Subscription' (Lloyds 1805, 71).

Access to Lloyd's was limited on purpose, and this applied not only to the profession. Thus Subscriber had to decide for or against Lloyd's, a parallel membership at Lloyd's and any other maritime insurer was not permitted. Once a trader decided to stay at Lloyd's as a subscriber, he could directly benefit from the information provided by this organization.

The world of commerce was a networked world, and as the complexity increased more and more over time, even an experienced businessperson needed help, which could be provided by a strong, worldwide operating information network. Lloyd's of London recognized these needs and established a comprehensive system to provide this information for a fee. This system was the Lloyd's List. The oceans were a transport full of uncertainties, and the Lloyd's List offered some degree of certainty to it. An example for these worldwide connections established by trade may be the Maury marine reports that show the main ship routes of the eighteenth and nineteenth century. Matthew Maury (1806-1873) was an US Navy officer and oceanographer who collected enormous amounts of ship logs during the nineteenth century and published tables about the winds and currents of the North Atlantic. Benjamin Schmidt from Northeastern University took this Data and visualized all voyages from the Maury collection and these results in a picture of a networked world highly connected by more or less frequented ocean routes.[5]

During this time, you can discover a global appearance of the maritime trading. Long distance trading was not only a matter of the British Empire or the other European powers. Often private merchants or companies organized themselves to earn some money far away.

Now, when a British merchant was a Subscriber at Lloyd's, he could use this information to improve his trading activities significantly. At first, he could see certain supply and demand situations by the attached price indexes of the individual ports to which he could respond. If he had booked a ship for transport, the successive issues of the Lloyd's List would track the route of the ship when they were heading for 'monitored' ports. Although the news of the ports needed of course days or weeks to reach their destination in London, they were still significantly faster than the monitored vessel. The so-called *'Packet Line Ships'* of course had to contend with the weather conditions, but their lightweight and compact build in comparison to the much heavier and slower merchant ships generally shortened their travel time (see Karagöl 2013, 51-52).

A ship was a very expensive medium of transport and its owners wanted to minimize the risk of a loss as far as possible. Ship owners and merchants were searching for the most detailed information on the position of the vessel to prepare in time their respective sales in the ports of destination.

---

5   See his Homepage for more information and the different visualisations itself: http://sappingattention.blogspot.ch/2012/11/reading-digital-sources-case-study-in.html [31.03.2016].

During a transport of goods over long distance, accurate timing was necessary for the company to make profit. The precise arrival time of a vessel with much-needed goods could decide between wealth and bankruptcy. One can certainly use the well-known quote that here, *'time is money'*. Depending on the destination, a trader could react in time with thus appropriate information and make an arrangement to sell his goods as successful as possible. For longer trips, for example to Asia or America, a notification by the merchant to his companions in the destination port was hardly possible, even if the fast post ships left their trading counterparts far behind. Nevertheless, this information was not worthless. A trader could be at least certain, that his goods had arrived unscathed to his partners. Without the Lloyd's List, he would only know after months of waiting and worrying.

The traders learned thus also in times when a ship has been damaged. The repair of the damage could greatly extend the journey or make it impossible at worst.

If you operated a well-established trade over the oceans, you have to accept the inconceivable risks of failure, because *'carriage by sea was, however, liable to interruption and delay'* (Ashton 1977, 72). In this case, the second part of being a Subscriber at Lloyd's comes into play, the role as an 'underwriter':

> *'Because interpreting all this information to determine premiums involved weighing numerous factors, underwriting was ultimately a matter of individual judgment, requiring experience and familiarity with the routes, vessels, people, and circumstances involved. Lloyd's attracted a wide variety of underwriters, many of whom were active or retired merchants, and whose specialist knowledge of particular kinds of risks enabled them to make these kinds of judgments.'* (Kingston 2007, 386).

An underwriter insured ships or cargo with his private assets against damage or total loss so that he gets a profit from the premium in the case of a successful crossing. However, he does not want to bear this risk alone, so that in most cases a group of underwriters join together and insured a ship. Not all of them wanted or could analyse the information of the Lloyd's List and other sources *en detail*, so usually a very well-informed underwriter drew an insurance policy for a supposedly 'safe' ride, and then a lot of 'free riders' also tried their luck, and thus shared the risk (see Kingston 2007, 386-387). The allocation depends of course on the size and value of a ship. However, popular were in particular 8, 16, 32 or 48 underwriters.[6]

If they found sufficient underwriter for an insurance policy, the ship was insured against the natural and human hazards at sea and the owners were in the comfortable position to send the ship away. Such insurance against peril on a long voyage was particularly one of the foundations of trade with partners in Asia and other distant areas. From the eighteenth century onwards the trade across the oceans grew, among other things, increasingly due to this fact (see Schulte Beerbühl 2007, 331 and Ashworth 2003, 135).

After the move to the Royal Exchange, Lloyd's Coffee House became a promising 'trading point' for maritime information in which the collected data was considered

---

6   See for further information Barbour 1928-1929, 569-570.

as a valuable commodity by all parties. The quantity of this data collection speaks for itself and we can assume that organizational structure behind it based on the following numbers: Within two months of the year 1829, 3558 shipping lists and 627 individual letters from agents or subscribers reached London where the information was evaluated, processed and afterwards published in 30 issues of Lloyd's List.

The Lloyd's List is a network of policyholders, insurers, investors, and objects. With the rapid growth in the British maritime trade (between 1780 to 1850 by about a factor of 10) and then telegraph as a fast communication medium, this network obtained a global scale. In such a capital-intensive sector as maritime insurance, the involved players always require accurate information in order to calculate their own risk. An advantage of the 'commodity information' often meant higher profits.

Through its own information, management a merchant or ship-owner was also informed about the operations of rival traders or trading companies in London. He developed an entirely new approach to deal with information. By using the already compiled data of Lloyd's List individually, they could forestall their competitors. Lloyd's had to establish this completely new data-management, there was no predecessor. *'The ultimate goal is to codify and enforce best practices for data management across the organization. Meeting this goal can be frustrating and elusive. There is no manual that lays out a step-by-step plan, so the path can seem confusing and difficult to manoeuvre.'* (Fisher 2009, 65).

However, this required different information and links to associate for example, the names of the ship owners to the client of individual captains. For this purpose, new publications were needed. In addition to Lloyd's List and the Lloyd's Register, they created 'Lloyd's Shipping Lists' with the classifications of single vessels, their captains with their individual career track and – based on the data of the List – map-based registers of damaged ships and wrecks. These losses of ships and cargoes represent 'fractures' in the ordinary everyday business of a merchant community and underpin the need for tools such as the Lloyd's List in order to minimize future hazards. The different casualty types were ordered by date and area, so Lloyd´s could set a specific risk for every region by the time the ship sailed there.

The collection and processing of such huge amounts of data within a few days required a considerable logistic capacity that continuously grew even bigger. During the eighteenth and nineteenth century, London had become the centre of the trade and finance of Europe and the Lloyd´s List had to grow with it and differentiate their focus. Lloyd's had to change their content in the following decades. The collecting of information became a business itself and therefore a new sub-company, the *'Lloyd's List'*, was established. The process and the change in aggregation through technological innovations, such as the telegraph, or the improved postal services, but also the slow transition from sail to steam ships to the use of the ship's propellers had an impact on travel routes, communication times and ultimately on the standards of information gathering.

Over time, also the trade with ports under direct British control expanded. Information from far remote areas was passed through several stops, which have not always worked accurately and reliably. They could not, as previously, rely solely on the generated lists, but needed more sources of information.

The agents of Lloyd's

The second 'stage of professionalization' was the development of a global agent network, which allows a much more accurate grade of information collection as would have been possible by Sound and Marine Lists. An agent of Lloyd's was and still is the local single point of contact in an insurance case. He regulates the communication with the owners, other involved people and Lloyd's. He also checks whether the case is a legal insurance case. Although historical reports of Lloyd's dated the founding if the agent service not before the mid-nineteenth century, an agent list for 1821 was confirmed in the archive (see Lloyd's of London 1822). Individual entries within the protocols of the General Meeting in August 1800 even point to a prior organization (Lloyd's 1804, 271). Presumably, the first agents were initially 'only' simple suppliers of Shipping Intelligence (the extracted and summarized data from the Sound and Marine-Lists) and further information. These reports of passages are still the 'bread and butter' of the daily merchant business. With additional sources, a trader could forecast a supply or a demand in different ports, colonies or even countries, and therefore, make profit with this knowledge.

Later an agent was responsible for the acquisition of valid and trustful information, and in this case he was much more reliable than previous sources. In addition, they collected a new type of information – the so-called *'Speakings'*- maybe the most important section of the List. Although the oceans cover a huge area, the ships moved on more or less regular routes. Thus, it was not unusual that two ships met on their respective route. A common maritime term for this was *'to speak'*. This could be an actual verbal communication, but often they communicated through standardized single flag signals (see Laakso 2008, 148). The Committee of Lloyd's paid, therefore, private captains and navigators to keep a record of Sightings of other ships on the oceans. These notes were taken in a second, a private logbook. The data of this log was then transmitted as soon as possible after the arrival in a port to Agent and through him further reported to Lloyd's in London. This practice was not new but has been professionalized by Lloyd's, institutionalized and thus raised to a new level. As reported by Karel Davids, such records can be backdated to the seventeenth century (Davids 1997, 83).

With this innovation we have a new quality of information – the ocean was, based loosely on Roland Wenzlhuemer, no longer a 'black box', a trader could now at least keep track of the route of his ship. With this information, the merchants got an even better overview of the actual positions of their ships. During the early years, they had of course only a rough idea of the position, but later a ship was sighted nearly every day. Now we can, with the Lloyd's List as an historical source, trace the route of a ship more or less accurately.

The sources indicate as well some agents in quite prominent positions such as a consul, a governor or a higher officer in the British Navy, thus a representative of the British government in the specific port city. Nowadays, you can still discover different emblems of Lloyd's agents on buildings of ports which were significant trading points in the past. Perhaps there are even the same companies or families, which continues to work for Lloyd's for centuries. Even in the days of faster communication and GPS-equipped ships, a ship-owner or merchant still wants a local contact who takes care of all odd jobs and trouble (Umbach 2008, 14).

Lloyd's also used these connections to support their own political ambitions. Around 1807 some legislative proposals concerning an increased subscription tax for maritime insurance policies were launched in the British Parliament, which would have a direct negative impact on Lloyd's. In addition to many other efforts, Lloyd's requested a favour to those subscribers who sat in Parliament: *'That the Members of the City of London, and such Subscribers to this House who are Members of Parliament, be requested to watch the progress of the Bill intended to be brought in'* (Lloyd's of London 1810, 302).

This, by the way partly successful exertion of influence, is a perfect example of a variety of political efforts by Lloyd's of London. In addition to collecting information, Lloyd's used its network thus also for other purposes. It is conceivable that they are already using existing structures of the East India Company, in order to develop their own network of agents. More research in this areas is required for a better understanding of this network. It is the opinion of the author, that this network of agents is one of the main factors of the success of Lloyd's of London.

Conclusion

This contribution could only give a small glimpse of the formation, structure and especially the impact of the Lloyd's List on the global trade and thus the logistics. However, the importance of information and its usage as a commodity was pointed out and can be considered as an important component of this system. The Lloyd's List is considered as a 'communication system' which collect and processed information in a global scale and offer this product to a more or less closed community.[7]

The 'danger zone sea' and the risk within gets more calculable with this information and could now be rated with numbers – ideal for an insurance policy. The impact of cheaper, faster, and better information cannot be underestimated. Moreover, this is one of the reasons the Lloyd´s List is a very valuable source for us today. With the lists, you can map and visualize trade routes all over the world. The latitude/longitude coordinates still keep an uncertainty, but considering the huge amount of data we get from the List, it is quite useful. However, of course, it can only be an indication for further research projects. There are some possible approaches how to use the List as a primary Source or a reference to additional source material. Besides these three main sections, the lists contain also stock prices, maritime news, advertisements and you could even find sale and purchase offers for ships. Some of the data is already in use by different projects. But, we know little about the Lloyd´s List itself. Of course, we have the Lists in different libraries and archives, and most of them are nowadays digitized and available. The details about the collection, the processing and validating of the information from which the weekly or later daily list was created, remains unknown. Earlier or in fact, present works too were often mainly concerned with aggregate data, the general movement of ships and goods, and changes in economic trends, or with collective political, cultural and social portraits of merchants groups, while the basics of the Lloyd´s List are almost unknown.

---

7   See Shannon 1948, 2 and Headrick 2000, 3-4 for some definitions of *'communication system'*.

Here lies the focus of my PhD-Project. I want to understand how the Committee of Lloyd´s and before them the different masters of the coffee house identified a need for such a newspaper. How they organize the collection of the information in a worldwide communication system still based on mail, and how they manage to establish such a network even in times of war and competition.

References

Ashton, Th. 1977. *An economic history of England. The 18th Century.* London: Methuen.

Ashworth, W. 2003. *Customs and excise. Trade, production and consumption in England 1640-1845.* Oxford: Oxford University Press.

Aven, T.; Renn, O. 2010. *Risk Management and Governance. Concepts, Guidelines and Applications.* Heidelberg: Sprinter.

Barbour, V., 1928-1929. Marine risks and insurance in the seventeenth century. *Journal of Economic and Business History* 1, 561-596.

Borscheid, P. 2012. Europe. Overview, in: Borscheid, P. and Haueter, N. (eds.). *World Insurance. The evolution of a global risk network.* Oxford: Oxford University Press.

Burke, P. 2014. *Die Explosion des Wissens. Von der Encyclopédie bis Wikipedia.* Berlin: Wagenbach.

Centre for Port & Maritime History 2004. *Infosheet 52,* Lloyd's Marine Insurance Records, Merseyside Maritime Museum. Liverpool.

Davids, K. 1997. Sources of Knowledge. Journals, Logs, and Travel Accounts, in: Hattendorf, J. (ed.). *Maritime history. Volume 2: The eighteenth century and the classic age of sail.* Malabar: Krieger Pub. Co, 79-86.

Davis, R. 1972. *The rise of the English shipping industry. In the seventeenth and eighteenth centuries.* Newton Abbot: David & Charles.

Fisher, T. 2009. *The Data Asset. How Smart Companies Govern Their Data for Business Success.* New Jersey: Wiley.

Headrick, D. 2000. *When Information came of age.* Oxford: Oxford University Press.

Karagöl, J. 2013. *Girdling the Globe, networking the world. A discourse analysis of the media representation of nineteenth-century transport and communication technologies in Victorian Britain, 1838-1871.* PhD-Thesis, Heidelberg.

Kingston, Ch. 2007. Marine Insurance in Britain and America, 1720-1844. A Comparative Institutional Analysis. *The Journal of Economic History* 67/2, 379-409.

Kyriakou, M. 2002. *From discreteness to cooperation. Relational contracting in the London marine insurance market.* PhD-Thesis. London.

Laakso, S.-R. 2002. *Across the Oceans. Development of Overseas Business Information Transmission, 1815-1875.* PhD-Thesis, Helsinki.

Leonard, A. 2014. *Gresham and Defoe (underwriters). The Origins of London Marine Insurance,* Gresham College Lecture, Thursday 13 March 2014 (Transcript), London.

Llorca-Jaña, M. 2010. The Marine Insurance Market for British Textile Exports to the River Plate and Chile. 1810-50, in: Pearson, R. (ed.). *The development of international insurance.* London: Pickering & Chatto, 25-36.

Lloyd´s of London 1805. *Minutes of the Committee of Lloyd´s. Dec 1771 – Aug 1804.* Guildhall Library/MS31571-001. London.

Lloyd´s of London 1810. *Minutes of the Committee of Lloyd´s. Aug 1804 – Dec 1809.* Guildhall Library/MS31571-002. London.

Lloyds of London 1822. *A List of the subscribers to Lloyd's. Also a list of the agents and a copy of their appointment and instructions, December 31, 1821.* London.

Lloyd's of London 1934. *Lloyd's List & Shipping Gazette. 1734-1934, 200 years of shipping news*, Guildhall Library (Fo Pamphlet 288). London.

Lloyd's Register of Shipping 1884: *Annals of Lloyd's Register. Being a sketch of the origin, constitution, and progress of Lloyd's Register of British & foreign shipping.* London.

Nonaka, I. 1994. A Dynamic Theory of Organizational Knowledge Creation. *Organization Science* 5.1, 14-37.

Schulte Beerbühl, M. 2007. *Deutsche Kaufleute in London. Welthandel und Einbürgerung (1660-1818).* München: Oldenbourg (Veröffentlichungen des Deutschen Historischen Instituts London 61).

Shannon, C.E. 1948. *A Mathematical Theory of Communication.* Urbana: ACM.

Umbach, K. 2008. *Das grenzüberschreitende Geschäft in der See- und Transportversicherung von Ende des 19. Jahrhunderts bis in die 1990er Jahre. Ein internationaler Gewerbezweig auf dem Weg hin zu «globalisierten» Verhältnissen?* PhD-Thesis, Marburg.

Zwierlein, C. 2011. *Der gezähmte Prometheus. Feuer und Sicherheit zwischen Früher Neuzeit und Moderne.* Göttingen: Vandenhoeck & Ruprech.

Cultural Exchange in Early Modern Shipbuilding

Anne-Kathrin Piele

Abstract

Already in the beginning of the early modern age, trading contacts with northern Europe caused changes in shipbuilding in the Mediterranean. Like other seafaring nations in northern Europe, people in the Mediterranean started to use square sails instead of lateen sails, which were common in the Mediterranean since Roman antiquity. These changes were the result of trade contacts which were accredited to the Dutch. In the following centuries, the Netherlands still had a leading position in shipbuilding and they passed on not only their construction techniques but also sold complete ships to other seafaring nations in Europe. As Kurbrandenburg (Electorate of Brandenburg) acquired Hinterpommern (Farther Pomerania) and gained access to the coast of the Baltic Sea in the seventeenth century, they hired a Dutch naval architect and bought several ships in the Netherlands in order to build up an own merchant fleet including the slave trade. In the eighteenth century, Austria also trusted in shipbuilders which build in Dutch tradition and with help of two of them they wanted to remodel shipbuilding on the Danube. This is reflected by a shipbuilding tradition which is typical for the coast of the North Sea.

Keywords: shipbuilding, Dutch shipbuilding, shipping, shipwreck, modernisation, cultural exchange, knowledge transfer, Early Modern Age, Danube, Johannes Mattheus Hepp, Maria Theresia

Using the example of Dutch shipbuilding

In the sixteenth century, the Portuguese and the Spanish were the dominating forces in East Asian trade but knowledge of the seaways to reach the treasures of East Asia increased significantly in the Netherlands at the end of the sixteenth century. Important scholars like the student of Mercator, Petrus Plancius, served as an advisor on the first voyages and thanks to them, Dutch cartography got a leading position in Europe. Essential basics for charts were delivered from reports of seamen which travelled on

in: Kahlow, S. (ed.) 2018: *Transfer between sea and land. Maritime vessels for cultural exchanges in the Early Modern Period*, Sidestone Press (Leiden), pp. 131-142.

Portuguese ships to Asia (Nagel 2011, 100). The first voyage of a Dutch company ship took place in 1595 (*ibid.*, 101). In the year 1603, the first ship of the VOC (*Verenigde Oostindische Compagnie*) set sail. The Dutch took action against the Portuguese and slowly adopted the leading position in East Asia trading (Nagel 2011, 103). In the aftermath, more East-Indian Companies were founded (Denmark, Sweden, Brandenburg). They corresponded to the Dutch example (*ibid.*, 127-140) and ship types were also based on the Dutch equivalents (for example the Swedish ship Götheborg was similar to the Dutch ship Batavia).

Kurbrandenburg and the Sea

The Dutch shipbuilding tradition was also appreciated in other countries of Europe like Kurbrandenburg. Elector Friedrich Wilhelm the Great of Brandenburg spent four years of his youth in the Netherlands and he realized whereon their power was founded: Exploitation of the colonies and maritime trade and both was only possible with a great powerful fleet. Until his death in 1688, Wilhelm tried to emulate the Dutch example. The Brandenburg fleet should be appointed for capturing other ships, maritime trade and for the appropriation of colonies. Because of the lack of suitable ships in Königsberg, today Kaliningrad and other Prussian harbours, the elector sent delegates to the Netherlands, instructed shipowner Benjamin Raule and rented Dutch Frigates. He bought eight ships from Raule to build up his own fleet in 1684. In 1682 the *'Brandenburgisch-Africanische Compagnie'* (BAC) was founded by Raule but for competing with important naval powers like the Netherlands or Great Britain, the BAC was too small (Feige 2005, 20-22.).

Modernization of Danube shipping by Maria Theresia

In inland water transport, the Dutch shipbuilding tradition was also successful and often used as an example like in the following way. Modernization of shipping was started by Charles VI. of Austria (1685-1740) and still pursued by his daughter, Empress Maria Theresa (1717-1780). After the Seven Years War (1756-1763), which was a war between Prussia, Great Britain, and Kurhannover (Electorate of Hannover) against Austria, Russia, France and the Holy Roman Empire about the predominance not only in Central Europe but also in North America and India, Austria lost Silesia and therefore trade routes changed. Amongst other things, there was more passenger traffic on the water, especially in the direction of Germany (Slezak 1971, 58).

In 1764, the shipwright Johannes Mattheus Hepp transported the equipage of the Earl of Pergen and the Prince of Esterhàzy from the Austrian Netherlands to Vienna. On his way to Austria, he made observations about shipping on the Danube. In comparison with his home, handling plants on the Danube were antiqued and backwardly. During his stay in Vienna in 1765, Hepp made ideas for improving shipbuilding and provided them to the Austrian court. Due to his experience on the Rhine between Amsterdam and Strasbourg, he wanted to reform shipping. On the Rhine, it was common in that time to build in Dutch tradition, so Hepp designed and constructed ships in that tradition too. A ship build of oak could last for some 20 years, the common softwood ships on the Danube on the other hand only for a short time. It was not allowed to use them more than three years. Construction costs (without timber) were

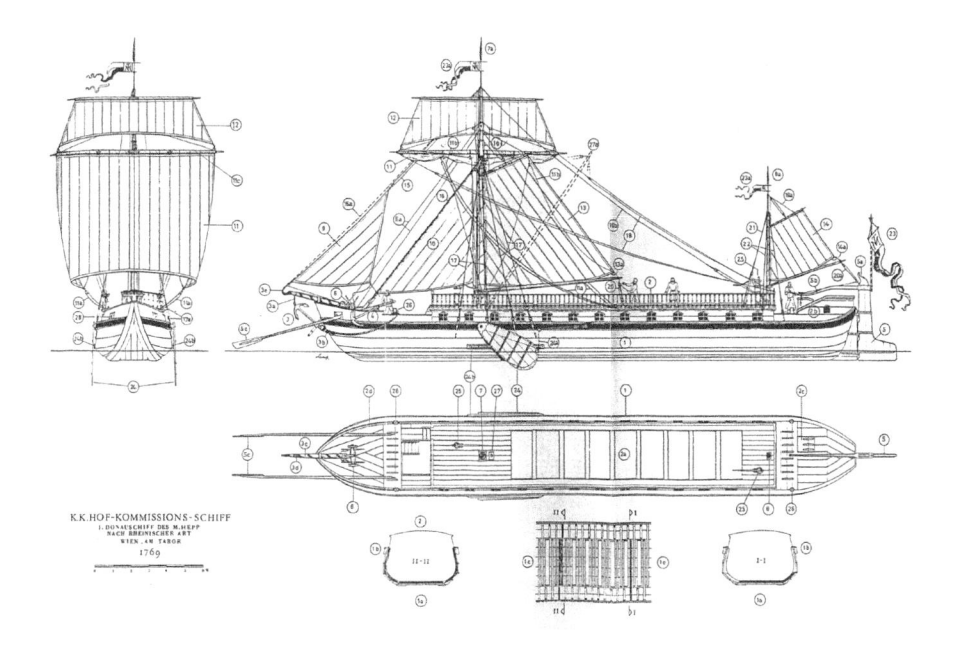

Figure 1: Design drawing of the first ship build by Hepp in Vienna 1769.

800 guldens (fl.). Maria Theresa sent Hepp's ideas for improvement to the Austrian councillor of commerce in 1765, but because there were disunity and discussion about giving Hepp advanced money for constructing the ship, it resulted in delay (Slezak 1971, 59).

Hepp provided a construction drawing with a ship in the Dutch tradition (Fig. 1). No special name is known for this type from the Danube. Comparable types from the Rhine from that period are known as *'Keulsche Aak'* and *'Samoreus'* (Fig. 2 and 3). A ship constructed by Hepp would be able to carry a burden of 1,200 hundredweight and a 40 men crew (Slezak 1971, 59).

The shipyard in 1767 lay on the place where is now the *'Augarten'* in Vienna. On Hepp's ship, there were some innovations which were not common in Danube shipping before like mast and sail, pumps, winches, and anchors. He also provided cranes for the handling of cargo like they were common on the Rhine and in the Netherlands. Empress Maria Theresa advocated his ideas. The masts and sails were produced in Mainz and Hepp also recruited his craftsmen from his homeland. Travel expenses for the craftsmen and the delay of the appropriation of construction material (60 trunks of oak) increased the price for the construction of the ship threefold. It was calculated that for the distance between Vienna and Linz with a cargo of 1,000 hundredweight it would take ten days instead of three or four weeks. This only with seven to eight horses, four men crew and one boy instead of 12 to 14 horses and same number men as a crew (Slezak 1971, 60).

In February 1776 Hepp's 'Rhenish Ship' was finished. It had a cargo capacity of 1200 to 1500 hundredweight which matched with a middle 'Klobzille' (barge type from the Danube) and the towed barge was equal in size and cargo capacity of 300 hundredweight to a middle 'Gamszille'. Hepp's ship had a length of 96 Schuh and 6

Figures 2 and 3: Similar types of the Rhine: Samoreus and Keulsche Aak.

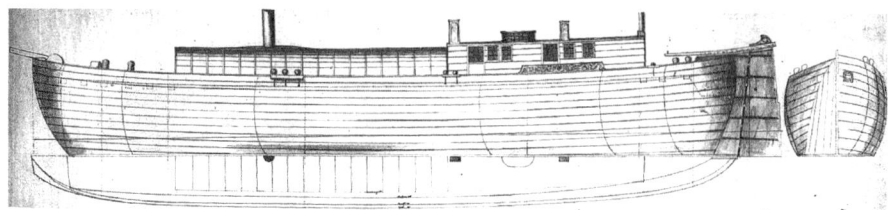

Figure 4: Local ship type used for the salt transport in Gmunden, Austria.

Zoll, which can be converted to about 30 m. The height including the superstructure was 8 Schuh. Common ships from the Danube had a height of 4.5 Schuh (circa 1.35 m) and had to weather a storm in the harbour whereas Hepp's ship could sail with every strength of wind. It was equipped with three anchors, one at the bow, a second one at the forecastle and a third one amidships on the gallery. Also new was the Dutch type of rudder Hepp's ship used and the winch served not only for mounting the mast and hoisting the anchors but also for freeing the ship from sandbanks. Hepp's ship

TRANSFER BETWEEN SEA AND LAND

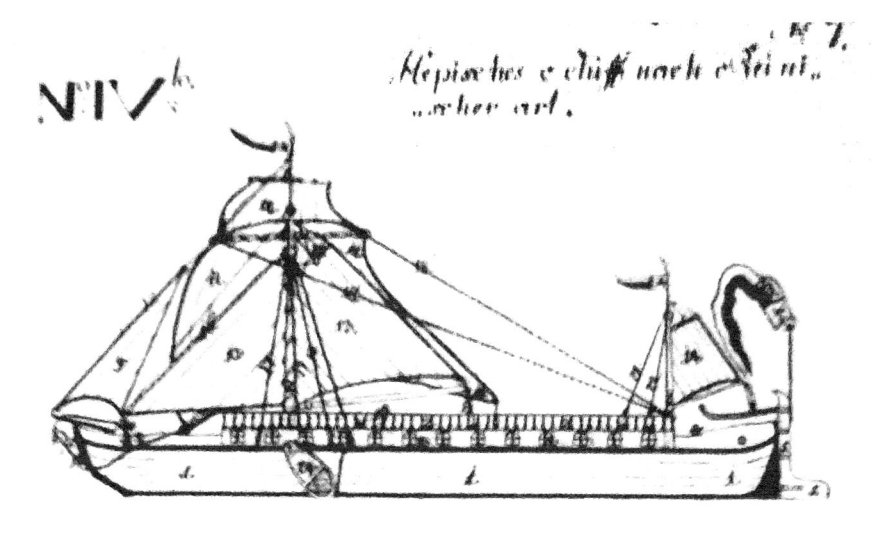

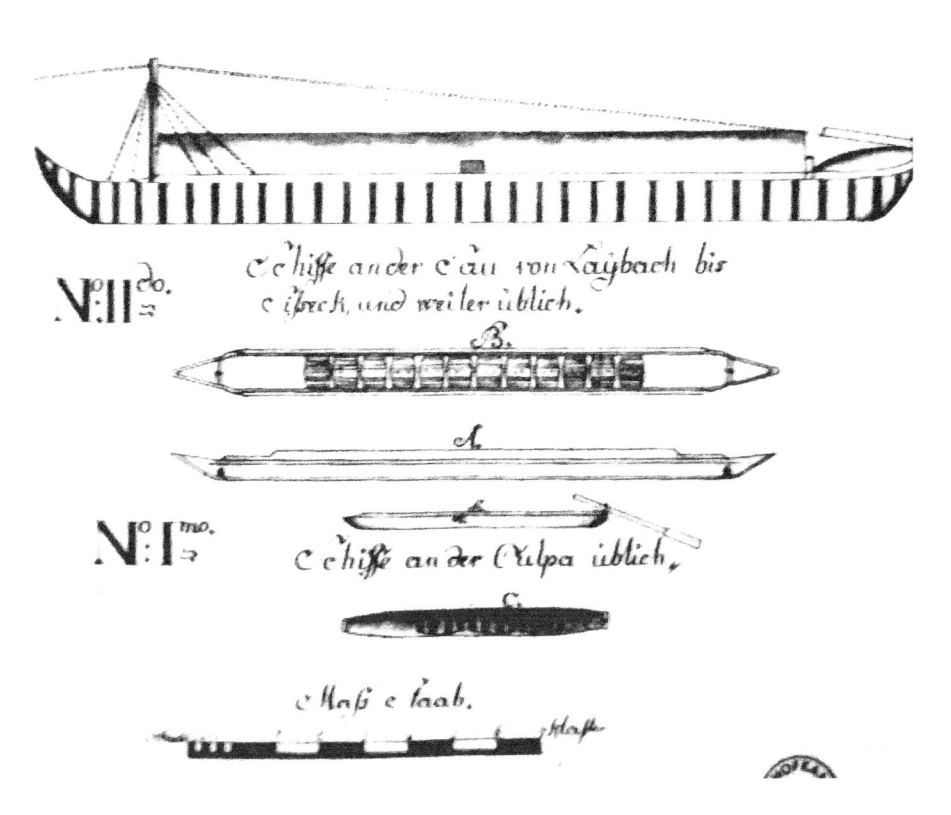

Figure 5: Hepp's ship and local ship types.

Figure 6: Depiction of a 'Zille', Vilshofen on the Danube.

had two masts with six sails and the mizzen served as support for the rudder (Fig. 5) (Slezak 1971, 60).

There are three similar ship types of ships at that time in Austria: the *'Culpa-Korabe'*, the *'Save-Softwoodship'* and a ship made from fir wood, named *'Kehlheimer'* or *'Klobzille'* (Fig. 4 to 6) (Slezak 1971, 61).

The *'Culpa-Korabe'* was a holed oak tree with an additional plank for getting more freeboard. This ships operated between Karlstadt (Croatia) and Sisseg (Croatia). Upstream (pulled by men) they could carry a burden of 60 hundredweight, downstream a burden of 30 to 35 hundredweight. A ship of this type could be used for the maximum of six years (Table 1) (Slezak 1971, 61).

Between Salloch (near to Laibach, Slovenia) and Sisseg, the *'Save-Softwoodship'* was in use. It could carry a burden of 200 hundredweight upstream and a burden of 140 hundredweight downstream (Slezak 1971, 61).

On the Danube, the *'Kehlheimer'* or *'Klobzillen'* were the common types of ship (Fig. 6). They were built in Austria (Salzburg) and Bavaria (Passau for example) and were made from fir wood. A ship of that type was in use for a maximum of three years. Upstream they could carry a burden of 2,300 hundredweight and downstream a burden of 2,000 hundredweight (Slezak 1971, 61).

Hepp's ship could be in use up to 40 years and it was coated with tar like a real seagoing ship. Unloaded it was able to operate in water with a depth of only 30 cm. With a draught of 80 cm, it was able to carry a burden of 1,500 hundredweight. Fully loaded (2,000 hundredweight burden) the depth of the water had a draught of 1 m. The towed barge could carry a burden of 600 to 800 hundredweight.

By order of Maria Theresa, Hepp made a test run to Regensburg in June 1769, most likely loaded with copper. The test was a success. Therefore, Maria Theresa grant-

Type	Lenght	Breadth (bottom/above)	Draught (fully loaded)	Cost
Korbe	36	-/3.5	1,5	60-70 fl.
Saveschiff	82	-/5.75	2	200 fl.
Klobzille	120	18/22	4	300-400 fl.
Hepp-Schiff	96,5	8/12	4	3000-9000 fl.

(Measurements in Schuh, 1 Schuh = 12 Zoll à 26.34 mm).

Table 1: Different ship types of the Danube.

ed Hepp the right to build ships in Vienna. Furthermore, he got a yearly salary of 300 fl. on condition that he takes care of the new shipbuilding and for educating other shipwrights. Until the beginning of autumn, both ships (the towed barge) were finished and were also given to Hepp as a gift and as a source of income (Slezak 1971, 61).

The shipwrights from Vienna opposed Hepp and the new ways of shipping. For them, Hepp was an irritating rival and they thought the new vessels were not suitable for shipping on the Danube (Slezak 1971, 62).

In spite of this Hepp started in 1769 to design a personal ship for Maria Theresa. One year later, he began to build the ship but in 1771, the shipyard caught fire and nothing from the vessel was left (*ibid.*).

Franz Anton von Raab, an advisor of Maria Theresa, praised the Dutch example and the assignment of Hepp. Together with a Walloon, he was in charge of the improvement of shipping on Save and Culpa. He appreciated Hepp's professional experience of 40 years and had an eye for the fact, that the new ship had none of the disadvantages of the common ships on the Danube. In his opinion, the other shipwrights in Vienna had to end their jealousy and their prejudice and had to accept the new way of shipping and see the advantages (Slezak 1971, 63-64).

The court of Vienna also hoped for some proposals for the problems of shipping on the Danube and its confluence. Thereupon Hepp went on a journey to the Traun, a confluence of the Danube in Austria and to the Salzkammergut at the northern edge of the Alps. Hepp observed that the sailors on the Hallstädter See and Traunsee used sails but rather to their disadvantage and had to be taught in trimming their sails right. Furthermore, he suggested reducing the height of the weirs of the six mills, to blow up some rocks and to build watergates and hoists at the Traunfall to reduce the number of horses for hauling the vessels. In addition, it should be considered to plug the shores downriver of Lambach but the residents did not accept his ideas. By reason of justified objections, nothing more was undertaken. He made a similar suggestion for a channel bypassing the Culpa cataract lined with wood like those of the Main and Lahn (Slezak 1971, 64-65).

On his voyages, he presumably used conventional vessels and explored not only the consistency of the waters with regard to his new oak ship but also the possibilities for building Rhenish ships in the oak forests of Croatia (*ibid.* 66).

In 1771, the first voyage of the commission of the court took place. The route (along with the Danube and Traun) was Vienna-Linz-Gmunden (Traun)-Linz-Passau-Vienna. During the journey, rock barriers in the river and other places like the Traunfall-Channel were inspected. On the second voyage in the same year, the route took course from Vienna to Preßburg (Bratislava) on the Danube and thereon along Save and Kulpa to Karlstadt (Karlovac). At this opportunity, the Kulpa cataract was also visited with regard to the changes Hepp suggested. Because the shipyard in Vienna was too expensive, Hepp also changed the position to Karlstadt. For the present, two Rhenish ships should be built there together with two towed ships. Both vessels should serve in the Hungarian Salttransport. Every ship was planned 120 feet in length, 12 feet in breadth and each of them with a cargo capacity of 3,000 to 4,000 hundredweight together with the towed ship. As Hepp's first ship was built, the local shipwrights were in doubt about the availability in use on the Danube, but the new ship could sail even when the water level was low and local ships had to wait for a higher tide. The ship was also resistant enough to survive collisions with trunks which lay underwater on the riverbed. Two Rhenish could serve 30 years (each) and manage the burden of all the 20 local ships used for the transport of salt and which would not be used for more than three years. Because of the conflicting opinions, a test run with the Rhenish ship from 1769 was made. In 1773 it sailed to Semlin (Zemun/Serbia) and from there on Danube and Theiss to Szeged (Hungary), where it was loaded with a cargo of salt and by the use of a removable deck, the charging was easy. From Semlin to Szeged and back to Semlin Hepp needed only 12 days and a half whereas local ships were on the move for five weeks. Thereby he persuaded the Earl of Starhemberg and was authorized for the transport of salt from Szeged to Semlin (Slezak 1971, 66-69).

The launching from the first ship took place in 1774 in Karlstadt, a second one was finished in 1775 and a third one was launched in the same year in Eckartsau on an anabranch of the Danube close to Vienna. As the ships were finished the Rhenish carpenters were paid and discharged so they could go back to their homeland. Meanwhile, the better shipbuilding with oak was spread by itself (Slezak 1971, 69-70).

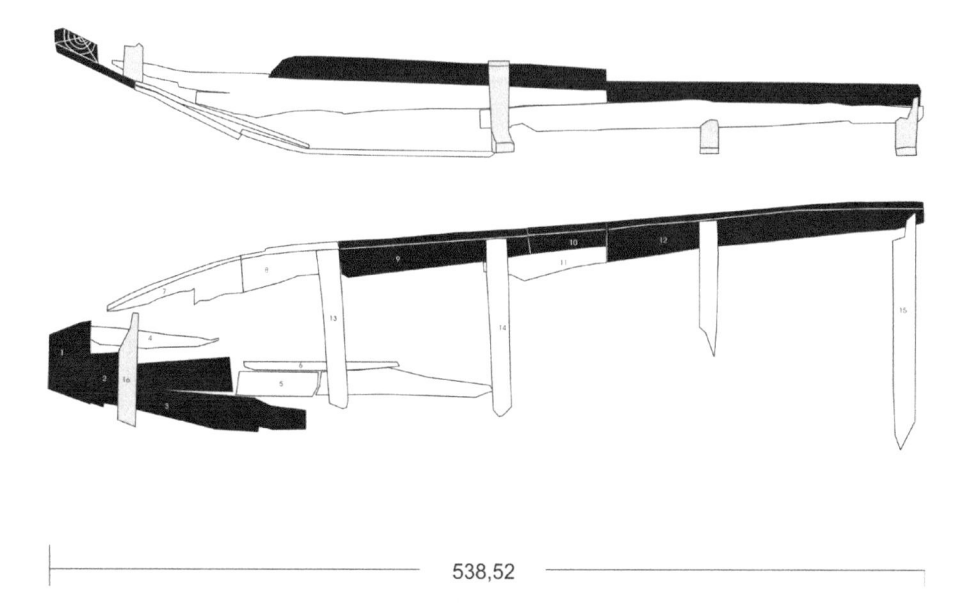

538,52

Figure 7: Wreck of Kehlheim-Kehlheimwinzer.

Figure 8: Cockle boat at Strassbourg, engraving by W. Hollar, circa 1630.

Figure 9: Wreck of Kehlheim-Kehlheimwinzer.

In the 1770's Hepp also travelled to the Vltava to take care for a better shipping. A test run was made in 1772 and 1775. Hepp built two pointed ships to ferry across the river. He also travelled to Galicia in March 1776 together with two ship carpenters and build a test ship.

A document from the year 1780 reported the death of Johann Matthäus Hepp in Hungary. Because his son did not want to take over the contract, the three ships from Hepp came under their own administration. They were managed by the salt officials from Semlin (Slezak 1971, 72).

In the year 1976, the wreck of a boat was found on the Danube which was built in the Rhenish type and which is interesting in this context (Fig. 7 and 9). It was discovered during the construction of the Rhein-Main-Donau-Channel (Herzig and Weski 2009, 85.). A sample for radiocarbon dating was taken and produced a date 120+/- 60 BP. Because the find spot was registered as dry land in the cadastre, the age supposed to be between 1640 and 1800 AD. The preserved fragments were from oak and measured 5.85 m in length with a breadth of 1.40 m and a height of 0.50 m.

Significant features are the flat bottom, the double cracked ribs and the flat and peaked endings on both sides. Originally the boat had a breadth of 2.70 m but the original length was undeterminable (Herzig and Weski 2009, 86). Sawn planks were used and the planks and frames were connected by iron nails. There was a layer of moss impregnated with tar between the planking and the plank scarfing lead to the interpretation that it was the stern of the boat. Analysis of the oak wood showed, that it was cut between the northern part of Baden-Württemberg and the Rhineland, not before 1775+/-10 AD (Herzig and Weski 2009, 87). This type of boat is clearly different from the common boats used on the Danube which were built from spruce wood in the shell construction technique. The reconstructed form of the hull with double cracked ribs, constructed frame first, caulked with moss and made of oak fits better with boats from the Rhine called cockle boats, see Fig. 8, so it is probable that the boats origin has to be searched in this region (Herzig and Weski 2009, 87-88). Maybe the wreck from Kehlheim-Kehlheimwinzer could be linked with Mattäus Hepp and the transportation of the equipages of the Earl of Pergen and the Prince of Esterhazy 1764. In the eighteenth century, there was an active movement of travellers of distinguished people. It was about imperial legates which had extensive luggage that had to be transported. They were on their journey to the Reichstag in Regensburg or also to the coronation of the emperor in Frankfurt and in the context of this events it would be possible that the boat was carried on a carriage and transported over the watershed (Herzig and Weski 2009, 89-90).

Conclusion

The innovations which were brought with the ships from Hepp are still in use today (anchors, winch, pumps, stem rudder, hatchway, cargo hold on the bow, crew accommodation aft). From the middle Danube, there are types known which were very similar to the ships from Hepp and probably lead back to the ships build in Karlstadt.

For further research, it would be interesting to examine, how later ship types on the Danube had been influenced by Hepp and his innovations in shipbuilding and shipping, especially on the middle Danube where ships were built which looked very

TRANSFER BETWEEN SEA AND LAND

similar to the ships from Hepp. Thus it would be possible to see, which features from the Rhenish ships were especially preferred for the later types. Although the new type of ship was not able to become accepted completely, Hepp's project can be still seen as a success. Not only because his ships succeeded in their test runs and because they were accepted as suitable for the shallow waters and because some ships of the new type were built and inserted for the salt shipping but also due to the later build ship types which showed clear similarity to the predecessors build by Hepp. After 1774 nothing is known about the fate of the ship from 1769. The three ships used for the salt transport were still in use 1782. Because of a request from the Willeshovenschen Kompanie, one ship was given to them for operating in the Black Sea (Slezak 1972, 72).

References

Dessens, H., 1995. European Inland Sailing Craft. In: R. Gardiner, P. Bosscher, *The Heyday of Sail. The Merchant Sailing Ship 1650-1830*. London 1995: Chartwell Books, 105-123

Feige, T. 2005. Kurbrandenburg zur See. Handel und Seefahrt im Zeitalter des Barock. *Deutsches Technikmuseum Berlin* 5, 20-22.

Herzig, F. and Weski, T. 2009. Neues zu Altfunden von Booten aus Bayern. *Nachrichtenblatt Arbeitskreis Unterwasserarchäologie* 15, 79-90.

Nagel, J. 2011. *Abenteuer Fernhandel: Die Ostindienkompagnien*. 2.Auflage Darmstadt: Wissenschaftliche Buchgesellschaft.

Sarrazin, J. 1996. *Schopper und Zillen: eine Einführung in den traditionellen Holzschiffbau im Gebiet der deutschen Donau*. Hamburg: Kabel.

Schaefer, K. 1985. Architectura Navalis Danubiana. Dissertation. Technische Hochschule Wien.

Slezak, F. 1971. Matthäus Hepp. Vom Mainzer Schiffer zum kaiserlichen Leibschiffmeister. *Mainzer Zeitschrift* 66, 58-72.

Index

B

C

N

O

P

Ferdinand I, 93
Flower, Henry, 108
Frederick Henry, Prince of Orange, 98
Frederick Wilhelm the Great, 132
Fuchs, Herman, 67, 71, 78
Fugger, 17-18, 50, 101
Gardie, Magnus Gabriel De la, 65, 82
George, Wilma, 94
Gessner, Conrad, 98
Grim, Herman Nicolai, 79
Gustav II Adolf, 66
Gustav Vasa, 65
Hakon III, 96
Henry I, 91
Henry III, 96
Henry VIII, 81
Hepp, Johannes Mattheus, 131-132
Heraeus, Christian, 66-67, 78
Heraeus, Johan, 66
Hornstedt, Clas Fredrik, 100
Johann Albrecht II of Mecklenburg-
  Güstrow, 66
Katharina of Austria, 93
Katzenelnbogen, Philip of, 29
Khevenhüller, Hans, 101
King Louis, 29
King Manuel, 107
Landgraves of Hesse, 29
Lauffer, Cornelius, 53
Leo X, 107
Linneaus, Carl, 79
Marcusz, Andries, 104
Maria Theresa, 131-133, 136-137
Matthias of Hungary, 33
Maury, Matthew, 124
Mercator, 131
Metrà, Andrea, 45
Murad III, 47
Müller, Georg Franz, 106
Nestorian Christian, 29
Paracelsus, 63, 66, 81
Plancius, Petrus, 131
Polo, Marco, 33, 35-36
Pope, 29, 107
Prince of Esterhàzy, 132
Raule, Benjamin, 132

Rietz, Grégoire François Du, 65-66
Rudolf II, 93, 101
Ryff, Walther Hermann, 79
Schallerus, Peter, 65
Sheldon the Elder, Francis, 64
Sparman, Anders, 66
Steckert, Alexander, 67, 71, 78
Struan, Jacob Robert of, 66
Sybelist, Wedelin, 82
Tartaglini, Leone, 102
Trotzig, Peter, 68, 77
Tulp, Nicolaes, 97
Tyson, Edward, 108
van Kippen, Barend Jansz., 104
von Bretten, Michael Heberer, 45
von Raab, Franz Anton, 137
Vosmaer, Arnout, 108
Wattrang, Zacharias, 66
Weinmann, Christoph, 74, 80
Woldran zu Genua, Johann, 51
Wrangel, Carl Gustaf, 65-66, 68
pestle, 72; see also mortar
pet, 89, 92, 110-112
pharmacie, 67; see also Dispensatorium
  Hafniensae; Dispensatorium
  Nürnbergiensis; Pharmacopoeia
  Holmiensis
Pharmacopoeia Holmiensis, 66, 77, 83;
  see also Galeno-Chymica
pilgrimages, 31
pills, 64, 74, 80-81, 83
pine resin, 74, 76
pins, 43-44, 53, 58
plants, 20, 35, 93, 132
plaster, 68, 77, 81
port, 13, 20, 26-27, 29, 50, 57, 69, 77,
  89, 101-103, 109-111, 120, 122-127
portrait, 96, 128
powder, 71
preparation, 35, 66, 68, 76, 78
prestige, 16, 18, 20, 90, 100
professionals
  botanist, 94
  medical professional, 98
    apothecary, 64-65, 67, 69, 74, 78,
    80, 82

R

S

TRANSFER BETWEEN SEA AND LAND

T

U

V

W

Z